The Model Financial Reporting Handbook

The Model Financial Reporting Handbook

David Chitty
Chantrey Vellacott DFK

Accountancy
BOOKS

40 Bernard Street
London
WC1N 1LD

Tel: +44 (0)20 7920 8991
Fax: +44 (0)20 7920 8992

E-mail: info@accountancybooks.co.uk
website: www.accountancybooks.co.uk

Contents

Contents

Preface and acknowledgements

The *Model Financial Reporting Handbook* is intended to assist those who have responsibility for preparing and reporting on the financial statements of private companies with the application and interpretation of the growing volume of financial reporting disclosures.

The book has evolved in Chantrey Vellacott DFK over several years and has proved to be a successful practical aid both in preparing and auditing financial statements. It deliberately focuses on the reporting needs of private companies which are exempt from preparing group accounts and which are eligible to file abbreviated accounts with the Registrar of Companies. This deliberate focus helps to enhance practicality.

The author is grateful to many colleagues in Chantrey Vellacott DFK for their assistance in the preparation and publication of this book. Particular mention should be made of the co-author of the first edition, David James, and of Michael Wheeler and William Bullock who prepared the original internal versions of this publication. Julia Penny performed an invaluable review of the manuscript and made many worthy suggestions for its improvement.

David Chitty
Chantrey Vellacott DFK
July 1999

Introduction and how to use the book

The purpose of the *Model Financial Reporting Handbook* is to assist those who have responsibility for preparing or reporting on financial statements in applying the requirements of company law, accounting standards and other pronouncements by professional bodies. This book concentrates on the preparation and presentation of the directors' report and financial statements of limited companies which are neither plcs nor the subsidiaries of plcs.

The book contains a specimen set of financial statements for a private limited company together with supporting explanatory notes explaining the detailed financial reporting requirements. The model financial statements for Russell Square Enterprises Limited contain a directors' report, auditors' report, primary statements and notes. Russell Square Enterprises Limited is privately owned and is the parent company of a group. Russell Square Enterprises Limited and the members of its group qualify as small companies, and advantage has been taken of the exemption for small companies from preparing group financial statements. They have elected to prepare abbreviated accounts for filing with the Registrar of Companies which are also illustrated in this book. The model financial statements have been prepared using the full United Kingdom reporting framework. However, where alternative reduced disclosures are available, under Schedule 8 of the Companies Act 1985 and the Financial Reporting Standard for Smaller Entities (FRSSE), these are shown.

The model financial statements have been prepared to include as many items as possible for which there are statutory or quasi-statutory disclosure requirements. The financial statements and abbreviated accounts (pp. 1-47) are cross-referenced to the explanatory notes (pp. 49-220), which are in turn cross-referenced to the statutory or professional authority which sets out the specific requirement. These cross-references are shown in *italics* in the right-hand column of each page. Cross-references in the explanatory notes to other sections of the explanatory notes are shown in **bold**.

The *Model Financial Reporting Handbook* can be used to assist in drafting disclosures for inclusion in a set of financial statements. It can also be used to obtain an understanding of the details of a specific disclosure requirement, or to identify a specific authority. The book is intended to be of practical assistance to its readers and to help them apply the financial reporting requirements of company law and professional standards correctly in the financial statements of private limited companies.

References in this book are to:

- Companies Act 1985 (as amended by Companies Act 1989) – section references   *CA 1985*
  only are given.

- Financial Reporting Standards and Statements of Standard Accounting Practice   *FRS/SSAP*
- Financial Reporting Standard for Smaller Enterprises   *FRSSE*
- Financial Reporting Exposure Drafts issued by the Accounting Standards Board   *FRED*
- Urgent Issues Task Force   *UITF*
- International Accounting Standards   *IAS*
- Statements of Auditing Standards   *SAS*
- Practice Notes issued by the Auditing Practices Board   *PN*
- Accounting Recommendations issued by the Institute of Chartered Accountants in England and Wales   *AR*
- Institute Statements   *IS*
- The Stock Exchange requirements for listed companies   *SE*

The *Model Financial Reporting Handbook* has been prepared using United Kingdom statutory financial reporting requirements and accounting standards disclosures which are extant at 30 June 1999. The book includes all Financial Reporting Standards to FRS 15 *Tangible fixed assets* and all developments in company law to SI 1997/936 The Companies Act 1985 (Audit Exemption) (Amendment) Regulations 1997.

The terms 'accounts' and 'financial statements' are generally interchangeable. The latter terminology is used in the examples in this book but there is no reason why a company cannot adopt the word 'accounts'.

When this book went to press, a draft Statutory Instrument to raise the small and medium-sized company thresholds was under consideration. Increases in the existing thresholds of up to 40 per cent are expected later in 1999. A process of consultation was also beginning with the intention of raising the audit exemption threshold from the existing level of £350,000. No timetable for amending the legislation had been issued, and although there had been widespread speculation as to the new audit exemption threshold, no clear proposals had been issued.

RUSSELL SQUARE ENTERPRISES LIMITED

Financial Statements
30 September 1999

Marginal references on pp. 1-47 refer to the explanatory notes which begin on p.49.

RUSSELL SQUARE ENTERPRISES LIMITED

Financial statements for the year ended 30 September 1999

Contents   *Pages*

A list of contents is optional. Its inclusion is recommended if the financial statements are lengthy.

*A five-year summary of key ratios, profit and loss account and balance sheet information may be included.

3

RUSSELL SQUARE ENTERPRISES LIMITED

Directors, officers and advisers

Directors
K L Hill (Chairman)
D M Hill (Managing Director)
T R Hill
M J Wood
A King (Non-Executive)

Secretary and registered office
K R Wright
Whitefriars House
125 Thames Street
Reading
Berkshire
RG1 7VP

Registered number*
19961997

Auditors
Burlington & Greenslade
Chartered Accountants
Viking House
17 John Street
London
WC1B 3SD

Bankers
Western Counties Bank plc
St Peter's House
245 Thames Street
Reading
Berkshire
RG1 1LC

Solicitors
Birkett & Button
16 Canterbury Square
London
WC1D 6FR

An introductory page giving details of officers and advisers is optional. If it is included, the directors listed should normally be those at the date of the report. It is not appropriate to record appointments and resignations on this page.

*The company's registered number should also be shown in the top right corner of the cover page on the copy of the financial statements which is sent to Companies House for filing.

RUSSELL SQUARE ENTERPRISES LIMITED

Directors' report for the year ended 30 September 1999 [Full version]

The directors present their report and the financial statements of the company for the year ended 30 September 1999.

1.1

Review of the business

The principal activity of the company is the manufacture and selling of musical instruments. In November 1998 the company started manufacturing and selling furniture. The subsidiaries are principally concerned with the manufacture and wholesaling of car components.

1.2.1

Turnover has increased by 30 per cent to £2,081,959 during the year, partly due to the new trade in furniture although sales of musical instruments have continued to increase. The directors believe this was a creditable performance against the background of a difficult and increasingly competitive marketplace brought about by the general economic climate. With this in mind the directors looked carefully at the company's manufacturing facilities and have decided with reluctance to close the Brentford factory. The directors have estimated that the costs associated with the closure will be in the region of £77,500, including several redundancies.

1.2.2

The directors consider that the year-end financial position was satisfactory and that the company is now well placed to sustain the present level of activity in the foreseeable future, particularly in view of the company's recent move into the North American market.

1.2.3

Results and dividends

The results for the year ended 30 September 1999 are shown in the profit and loss account on page 6. The profit for the year after taxation was £166,615 after charging exceptional items of £20,300 which are detailed in note 8 to the financial statements and the factory closure costs noted above.

1.3

It is recommended that a final dividend of £43,800 should be paid on the ordinary shares, making a total for the year of £73,000, which with preference dividends of £3,150 leaves profit to be retained of £90,465.

Post balance sheet events

In line with the company's policy of long-term expansion and diversification through the acquisition of soundly based companies, the whole of the issued share capital of Clarendon Limited was acquired for £95,000 on 15 October 1999.

1.4

Clarendon Limited manufactures and sells office equipment and in the year to 31 March 1996 made an operating profit before tax of £21,000 on a turnover of £336,000.

Year 2000 and the euro

Year 2000

During the year the directors conducted an extensive review of the potential impact of the year 2000 'millennium bug' upon the group. Most existing systems and processes

14.1

RUSSELL SQUARE ENTERPRISES LIMITED

appear to be millennium compliant and a programme to modify the remaining systems and processes has been completed. The final reviews and testing of systems was completed shortly after the year end.

In 1999 the group incurred £100,000 costs in respect of year 2000 related projects. The directors do not anticipate that any further year 2000 systems modification costs will be incurred.

The company's programme has included working with its leading customers and suppliers to minimise the risks to the business from third-party systems. Actions taken have included requesting confirmation on the status of third parties' programmes to address the problem, and commissioning suppliers to test equipment that they have supplied to the company.

The euro

The directors have considered the implications of the introduction of the euro upon the activities of the company. The existing systems allow transactions to be recorded in euros. It is anticipated that contracts with several European customers will, in future, be priced in euros.   *14.2*

Next year, the systems of Russell Square Enterprises GmbH will be converted to enable all activities to be conducted using the euro. The expected cost of the sytems changes required and the retraining of staff is £15,000.

Directors

The directors who served during the year were: *1.5.1*

K L Hill (Chairman)
D M Hill
T R Hill
M J Wood
A King (appointed 12 March 1999)   *1.5.2*
A R Hill (resigned 14 June 1999)

Mr A King having been appointed since the last annual general meeting retires and,   *1.5.2*
being eligible, offers himself for re-election. The director retiring by rotation, in
accordance with the articles of association, is Mr T R Hill who, being eligible,
offers himself for re-election.

Directors' responsibilities

Company law requires the directors to prepare financial statements which give a   *1.1(b)*
true and fair view of the state of affairs of the company at the end of its financial
year and of the profit or loss of the company for the year then ended. In preparing
those financial statements, the directors are required to:

- select suitable accounting policies and apply them consistently;
- make judgements and estimates that are reasonable and prudent;
- state whether applicable accounting standards have been followed, subject to any
  material departures disclosed and explained in the financial statements*;

Page 2

Not mandatory for companies entitled to file abbreviated accounts.

RUSSELL SQUARE ENTERPRISES LIMITED

- prepare the financial statements on the going concern basis unless it is inappropriate to presume that the company will continue in business.

The directors are responsible for keeping proper accounting records which disclose with reasonable accuracy at any time the financial position of the company and to enable them to ensure that the financial statements comply with the Companies Act 1985. They are also responsible for safeguarding the assets of the company and hence for taking reasonable steps for the prevention and detection of fraud and other irregularities.

Directors' interests in shares and debentures*

The beneficial interests of the directors and their families in the share capital of the company were as follows:

1.6

	30 September 1999		1 October 1998	
	Ordinary	*3.15% preference*	*Ordinary*	*3.15% preference*
K L Hill	110,575	20,000	110,575	20,000
D M Hill	51,460	15,000	56,390	30,000
T R Hill	2,025	–	525	–
M J Wood	27,500	–	20,000	–
A King	500	–	†500	–

† held on appointment on 12 March 1999.

Interests in land

The directors are of the opinion that, on an existing use basis, the value of land and buildings is £285,000 in excess of book values. If the properties were disposed of at the estimated values, tax payable on the capital gain arising would be approximately £78,000. At present the directors have no plans to make any major sales.

1.7

Research and development

The company continues to be committed to research and development in order to maintain its position as market leader in sectors of the percussion instrument market. The expenditure written off this year includes the costs of a three-year research project into the use of plastics in the production of percussion instruments.

1.8

Employees**

Arrangements exist to keep all employees informed on matters of concern to them and information on company performance and prospects is disseminated widely. Employees are encouraged to be concerned with the performance and efficiency of the company and various profit-sharing and bonus schemes, including a profit-related pay scheme, operate to emphasise and reinforce this.

1.9

Page 3

*May alternatively be dealt with in the notes to the financial statements.

**Mandatory for companies with more than 250 employees, otherwise disclosure is optional.*

Disabled employees*

Disabled employees are employed by the company having regard to their aptitudes and abilities. There is a training scheme in operation so that employees who have been injured or become disabled can, where possible, continue employment within the company.

1.10

Political and charitable contributions

Contributions made by the company during the year for political and charitable purposes were:

1.11

Political – Aims for Industry   £250
Charitable   £4,675

Auditors

A resolution to reappoint Burlington & Greenslade as auditors of the company will be proposed at the forthcoming annual general meeting.

1.12

[OR where advantage is taken of the Companies Act dispensation not to reappoint auditors annually

The company has elected to dispense with the annual requirement to reappoint auditors and accordingly Burlington & Greenslade will continue to act as auditors to the company.]

Signed on behalf of the board

K R WRIGHT
Secretary

Approved by the Board on 29 November 1999.

1.14

Additional disclosures in the directors' report will arise where a company has purchased or has an interest in its own shares.   *1.13*

*Mandatory for companies with more than 250 employees, otherwise disclosure is optional.

RUSSELL SQUARE ENTERPRISES LIMITED

Directors' report for the year ended 30 September 1999 [Simplified version]

The directors present their report and the financial statements of the company for the year ended 30 September 1999.

16.2

Principal activity

The principal activity of the company is the manufacture and selling of musical instruments. In November 1998 the company started manufacturing and selling furniture. The subsidiaries are principally concerned with the manufacture and wholesaling of car components.

Directors

The directors who served during the year were:

1.5.1

K L Hill (Chairman)
D M Hill
T R Hill
M J Wood
A King (appointed 12 March 1999)
A R Hill (resigned 14 June 1999)

1.5.2

Mr A King having been appointed since the last annual general meeting retires and, being eligible, offers himself for re-election. The director retiring by rotation, in accordance with the articles of association, is Mr T R Hill who, being eligible, offers himself for re-election.

1.5.2

Directors' responsibilities

Company law requires the directors to prepare financial statements which give a true and fair view of the state of affairs of the company at the end of its financial year and of the profit or loss of the company for the year then ended. In preparing those financial statements, the directors are required to:

1.1(b)

- select suitable accounting policies and apply them consistently;
- make judgements and estimates that are reasonable and prudent;
- prepare the financial statements on the going concern basis unless it is inappropriate to presume that the company will continue in business.

The directors are responsible for keeping proper accounting records which disclose with reasonable accuracy at any time the financial position of the company and to enable them to ensure that the financial statements comply with the Companies Act 1985. They are also responsible for safeguarding the assets of the company and hence for taking reasonable steps for the prevention and detection of fraud and other irregularities.

RUSSELL SQUARE ENTERPRISES LIMITED

Directors' interests in shares and debentures*

The beneficial interests of the directors and their families in the share capital of the company were as follows:

1.6

	30 September 1999		1 October 1998	
	Ordinary	3.15% preference	Ordinary	3.15% preference
K L Hill	110,575	20,000	110,575	20,000
D M Hill	51,460	15,000	56,390	30,000
T R Hill	2,025	–	525	–
M J Wood	27,500	–	20,000	–
A King	500	–	†500	–

† held on appointment on 12 March 1999.

Political and charitable contributions

Contributions made by the company during the year for political and charitable purposes were:

1.11

Political – Aims for Industry	£250
Charitable	£4,675

Auditors

A resolution to reappoint Burlington & Greenslade as auditors of the company will be proposed at the forthcoming annual general meeting.

1.13

[OR where advantage is taken of the Companies Act dispensation not to reappoint auditors annually

The company has elected to dispense with the annual requirement to reappoint auditors and accordingly Burlington & Greenslade will continue to act as auditors to the company.]

The above report has been prepared in accordance with the special provisions of Part VII of the Companies Act 1985 relating to small companies.

Signed on behalf of the board

K R WRIGHT
Secretary

Approved by the Board on 29 November 1999.

1.15

May alternatively be dealt with in the notes to the financial statements.

Auditors' report to the members of Russell Square Enterprises Limited

2.1–2.3

We have audited the financial statements on pages 6 to 26 which have been prepared under the historical cost convention, as modified to include the revaluation of certain freehold land and buildings, and the accounting policies set out on pages 10 to 12.

Respective responsibilities of directors and auditors

As described on page 2 the company's directors are responsible for the preparation of financial statements. It is our responsibility to form an independent opinion, based on our audit, on those statements and to report our opinion to you.

Basis of opinion

We conducted our audit in accordance with auditing standards issued by the Auditing Practices Board. An audit includes examination, on a test basis, of evidence relevant to the amounts and disclosures in the financial statements. It also includes an assessment of the significant estimates and judgements made by the directors in the preparation of the financial statements, and of whether the accounting policies are appropriate to the company's circumstances, consistently applied and adequately disclosed.

We planned and performed our audit so as to obtain all the information and explanations which we considered necessary in order to provide us with sufficient evidence to give reasonable assurance that the financial statements are free from material misstatement, whether caused by fraud or other irregularity or error. In forming our opinion we also evaluated the overall adequacy of the presentation of information in the financial statements.

Opinion

In our opinion the financial statements give a true and fair view of the state of the company's affairs at 30 September 1999 and of its profit for the year then ended and have been properly prepared in accordance with the Companies Act 1985.

BURLINGTON & GREENSLADE

Chartered Accountants
Registered Auditors

LONDON

29 November 1999

Page 5

11

RUSSELL SQUARE ENTERPRISES LIMITED

Profit and loss account for the year ended 30 September 1999 [Format 1]

4.1.1

	Notes*	1999 £	As restated 1998 £	
Turnover	2	**2,081,959**	1,600,091	4.2
Cost of sales		**1,361,601**	1,104,063	4.3
Gross profit		**720,358**	496,028	
Distribution costs		**104,319**	62,387	4.5.1
Administrative expenses		**352,272**	178,967	4.5.2
		456,591	241,354	
Other operating income	3	**(95,383)**	(42,800)	4.5.3
Net operating expenses		**361,208**	198,554	4.5
Operating profit		**359,150**	297,474	4.1.7
Provision for closure of factory	19	**(77,500)**	–	8.12
Income from fixed asset investments		**2,650**	1,512	4.7
Interest payable and similar charges	4	**(11,801)**	(5,219)	4.16
Profit on ordinary activities before taxation	5	**272,499**	293,767	4.6
Tax on profit on ordinary activities	9	**105,884**	118,654	4.19
Profit for the financial year		**166,615**	175,113	4.21
Dividends (in respect of equity and non-equity shares)	10	**76,150**	76,150	4.22
Retained profit for the year	21	**90,465**	98,963	4.23

None of the company's activities was acquired or discontinued during the above two financial years.

4.1.5

The notes on pages 10 to 26 form part of these financial statements. Details of the restatement of the 1998 figures and a prior year adjustment are given in note 14.

Sundry matters relating to the profit and loss account are set out in the explanatory notes, pp. 67-96.

*Notes refers to the notes to the accounts on pages 10 to 26.

The disclosures in the shaded boxes are not required if the FRSSE is adopted.

RUSSELL SQUARE ENTERPRISES LIMITED

Profit and loss account for the year ended 30 September 1999 [Format 2]

4.1.1

	Notes	1999 £	As restated 1998 £	
Turnover	2	**2,081,959**	1,600,091	4.2
Change in stocks of finished goods and work in progress		**61,330**	140,238	4.4(a)
		2,143,289	1,740,329	
Other operating income	3	**95,383**	42,800	4.5.3
		2,238,672	1,783,129	
Raw materials and consumables		**526,889**	239,279	4.4(c)
Other external charges		**10,516**	6,332	4.5.4
		537,405	245,611	
		1,701,267	1,537,518	
Staff costs	7	**1,003,875**	1,064,587	4.17
Depreciation and amortisation		**53,603**	39,766	4.10
Other operating charges		**284,639**	135,691	4.5.4
		1,342,117	1,240,044	
Operating profit		**359,150**	297,474	4.1.7
Provision for closure of factory	19	**(77,500)**	–	8.12
Income from fixed asset investments		**2,650**	1,512	4.7
Interest payable and similar charges	4	**(11,801)**	(5,219)	4.16
Profit on ordinary activities before taxation	5	**272,499**	293,767	4.6
Tax on profit on ordinary activities	9	**105,884**	118,654	4.19
Profit for the financial year		**166,615**	175,113	4.21
Dividends (in respect of equity and non-equity shares)	10	**76,150**	76,150	4.22
Retained profit for the year	21	**90,465**	98,963	4.23

None of the company's activities was acquired or discontinued during the above two financial years.

4.1.5

The notes on pages 10 to 26 form part of these financial statements. Details of the restatement of the 1998 figures and a prior year adjustment are given in note 14.

Page 6A

Sundry matters relating to the profit and loss account are set out in the explanatory notes, pp. 67-96.

The disclosures in the shaded boxes are not required if the FRSSE is adopted.

RUSSELL SQUARE ENTERPRISES LIMITED

Statement of total recognised gains and losses*

	1999 £	As restated 1998 £
Profit for the financial year	**166,615**	175,113
Exchange adjustment on net investments in overseas operations	**11,075**	–
Total recognised gains and losses relating to the year	**177,690**	175,113
Prior year adjustment relating to 1998 and before (as explained in note 14)	**40,841**	
Total gains and losses recognised since last annual report	**218,531**	

Note of historical cost profits and losses**

	1999 £	As restated 1998 £
Reported profit on ordinary activities before taxation	**272,499**	293,767
Difference between a historical cost depreciation charge and the actual depreciation charge of the year calculated on the revalued amount	**1,199**	1,199
Historical cost profit on ordinary activities before taxation	**273,698**	294,966
Historical profit for the year retained after taxation and dividends	**91,664**	100,162

The notes on pages 10 to 26 form part of these financial statements. Details of the restatement of the 1998 figures and a prior year adjustment are given in note 14.

Page 7

Other items which might feature here include unrealised surplus (or deficit) on revaluation of properties and unrealised gains (or losses) on investments. Where there are no gains or losses other than the profit or loss for the period a statement of this fact should immediately follow the profit and loss account. The following wording is suggested:
    'The company has no recognised gains and losses other than those included in the profits above and therefore no separate statement of total recognised gains and losses has been presented.'

Such a statement is not required when the accounts are prepared in accordance with the FRSSE.

**This statement is included for illustrative purposes only as in normal circumstances details would only be given where there was a material difference between the actual results and the results restated on an unmodified historical cost basis. The major category of items likely to be included here is the realisation of property revaluation gains of previous years. Where a note of historical cost profits and losses is not required the following wording is suggested:*
    'There is no difference between the profits shown above and their historical cost equivalents.'

The FRSSE does not require the presentation of a note of historical cost profit and losses, or the wording explaining why it is not required.

RUSSELL SQUARE ENTERPRISES LIMITED

Balance sheet at 30 September 1999

	Notes	1999 £	As restated 1998 £	
Fixed assets				6
Intangible assets	11	**10,000**	13,000	6.3
Tangible assets	12	**191,690**	92,483	6.5
Investments	13	**103,950**	94,700	6.8
		305,640	200,183	
Current assets				7
Stocks	14	**420,792**	288,898	7.2
Debtors	15	**656,137**	456,932	7.3
Cash at bank and in hand		**12,239**	39,050	7.6
		1,089,168	784,880	
Creditors: amounts falling due within one year	16	**(500,436)**	(392,677)	8.1.1
Net current assets		**588,732**	392,203	8.8
Total assets less current liabilities		**894,372**	592,386	8.9
Creditors: amounts falling due after more than one year	17	**(134,000)**	(37,000)	8.1.2
Provisions for liabilities and charges				8.12
Deferred taxation	18	**(19,592)**	(5,286)	8.13
Reorganisation provision	19	**(77,500)**	–	8.12
		(97,059)	(5,286)	8.13
Accruals & deferred income				
Deferred government grants		**(18,900)**	(7,260)	8.14
		644,380	542,840	8.15
				10.1
Capital and reserves				
Called-up share capital	20	**375,000**	375,000	10.3 & 10.4
Share premium account	21	**20,000**	20,000	10.5
Revaluation reserve	21	**65,415**	66,614	10.6
Profit and loss account	21	**183,965**	81,226	10.5
Shareholders' funds (including non-equity interests)	22	**644,380**	542,840	10.2

[The financial statements have been prepared in accordance with the special provisions of Part VII of the Companies Act 1985 relating to small companies] [and in accordance with the Financial Reporting Standard for Smaller Entities].*

Approved by the Board on 29 November 1999 and signed on its behalf.

.... **K L HILL – Director**

11.1

The notes on pages 10 to 25 form part of these financial statements. Details of the restatement of the 1998 figures and a prior year adjustment are given in note 14.

Page 8

The FRSSE does not require the disclosure of shareholders' funds.
*These statements should be included if advantage has been taken of the simplified accounts provisions and if the FRSSE has been adopted.

RUSSELL SQUARE ENTERPRISES LIMITED

Cash flow statement for the year ended 30 September 1999

	Notes	1999 £	As restated 1998 £
Operating activities			
Net cash inflow from operating activities	23a	**144,927**	96,134
Returns on investments and servicing of finance			
Dividends received		**2,120**	1,512
Preference dividends paid		**(3,150)**	(3,150)
Interest paid		**(10,951)**	(4,277)
Interest element of finance lease payments		**(850)**	(942)
Net cash outflow from returns on investments and servicing of finance		**(12,831)**	(6,857)
Taxation			
Corporation tax paid		**(54,289)**	(11,327)
Capital investment and financial investment			
Payments to acquire tangible fixed assets		**(164,965)**	(20,762)
Grants received in respect of capital expenditure		**14,340**	–
Payments to acquire listed investments		**(9,250)**	–
Receipts from sale of tangible fixed assets		**18,007**	7,500
Net cash outflow from investing activities		**(141,868)**	(13,262)
Equity dividends paid		**(71,200)**	(31,000)
Net cash flow before financing		**(135,261)**	33,688
Financing			
Issue of debenture stock		**100,000**	–
Increase in short term loans		**500**	–
Long term debt repaid		**(2,000)**	(5,000)
Finance leases – capital repayments		**(1,150)**	(1,250)
Net cash inflow/(outflow) from financing		**97,350**	(6,250)
(Decrease)/increase in cash	23c	**(37,911)**	27,438

The notes on pages 10 to 25 form part of these financial statements. Details of the restatement of the 1998 figures and a prior year adjustment are given in note 14.

Page 9

As *Russell Square Enterprises Limited is a small company it is not required to prepare a cash flow statement. The above example is prepared for illustrative purposes only.*

The FRSSE encourages the presentation of cash flow statements and contains an illustrative simplified cash flow statement. There is no compulsion for entities to present a cash flow statement, and in practice the simplified statement is very rare.

RUSSELL SQUARE ENTERPRISES LIMITED

Notes to the financial statements for the year ended 30 September 1999

1 Accounting policies

11.9

Basis of accounting

11.10

The financial statements are prepared on the historical cost basis of accounting, as modified to include the revaluation of certain freehold land and buildings [and are prepared in accordance with applicable accounting standards]* [and in accordance with the Financial Reporting Standard for Smaller Entities].**

Consolidation

6.8.1

The company and its subsidiaries comprise a small group. The company has therefore taken advantage of the exemption provided in section 248 of the Companies Act 1985 not to prepare group financial statements and accordingly these financial statements present information about the company as a single undertaking.

Depreciation of tangible fixed assets

4.11

Depreciation is not charged on freehold land nor on expenditure on assets not yet in use. Depreciation on other tangible fixed assets is charged so as to write off their full costs or valuation less estimated residual values over their expected useful lives at the following rates:

Freehold buildings	– $2\frac{1}{2}$% of cost or valuation per annum
Leasehold property	– by equal annual instalments over the term of the lease
Plant and machinery	– 15% of cost per annum
Motor vehicles	– 25% of cost per annum
Fixtures, fittings, tools and equipment	– 10% of cost per annum

Goodwill

6.4

Goodwill representing the excess of the purchase price over the fair value of the net assets of and unincorporated business acquired in 1992 is amortised by equal annual instalments over its expected useful economic life of 10 years.

Stocks

7.2

Stocks and work in progress are valued at the lower of cost and net realisable value.

Cost of raw materials is determined on the first in first out basis. In the case of work in progress and finished goods, cost includes all direct expenditure and production overheads based on the normal level of activity. Net realisable value is the price at which the stock can be realised in the normal course of business, less further costs to completion and sale.

Page 10

*Not mandatory for companies entitled to file abbreviated accounts.

**This statement is required when the accounts are presented in accordance with the FRSSE.

The shaded accounting policies on pages 10–12 are not required to be presented if the accounts are prepared under the FRSSE. However, their disclosure may be appropriate to show the true and fair view or because the policies are material or critical to preparing the accounts.

RUSSELL SQUARE ENTERPRISES LIMITED

8.13

Deferred taxation

Deferred taxation is provided under the liability method in respect of all material timing differences between the profits as computed for taxation purposes and the profits as stated in the financial statements, to the extent that it is probable that a liability or asset will crystallise. The rate of tax used is that which is expected to be applied when the liability or asset is expected to crystallise.

4.8

Deferred government grants

Government grants in respect of capital expenditure are treated as deferred income and are credited to the profit and loss account over the estimated useful life of the assets to which they relate.

4.26

Foreign currencies

Assets and liabilities denominated in foreign currencies are translated into sterling at the rates ruling at the year end. The trading results of overseas operations are translated at average rates of exchange for the year.

Exchange differences arising from the retranslation of the opening net investment in overseas operations and from translating their trading results at average and closing rates of exchange are taken directly to retained profits. All other gains and losses on exchange are dealt with in the profit and loss account.

4.9

Research and development expenditure

Research and development expenditure is written off as it is incurred, with the exception of certain machinery and equipment which is capitalised and depreciated over its expected useful life.

9.2

Hire purchase and lease transactions

Assets acquired under hire purchase agreements and finance leases are capitalised in the balance sheet and are depreciated in accordance with the company's normal policy. The outstanding liabilities under such agreements less interest not yet due are included in creditors. Interest on such agreements is charged to profit and loss account over the term of each agreement and represents a constant proportion of the balance of capital repayments outstanding.

Rentals under operating leases are charged to the profit and loss account as they fall due.

RUSSELL SQUARE ENTERPRISES LIMITED

4.18

Pensions

EITHER – for defined benefit scheme
The company provides a defined benefit pension scheme, the assets of which are held separately from those of the company in an independently administered fund. Contributions to the scheme are charged to profit and loss account so as to spread the regular cost of pensions over the employees' service lives within the group. Variances from regular cost are spread over the remaining service lives of the current employees.

OR – for defined contribution scheme
The company provides a defined contribution pension scheme, the assets of which are held separately from those of the company in an independently administered fund. Contributions to this scheme are charged to the profit and loss account as they become payable.

2 Turnover*

Turnover represents the amounts receivable for goods sold during the year, exclusive of VAT. 4.2

The contributions of the various activities of the company to turnover which are in respect of continuing activities are set out below: 4.2.2

	1999 £	1998 £
By activity:		
Musical instruments	**1,781,741**	1,600,091
Furniture	**300,218**	–
	2,081,959	1,600,091
By geographical market		
United Kingdom	**1,410,944**	1,098,449
Rest of European Union	**633,051**	501,642
North America	**37,964**	–
	2,081,959	1,600,091

Turnover attributable to geographical markets outside the United Kingdom amounted to 32% (1998 – 31%).

3 Other operating income

16

	1999 £	1998 £
Exchange gains	**44,700**	–
Government grants credited	**2,700**	1,100
Other income	**47,983**	41,700
	95,383	42,800

4.5.3
4.8

The shaded box sets the sole disclosure requirement when simplified accounts are prepared.

RUSSELL SQUARE ENTERPRISES LIMITED

4 Interest payable and similar charges

	1999 £	1998 £	
On bank loan and overdraft	**926**	2,212	4.16
On obligations under finance leases	**850**	942	
On other loans	**10,025**	2,065	
	11,801	5,219	

5 Profit on ordinary activities before taxation

This is stated after charging:	1999 £	1998 £	
Research and development expenditure*	**23,591**	67,757	4.9
Amortisation of goodwill	**3,000**	3,000	6.4
Depreciation	**50,603**	36,766	4.11
Loss on disposal of tangible fixed assets	**1,424**	1,250	
Operating lease rentals:**			4.12
Land and buildings	**26,500**	14,250	
Plant and machinery	**16,540**	8,790	
Directors' emoluments (note 6)	**253,485**	212,947	4.13
Auditors' remuneration:			4.14
In respect of audit services	**7,100**	6,500	
Other services***	**10,000**	4,000	
Exceptional items (note 8)	**20,300**	29,250	4.15

6 Directors' emoluments****

	1999 £	1998 £	
Emoluments*****	**253,485**	212,947	4.13
Company contributions paid to defined contribution pension scheme*****	**3,500**	3,000	

Three directors (1998 – 3) are members of the group's defined benefit pension scheme.

One director (1998 – 1) is a member of the group's defined contribution benefit pension scheme.

The highest paid director received remuneration of £70,317 (1998 – £60,708). The accumulated total accrued pension provision of the highest paid director was £37,205 at 31 December 1999 (1998 – £31,106).

Page 13

*Not required for a private company which is within 10 times medium-size criteria.

**Under the FRSSE there is no requirement to disclose operating lease rentals for the period.

***Not required if company is entitled to file abbreviated accounts.

****If directors' emoluments are under £200,000 these disclosures are not required.

*****A small company's individual accounts may give the aggregate in total of (a) directors' emoluments (for services as director or management of the company or any subsidiary), (b) amounts receivable under long-term incentive schemes, and (c) company pension contributions to money purchase schemes (s246(3) following SI 1997 No. 570).

The interest payable and similar charges note is not required when simplified accounts are prepared.

RUSSELL SQUARE ENTERPRISES LIMITED

Gresham Studios, a partnership in which Mr A King is a partner, received fees amounting to £2,000 in respect of the services of Mr A King as a non-executive director.

4.13.6

7 Employee information

4.17.2

	1999 £	1998 £
Staff costs:		
Wages and salaries	**881,402**	933,643
Social security costs	**83,322**	88,361
Other pension costs	**39,151**	42,583
	1,003,875	1,064,587

The average number of persons employed during the year, including executive directors, was made up as follows:

4.17.1

	1999 Number	1998 Number
Manufacturing	**30**	33
Distribution	**8**	9
Administration	**6**	7
	44	49

8 Exceptional items

4.14

Exceptional items which are summarised below have been classified within the profit and loss account under the appropriate heading and arise in respect of continuing operations.

	1999 £	1998 £
Cost of sales:		
Obsolete stocks written off	–	102,500
Provision for loss on contract no longer required	–	(73,250)
	–	29,250

	1999 £	1998 £
Administrative expenses:		
Bad debts provision	**65,000**	–
Realised profit arising from fluctuations in foreign exchange rates during the year	**(44,700)**	–
	65,000	29,250

When simplified accounts are prepared, the disclosures of employee information are not required.

RUSSELL SQUARE ENTERPRISES LIMITED

9 Tax on profit on ordinary activities

4.19

United Kingdom corporation tax at 30% (1998 – 31%)	**82,757**	99,020
Tax attributable to franked investment income	**530**	378
Double taxation relief	**(484)**	(150)
Overseas taxation	**1,217**	351
Deferred taxation (note 18)	**13,062**	3,480
Adjustment in respect of previous years*	**8,802**	15,575
	105,884	118,654

The effective rate of United Kingdom corporation tax for the current year and the preceding year is higher than normal by virtue of the disallowance of certain expenditure for tax purposes. The exceptional items arising in the year do not have a material effect on the corporation tax charge.

4.19.2

Unprovided deferred taxation for the year amounts to £28,200 in respect of accelerated capital allowances.

4.19.2

10 Dividends

4.22

	1999 £	1998 £
On equity shares:		
Interim of 2.655p per ordinary share paid 20 June 1999 (June 1998 – 2.818p)	**29,200**	31,000
Proposed final 3.981p per ordinary share payable 17 April 2000 (April 1999 – 3.818p)	**43,800**	42,000
Making a total of 6.636p per share (1998 – 6.636p)	**73,000**	73,000
On non-equity shares:		
Preference dividend paid 20 June 1999	**3,150**	3,150
	76,150	76,150

The FRSSE does not require the detailed supporting note to dividends paid and proposed.
*The FRSSE does not require the separate disclosure of corporation tax liabilities relating to different periods or under or over provisions in respect of previous periods.

RUSSELL SQUARE ENTERPRISES LIMITED

11 Intangible fixed assets

6.3–6.4

	Goodwill £
Cost:	
At 1 October 1998 and 30 September 1999	**30,000**
Amortisation:	
At 1 October 1998	17,000
Provision for the year	3,000
At 30 September 1999	**20,000**
Net book value:	
At 30 September 1999	**10,000**
At 30 September 1998	13,000

12 Tangible fixed assets

6.5

	Land and buildings Freehold £	Short leasehold £	Plant, machinery, & motor vehicles £	Fixtures, fittings, tools & equipment £	Total £
Cost or valuation:					
At 1 October 1998	158,824	37,545	72,253	6,730	275,352
Exchange adjustments	–	4,662	2,394	–	7,056
Additions	–	36,870	128,095	–	164,965
Disposals	–	(29,574)	(39,433)	–	(69,007)
At 30 September 1999	**158,824**	**49,503**	**163,309**	**6,730**	**378,366**
Depreciation:					
At 1 October 1998	79,783	30,470	66,020	6,596	182,869
Exchange adjustments	–	1,630	1,150	–	2,780
Provision for the year	2,859	4,950	42,661	133	50,603
Adjustments for disposals	–	(29,574)	(20,002)	–	(49,576)
At 30 September 1999	**82,642**	**7,476**	**89,829**	**6,729**	**186,676**
Net book value:					
At 30 September 1999	**76,182**	**42,027**	**73,480**	**1**	**191,690**
At 30 September 1998	79,041	7,075	6,233	134	92,483

RUSSELL SQUARE ENTERPRISES LIMITED

Cost or valuation of freehold land and buildings is as follows:	£	
		6.5.12
At cost	71,969	
At valuation		
1991 (open market for existing use)	30,000	
1995 (open market for existing use)	56,855	
	158,824	

Under the transitional provisions of FRS 15 *Tangible fixed assets* the book value of freehold land and buildings of £158,824 is to be retained and no further revaluations will take place. — 6.5.14

Included in the figure of cost or valuation is freehold land of £44,464 which is not being depreciated. On an historical cost basis, land and buildings would have been included as follows: — 6.5.12 / 5.4.3

	1999 £	1998 £
Cost	71,969	71,969
Accumulated depreciation	(61,202)	(59,542)
Net book value	10,767	12,427

Included within fixed assets are assets held under finance leases as follows:* — 9.3.1

	Plant and machinery £	Fixtures and fittings £
Net book value	5,420	1
Depreciation provided during the year	1,670	133

13 Investments

6.8

	Shares in subsidiary undertakings £	Listed investments £	Unlisted investment £	Total £
Cost:				
At 1 October 1998	70,500	14,200	10,000	94,700
Additions	–	9,250	–	9,250
At 30 September 1999	70,500	23,450	10,000	103,950

The following information relates to the fixed asset investments:

Subsidiary undertakings

6.8.2

Registered in England and Wales
Clutch Assemblies Limited (100% of equity capital owned)
Registered in Scotland
Clutch Plates Limited (50% of equity owned directly; 25% indirectly)
Incorporated in Germany
Russell Square Enterprises GmbH (51% of equity capital owned)

Page 17

The FRSSE permits the analysis required by this disclosure to be restricted to 1) land and buildings and 2) " other assets".

In this example, the disclosures for separate classes may therefore be combined. The draft 1999 FRSSE does not require the shaded disclosures.

RUSSELL SQUARE ENTERPRISES LIMITED

Clutch Assemblies Limited and Clutch Plates Limited operate mainly in Great Britain, Russell Square Enterprises GmbH operates mainly in Germany and Denmark.

The aggregate of the share capital and reserves as at 30 September 1999 and the profit or loss for the year ended on that date for the subsidiary undertakings were as follows:

	Aggregate of share capital and reserves £	Profit/ (loss) £
Clutch Assemblies Limited	52,739	8,412
Clutch Plates Limited	25,507	(7,195)
Russell Square Enterprises GmbH	80,170	30,467

Listed investments

The market value of the listed investments at 30 September 1999 was £41,430 (1998 – £28,000).

Unlisted investment

The unlisted investment represents the company's 15% interest in the equity capital of Airport Instruments Limited, which is registered in England and Wales.

14 Stocks

	1999 £	As restated 1998 £
Raw materials	132,760	62,196
Work in progress	79,193	56,213
Finished goods and goods for resale	208,839	170,489
	420,792	288,898

Finished goods would amount to £245,326 (1998 – £203,129) if valued at current production cost at 30 September 1999.

The basis of valuation of stocks and work in progress was changed during the year ended 30 September 1999 to include all overheads attributable to the stage of production reached, in accordance with Statement of Standard Accounting Practice 9.

To conform with this change in accounting policy, the valuation of stocks and work in progress at 30 September 1998 has been increased by £40,841 and the comparative figures in these financial statements have been restated accordingly. In restating the results for the year ended 30 September 1998, £13,904 has been credited to the profit for that year. The balance of increased profits relating to earlier years, £26,937, has been credited to retained profits at 30 September 1997.

The directors estimate that the effect of the changes in accounting policy on the profit for the year to 30 September 1999 is a credit to the profit of £16,500.

Page 18

The FRSSE does not require stocks to be subdivided

25

RUSSELL SQUARE ENTERPRISES LIMITED

15 Debtors

	1999 £	1998 £	
Trade debtors	275,675	211,650	
Amounts owed by subsidiary undertakings	356,555	229,800	7.4
Other debtors*	4,065	–	
Prepayments and accrued income	19,842	15,482	
	656,137	456,932	

Trade debtors includes an amount of £15,000 which is due after one year (1998 – £Nil).

7.3

Included in other debtors is a loan to a director, Mr M J Wood, which is an interest-free season ticket loan of £2,000 (1998 – £Nil), repayable by monthly instalments. The maximum sum outstanding during the year was £2,500.

7.5

16 Creditors: amounts falling due within one year [full accounts]

8.1.1

	1999 £	1998 £	
Current instalments due on long-term loans (secured – note 17)	3,000	3,000	
Bank overdraft (secured – note 17)	34,350	23,250	
Short-term loan	8,000	10,000	
Obligations under finance leases (note 17)	1,000	1,150	9
Loan from a former director	8,250	5,750	8.11
Trade creditors	96,334	72,423	
Amounts owed to subsidiary undertakings	69,930	52,645	
Corporation tax	170,300	133,541	
Other taxes and social security	24,670	19,845	
Proposed dividend (note 10)	43,800	42,000	8.7
Other creditors	13,157	10,041	
Accruals and deferred income	27,645	19,032	8.6
	500,436	392,677	

*Schedule 8 allows these items to be combined as 'other debtors'

RUSSELL SQUARE ENTERPRISES LIMITED

16 Creditors: amounts falling due within one year [simplified accounts and FRSSE]

16.1.3

	1999 £	1998 £
Bank loans and overdrafts	37,350	26,250
Obligations under finance leases	1,000	1,150
Trade creditors	96,334	74,423
Amounts owed to subsidiary undertakings	69,930	52,645
Taxation and social security	194,970	153,386
Other creditors	100,852	86,823
	500,436	392,677

9
8.10

RUSSELL SQUARE ENTERPRISES LIMITED

17 Creditors: amounts falling due after more than one year

8.1.2

	1999 £	1998 £
Amounts repayable after five years:		
8½% Debenture Stock repayable at par between 2012 and 2017 (secured)	100,000	–
8½% Mortgage repayable at par on 30 June 2008 (secured)	10,500	10,500
6% Unsecured loan repayable at par on 31 March 2005	10,500	10,500
	121,000	21,000
Amounts repayable within five years – bank loan (secured)	12,000	14,000
Total debt	133,000	35,000
Less: amounts included in current liabilities (note 16)	(3,000)	(3,000)
	130,000	32,000
Obligations under finance leases are payable:*		
Between one and two years	1,000	1,150
Between two and five years	3,000	3,850
	134,000	37,000

8.1.3

9

On 23 November 1999 the company issued at par £100,000 8½% Debenture Stock redeemable 2012/2017. This stock was issued for the purpose of providing the necessary capital to enable the company to start the manufacture of furniture.

8.2

The debenture stock, mortgage, bank loan and overdraft which total £167,350 are secured by a fixed and floating charge over the freehold properties and other assets of the company. Obligations under finance leases which total £5,000 are secured on the assets to which they relate (note 12).

8.1.4

The maturity of total debt may be analysed as follows:**

	1999 £	1998 £
In one year or less	3,000	3,000
Between one and two years	3,000	3,000
Between two and five years	6,000	8,000
Over five years	121,000	21,000
	133,000	35,000

8.2.1

Page 20

The FRSSE allows disclosure of a single aggregated figure for "obligations under finance leases".
**This disclosure is not required by the FRSSE.*

RUSSELL SQUARE ENTERPRISES LIMITED

18 Deferred taxation

| | 1999 | | 1998 | |
	Amount provided £	Amount not provided £	Amount provided £	Amount not provided £
Accelerated capital allowances	**31,453**	**39,200**	17,893	11,000
Other timing differences	**(911)**	–	(413)	–
	30,542	**39,200**	17,480	11,000
Advance corporation tax	**(10,950)**	–	(12,194)	–
	19,592	**39,200**	5,286	11,000

Movement during the year:	£
At 1 October 1998	5,286
Provision for the year	13,062
	18,348
Change in ACT recoverable	1,244
At 30 September 1999	**19,592**

The provision for deferred taxation has been calculated based on a corporation tax rate of 30% (1998 – 31%).

No account has been taken of potential taxation liabilities amounting to £18,500 (1998 – £19,000) which might arise on the disposal of properties at their revalued amounts as these properties are retained for use in the business and the likelihood of any material liability arising is remote.

If the company's listed investments were realised at their market value the liability to taxation on the capital gain would amount to approximately £5,300.

Deferred tax is also not recognised on earnings retained overseas in Russell Square Enterprises GmbH as these earnings are earmarked for the continued development of that company and will not be remitted in the foreseeable future.

8.13.1

Page 21

The shaded items above are not required if the FRSSE is applied.

RUSSELL SQUARE ENTERPRISES LIMITED

19 Provisions

	£	
Reorganisation provisions		8.12
Balance at 1st October 1998	–	
Profit and Loss Account Charge	77,500	
Balance at 30 September 1999	77,500	

On 21 September 1999, the directors announced their intention to close the company's factory at Brentford. It is estimated that the costs of closing the factory will amount to £77,500, including the cost of several redundancies.

*The amount provided is the directors' best estimate of the costs involved including redundancies. The expenditure is expected to be made within 12 months of the balance sheet date. Approximately £20,000 of the provision relates to expected costs regarding onermous contracts: however it is not known at present whether this sum will correctly reflect the eventual outcome as negotiations with contractors are still under way.

20 Called-up share capital

10.3 & 10.4

	1999 and 1998	
	Authorised	*Allotted and fully paid*
	£	£
Equity shares:		
1,200,000 ordinary shares of 25p each, of which 1,100,000 have been allotted	300,000	275,000
Non-equity shares:		
100,000 3.15% preference shares of £1 each	100,000	100,000
	400,000	375,000

The ordinary shares of the company rank after the preference shares as regards payment of dividends and return of capital but carry full voting rights at general meetings of the company. Voting rights are not available to the preference shareholders unless their dividend falls into arrears. Dividends payable on ordinary shares may fluctuate depending on the company's results whereas preference dividends are payable at a fixed rate and are cumulative.

10.3

*The disclosures shown in italics are not required under the draft FRSSE for 1999.

RUSSELL SQUARE ENTERPRISES LIMITED

21 Reserves

10.5 & 10.6

	Share premium account £	Revaluation reserve £	Profit and loss account £	
At 1 October 1998, as previously reported	20,000	66,614	40,385	
Prior year adjustment (note 14)	–	–	40,841	*4.24*
As restated	20,000	66,614	81,226	
Exchange adjustment on net investment in overseas operations	–	–	11,075	
Difference between an historical depreciation charge and the actual depreciation charge for the year calculated on the revalued amount	–	(1,199)	1,199	*6.2.3*
Profit retained for the year	–	–	90,465	
At 30 September 1999	**20,000**	**65,415**	**183,965**	

22 Reconciliation of movement in shareholders' funds

10.2

	1999 £	As restated 1998 £
Profit for the financial year	**166,615**	175,113
Dividends	**(76,150)**	(76,150)
	90,465	98,963
Other recognised gains relating to the year	**11,075**	–
Net addition to shareholders' funds	**101,540**	98,963
Opening shareholders' funds, as restated for prior year adjustment	**542,840**	443,877
Closing shareholders' funds	**644,380**	542,840
Shareholders' funds may be analysed as follows:		
Attributable to equity interests	**544,380**	442,840
Attributable to non-equity interests	**100,000**	100,000
	644,380	542,840

10.2

Page 23

The FRSSE does not require disclosure of a reconciliation of movements in shareholders' files.

RUSSELL SQUARE ENTERPRISES LIMITED

23 Notes to the cash flow statement

(a) Reconciliation of operating profit to net outflow from operating activities

	1999 £	1998 £
Operating profit	359,150	297,474
Depreciation and amortisation	53,603	39,766
Loss/(profit) on sale of tangible fixed assets	1,424	(1,250)
Exchange adjustments	6,799	(3,022)
Deferred grants released to profit and loss account	(2,700)	(1,240)
Increase in stocks	(131,894)	(135,279)
Increase in debtors	(199,205)	(91,028)
Increase/(decrease) in creditors	57,750	(9,287)
Net cash inflow from operating activities	144,927	96,134

(b) Analysis of changes in net debt

	At 1 October 1998 £	Cash flow £	Other non-cash changes £	At 30 September 1999 £
Cash at bank and in hand	39,050	(26,811)		12,239
Bank overdraft	(23,250)	(11,100)		(34,350)
	15,800	(37,911)		(22,111)
Debt due within one year	(18,750)	(500)	(3,000)	(22,250)
Debt due after one year	(32,000)	(98,000)	3,000	(127,000)
Finance leases	(6,150)	1,150		(5,000)
	(41,100)	(135,261)	0	(176,361)

(c) Reconciliation of net cash flow to movement in net debt

	1999 £	1998 £
(Decrease)/increase in cash	(37,911)	27,438
Cash inflow from loans	100,000	–
Repayment of loans	2,000	5,000
Repayment of capital elements of finance leases	1,150	1,250
Increase in short term loans	(500)	–
Change in net debt from cash flows	(135,261)	33,688
Movement in net debt	(135,761)	33,688
Net debt at 1 October	(41,100)	(74,788)
Net debt at 30 September	176,361	(41,100)

RUSSELL SQUARE ENTERPRISES LIMITED

24 Capital expenditure

11.2

	1999 £	1998 £
Contracted for but not provided for in the financial statements	24,500	20,600

25 Contingent liabilities

11.3

The company has guaranteed the overdraft of a subsidiary undertaking up to a maximum of £50,000. At 30 September 1999 the amount of the overdraft was £35,454.

There were contingent liabilities in respect of bills discounted amounting to £26,207 at 30 September 1999.

There is a claim against the company by a former employee for £100,000 relating to unfair dismissal. The information usually required by FRS 12 is not disclosed on the grounds that it can be expected to prejudice seriously the outcome of the litigation. The directors are of the opinion that the claim can be successfully resisted by the company.

26 Pension commitments* [for defined benefit scheme]

4.17

The company contributes to a pension scheme providing benefits based on final pensionable pay. The assets of the scheme are held separately from those of the company, being invested with insurance companies. Contributions to the scheme are charged to the profit and loss account so as to spread the cost of pensions over employees' working lives with the company and are based on pension costs across the group. The contributions are determined by a qualified actuary on the basis of triennial valuations using the projected unit method. The most recent valuation was at 30 September 1998. The assumptions which have the most significant effect on the results of the valuation are those relating to the rate of return on investments and the rates of increase in salaries and pensions. It was assumed that the investment returns would be 9 per cent per annum, that salary increases would average 7 per cent per annum and that present and future pensions would increase at the rate of 4 per cent per annum.

The pension charge for the year in respect of this scheme was £36,651 (1998 – £40,583). This is after the benefit of £5,200 (1998 – £5,000) in respect of the amortisation of experience surpluses that are being recognised over 10 years, the average remaining service lives of the employees. Contributions totalling £4,575 (1998 – £4,350) were payable to the fund at the year end and are included in creditors.

Page 25

*Certain of the detail can be omitted in subsidiary which is part of a group scheme, providing the financial statements state in which parent company's financial statements the information can be found.

If accounts are presented in accordance with the FRSSE, then the disclosures required in respect of defined benefit schemes are reduced substantially.

RUSSELL SQUARE ENTERPRISES LIMITED

The most recent actuarial valuation showed that the market value of the scheme's assets was £1,200,000 and that the actuarial valuation of those assets represented 104% of the benefits that had accrued to members, after allowing for expected future increases in earnings. The contributions of the company and employees will remain at 11 per cent and 5 per cent of earnings respectively.

The company also has unfunded pension commitments to former directors of £2,500 per annum. In view of the insignificant amounts involved these are written off to profit and loss account when paid.

26 Pension commitments [for defined contributions scheme]

The company operates a defined contribution pension scheme on behalf of its directors and certain employees. The assets of the scheme are held separately from those of the company in an independently administered fund. Contributions are paid based upon the recommendations of a qualified actuary. The annual commitment under this scheme is for contributions of £36,651 (1998 – £40,583).

Contributions totalling £4,575 (1998, £4,350) were payable to the scheme at the year end and are included in creditors.

27 Lease commitments

9.3.1

Operating leases*

The company's commitments for rental payments under non-cancellable operating leases payable during the year to 30 September 2000 are as follows:

	Land and buildings £	Other operating leases £
Leases expiring:		
Within one year	–	2,400
Between two and five years	–	9,300
Over five years	26,500	3,700
	26,500	15,400

Finance leases

At 30 September 1999 a finance lease had been signed for a new computer which is due for delivery on 1 February 2000. The annual rentals will amount to £87,500 inclusive of finance charges.

28 Directors' interests in contracts

7.5.2

Mr M J Wood is a director of Contour Plastics Limited and holds 10 per cent of that company's share capital. Contour Plastics Limited has been advising on the use of plastics in the production of musical instruments and has received fees amounting to £35,000 during the year for advice given.

No other director had any material interest during the year in any contract with the company.

Page 26

*The FRSSE permists this disclosure to be restricted to
'At 30 September 1999 the company had annual commitments of £41,900 under non-cancellable operating leases'.

RUSSELL SQUARE ENTERPRISES LIMITED

Historical and statistical information*

Profit and loss summary years ended 30 September

	1999 £	1998 £	1997 £	1996 £	1995 £
Turnover					
Continuing	**2,081,959**	1,600,091	1,485,317	1,510,296	1,575,563
Discontinued	–	–	–	167,839	407,131
	2,081,959	1,600,091	1,485,317	1,678,135	1,982,694
Operating profit					
Continuing	**359,150**	297,474	151,225	190,143	179,608
Discontinued	–	–	–	5,520	12,743
	359,150	297,474	151,225	195,663	192,351
Non-operating exceptional items					
Continuing:					
Provision for closure of factory	**(77,500)**	–	–	–	–
Discontinued:					
Loss on fixed asset disposals	–	–	–	(3,435)	(11,339)
Profit on sale/ termination	–	–	–	48,384	(25,175)
	(77,500)	–	–	44,949	(36,514)
Income from fixed asset investments	**2,650**	1,512	1,472	1,210	1,296
Interest payable and similar charges	**(11,801)**	(5,219)	(7,758)	(10,222)	(12,833)
Profit on ordinary activities before taxation	**272,499**	293,767	144,939	231,600	144,300
Tax on profit on ordinary activities	**(105,884)**	(118,654)	(54,576)	(91,540)	(55,479)
Dividends	**(76,150)**	(76,150)	(76,150)	(76,150)	(69,150)
Retained profit	**90,465**	98,963	14,213	63,910	19,671

The results for the five-year period include the restatement of earlier years' figures to reflect the change in accounting policy for stocks.

Page 27

Optional, and may incorporate ratios such as earnings per share and dividends per share.

RUSSELL SQUARE ENTERPRISES LIMITED

Balance sheet summary as at 30 September

	1999 £	1998 £	1997 £	1996 £	1995 £
Employment of capital					
Fixed assets	**305,640**	200,183	175,418	162,697	155,386
Net current assets (*less* provisions and deferred government grants)	**472,740**	379,657	305,869	306,226	249,765
	778,380	579,840	481,287	468,923	405,151
Capital employed					
Creditors falling due after more than one year	**134,000**	37,000	42,000	47,000	51,000
Capital and reserves	**644,380**	542,840	439,287	421,923	354,151
	778,380	579,840	481,287	468,923	405,151
Shareholders' funds					
Equity	**544,380**	442,840	339,287	321,923	254,151
Non-equity	**100,000**	100,000	100,000	100,000	100,000
	644,380	542,840	439,287	421,923	354,151
Net borrowings					
Cash at bank and in hand	**12,239**	39,050	62,812	22,767	12,662
Bank overdraft	**(34,350)**	(23,250)	(12,611)	(38,452)	(45,581)
Current instalments due on loans	**(3,000)**	(3,000)	(3,000)	(3,000)	(3,000)
Loans falling due after more than one year	**(130,000)**	(32,000)	(35,000)	(38,000)	(41,000)
Finance lease creditor	**(5,000)**	(6,150)	(8,150)	(11,750)	(14,150)
Short-term loan	**(8,000)**	(10,000)	(15,000)	(17,000)	(21,000)
Loan from a former director	**(8,250)**	(5,750)	–	–	–
	(176,361)	(41,100)	(10,949)	(85,435)	(112,069)

This may include gearing and other ratios, if appropriate.

Notice of annual general meeting

13.1

NOTICE IS HEREBY GIVEN that the thirtieth annual general meeting of the company will be held at Whitefriars House, 125 Thames Street, Reading, Berkshire on 15 January 2000 at 11.00am for the following purposes:

1   To receive the directors' report and financial statements for the financial year ended 30 September 1999 and the auditors' report thereon.
2   To declare a final dividend.
3   To re-elect A King as a director.
4   To re-elect T R Hill as a director.
5   To reappoint Burlington & Greenslade as auditors.
6   To authorise the directors to agree the remuneration of the auditors.

1.5.2

By order of the Board

K R WRIGHT
Secretary

14 December 1999

A member wishing to attend and vote at the above meeting is entitled to appoint one or more proxies to attend and vote instead of him. A proxy need not also be a member of the company.

Forms of proxy must be deposited at the company's registered office not less than 48 hours before the time fixed for the meeting.

Page 29

Registered Number: 19961997

RUSSELL SQUARE ENTERPRISES LIMITED

Abbreviated Accounts
30 September 1999

RUSSELL SQUARE ENTERPRISES LIMITED

Auditors' report to Russell Square Enterprises Limited under section 247B of the Companies Act 1985

We have examined the abbreviated accounts on pages 2 to 7, together with the financial statements of the company for the year ended 30 September 1999 prepared under section 226 of the Companies Act 1985.

Respective responsibilities of directors and auditors

The directors are responsible for preparing the abbreviated accounts in accordance with section 246 of the Companies Act 1985. It is our responsibility to form an independent opinion as to whether the company is entitled to deliver abbreviated accounts prepared in accordance with section 246(5) and (6) of the Act to the Registrar and whether the accounts to be delivered are properly prepared in accordance with those provisions and to report our opinion to you.

Basis of opinion

We have carried out the procedures we considered necessary to confirm, by reference to the financial statements, that the company is entitled to deliver abbreviated accounts and that the abbreviated accounts to be delivered are properly prepared. The scope of our work for the purpose of this report did not include examining or dealing with events after the date of our report on the financial statements.

Opinion

In our opinion the company is entitled to deliver abbreviated accounts prepared in accordance with section 246(5) and (6) of the Companies Act 1985, and the abbreviated accounts on pages 2 to 7 are properly prepared in accordance with those provisions.

BURLINGTON & GREENSLADE
Chartered Accountants
Registered Auditors

LONDON

29 November 1999

Page 1

41

RUSSELL SQUARE ENTERPRISES LIMITED
Abbreviated balance sheet as at 30 September 1999

15.0

	Notes	1999 £	1998 £
Fixed assets			
Intangible assets	2	**10,000**	13,000
Tangible assets	3	**191,690**	92,483
Investments	4	**103,950**	94,700
		305,640	200,183
Current assets			
Stocks		**420,792**	288,898
Debtors	5	**656,137**	456,932
Cash at hand and in bank		**12,239**	39,050
		1,089,168	784,880
Creditors: Amounts falling due within one year	6	**(577,936)**	(392,677)
Net current assets		**511,232**	392,203
Total assets less current liabilities		**816,872**	592,386
Creditors: Amounts falling due after more than one year	6&7	**(134,000)**	(37,000)
Provisions for liabilities and charges		**(19,592)**	(5,286)
Accruals and deferred income		**(18,900)**	(7,260)
		644,380	542,840
Capital and reserves			
Called-up share capital	8	**375,000**	375,000
Share premium account		**20,000**	20,000
Revaluation reserve		**65,415**	66,614
Profit and loss account		**183,965**	81,226
		644,380	542,840

The abbreviated accounts have been prepared in accordance with the special provisions of Part VII of the Companies Act 1995 relating to small companies.

15.4

Approved by the Board on 29 November 1999 and signed on its behalf.

.... **K L HILL – Director**

The notes on pages 3 to 7 form part of these abbreviated accounts.

RUSSELL SQUARE ENTERPRISES LIMITED

Notes to the abbreviated accounts for the year ended 30 September 1999

1 Accounting policies*

Basis of accounting

The financial statements are prepared on the historical cost basis of accounting as modified to include the revaluation of certain freehold land and buildings.

Consolidation

The company and its subsidiaries comprise a small group. The company has therefore taken advantage of the exemption provided in section 248 of the Companies Act 1985 not to prepare group financial statements and accordingly these financial statements present information about the company as a single undertaking.

Depreciation of tangible fixed assets

Depreciation is not charged on freehold land nor on expenditure on assets not yet in use. Depreciation on other tangible fixed assets is charged so as to write off their full costs or valuation less estimated residual values over their expected useful lives at the following rates:

Freehold buildings   – $2\frac{1}{2}$% of cost or valuation per annum
Leasehold property   – by equal annual instalments over the term of the lease
Plant and machinery   – 15% of cost per annum
Motor vehicles   – 25% of cost per annum
Fixtures, fittings, tools
and equipment   – 10% of cost per annum

Goodwill

Goodwill representing the excess of the purchase price over the fair value of the net assets of an unincorporated business acquired in 1992 is amortised by equal annual instalments over its expected useful economic life of 10 years.

Stocks

Stocks and work in progress are valued at the lower of cost and net realisable value.

Cost of raw materials is determined on the first in first out basis. In the case of work in progress and finished goods, cost includes all direct expenditure and production overheads based on the normal level of activity. Net realisable value is the price at which the stock can be realised in the normal course of business.

Page 3

As with the full accounts, the accounting policies may be reduced if those accounts were prepared under the FRSSE – see the footnote on page 17.

RUSSELL SQUARE ENTERPRISES LIMITED

Deferred taxation

Deferred taxation is provided under the liability method in respect of all material timing differences between the profits as computed for taxation purposes and the profits as stated in the financial statements, to the extent that it is probable that a liability or asset will crystallise. The rate of tax used is that which is expected to be applied when the liability or asset is expected to crystallise.

Deferred government grants

Government grants in respect of capital expenditure are treated as deferred income and are credited to profit and loss account over the estimated useful life of the assets to which they relate.

Foreign currencies

Assets and liabilities denominated in foreign currencies are translated into sterling at the rates ruling at the year end. The trading results of overseas operations are translated at average rates of exchange for the year.

Exchange differences arising from the retranslation of the opening net investment in overseas operations and from translating their trading results at average and closing rates of exchange are taken directly to retained profits. All other gains and losses on exchange are dealt with in the profit and loss account.

Research and development expenditure

Research and development expenditure is written off as it is incurred, with the exception of certain machinery and equipment which is capitalised and depreciated over its expected useful life.

Hire purchase and lease transactions

Assets acquired under hire purchase agreements and finance leases are capitalised in the balance sheet and are depreciated in accordance with the company's normal policy. The outstanding liabilities under such agreements less interest not yet due, are included in creditors. Interest on such agreements is charged to profit and loss account over the term of each agreement and represents a constant proportion of the balance of capital repayments outstanding.

Rentals under operating leases are charged to the profit and loss account as they fall due.

Pensions

The company provides a defined benefit pension scheme, the assets of which are held separately from those of the company in an independently administered fund. Contributions to the scheme are charged to profit and loss account so as to spread the regular cost of pensions over the employees' service lives within the group. Variances from regular cost are spread over the remaining service lives of the current employees.

RUSSELL SQUARE ENTERPRISES LIMITED

2 Intangible fixed assets

	£
Cost:	
At 1 October 1998 and 30 September 1999	**30,000**
Amortisation:	
At 1 October 1998	17,000
Provision for the year	3,000
At 30 September 1999	**20,000**
Net book value:	
At 30 September 1999	**10,000**
At 30 September 1998	13,000

3 Tangible fixed assets

	£
Cost or valuation:	
At 1 October 1998	257,352
Exchange adjustments	25,056
Additions	164,965
Disposals	(69,007)
At 30 September 1999	**378,366**
Depreciation:	
At 1 October 1998	164,869
Exchange adjustments	20,780
Provision for the year	50,603
Adjustments for disposals	(49,576)
At 30 September 1999	**186,676**
Net book value:	
At 30 September 1999	**191,690**
At 30 September 1998	92,483

4 Investments

	£
Cost:	
At 1 October 1998	94,700
Additions	9,250
At 30 September 1999	**103,950**

The following information relates to the fixed asset investments:

Subsidiary undertakings

Registered in England and Wales
Clutch Assemblies Limited (100% of equity capital owned)
Registered in Scotland
Clutch Plates Limited (50% of equity owned directly; 25% indirectly)
Incorporated in Germany
Russell Square Enterprises GmbH (51% of equity capital owned)

Page 5

RUSSELL SQUARE ENTERPRISES LIMITED

The aggregate of the share capital and reserves as at 30 September 1999 and the profit or loss for the year ended on that date for the subsidiary undertakings were as follows:

	Aggregate of share capital and reserves	*Profit/ (loss)*
	£	*£*
Clutch Assemblies Limited	52,739	8,412
Clutch Plates Limited	25,507	(7,195)
Russell Square Enterprises GmbH	80,170	30,467

Unlisted investment

This represents the company's 15 per cent interest in the equity capital of Airport Instruments Limited, which is registered in England and Wales.

5 Debtors

Debtors include £15,000 which is due after more than one year (1998 – £Nil).

Included in debtors is a loan to a director, Mr M J Wood, which is an interest-free season ticket loan of £2,000 (1998 – Nil) which is repayable by monthly instalments. The maximum sum outstanding during the year was £2,500.

6 Secured liabilities

The company's debenture stock, mortgage, bank loan and overdraft which total £167,350 are secured by a fixed and floating charge over the freehold properties and other assets of the company. Obligations under finance leases which total £5,000 are secured on the assets to which they relate.

7 Creditors falling due after more than five years

The total amount of creditors falling due after more than five years and not repayable by instalments is £121,000 (1998 – £21,000).

RUSSELL SQUARE ENTERPRISES LIMITED

8 Called-up share capital

	1999 and 1998	
	Authorised £	*Allotted and fully paid* £
1,200,000 ordinary shares of 25p each, of which 1,100,000 have been allotted	300,000	275,000
100,000 3.15% preference shares of £1 each	100,000	100,000
	400,000	375,000

9 Directors' interests in contracts

Mr M J Wood is a director of Contour Plastics Limited and holds 10 per cent of that company's share capital. Contour Plastics Limited has been advising on the use of plastics in the production of musical instruments and has received fees amounting to £35,000 during the year for advice given.

Explanatory notes

1 Directors' report

1.1 General

(a) The Companies Act 1985 requires that a report of the directors should be attached to every set of accounts prepared for every accounting reference period. *s234(1)* *s238*

(b) The directors are required to include in the accounts a summary of their responsibilities in relation to the preparation of the accounts. This may be incorporated into the directors' report, the audit report or be given as a separate statement. These disclosures arise from SAS 600 *Auditors' reports on financial statments* and, accordingly, if the company is exempt from audit there is no requirement to include this statement as such. This is effectively replaced by the directors' statements which are required at the foot of the balance sheet. *SAS 600, 3* *SAS 600, 20b* *SAS 600, Appendix*

(c) Auditors are required to consider whether the information given in the directors' report is consistent with the accounts and if there is any inconsistency they shall state that fact in their report. *s235(3)*

(d) Comparative figures are not required in the directors' report.

4(1), Sch 4

1.2 Review of the business

1.2.1 Principal activity

The Companies Act 1985 requires that the directors' report shall state the principal activities of the company and of its subsidiaries in the course of the financial year and significant changes in those activities in that year. This should also make reference to any branches outside the UK. *s234(2)*

6(d), Sch 7

The noting of significant changes is often overlooked and should not be restricted to the acquisition of new activities or cessation of an activity but include significant changes in the degree of continuing activities. It is important to ensure consistency with the accounts and the presentational and other disclosures required by FRS 3.

It is not always an easy matter to decide whether different types of business are sufficiently significant to require separate disclosure. Although no precise rule can be laid down it is suggested that the activities which constitute less than 10 per cent of the total of turnover or profits before taxation should be ignored.

1.2.2 Fair review

The Companies Act 1985 requires that the directors' report shall include a fair review *s234(1)(a)* of the development of the business of the company and its subsidiaries during the year and of the position at the year end. The Act contains no indication as to the form that the review should take, but it should include a commentary on the results for the year and a comparison with the previous year as well as factors such as trading conditions, acquisitions, closures, etc. Reference to the balance sheet position should not be overlooked.

1.2.3 Likely future developments affecting the company or its subsidiaries

The Act contains no amplification thus allowing directors as much freedom as possible *6a, Sch 7* to decide how best to meet the requirement. It is not practicable for these notes to give examples of wording as each company's future development is likely to be different.

1.3 Results and dividends

The Companies Act 1985 requires: *s234(1)b*

(a) a fair review of the development of the business and its subsidiaries during the financial year and of their position at the end of the financial year (see **1.2.2** above);

(b) the disclosure of the amount (if any) recommended to be paid by way of dividend.

The Companies Act 1985 prohibits the making of a distribution except out of profits *s263* available for the purpose. For all companies (with the exception of public investment companies) profits available for distribution, in this context, are the accumulated realised profits of a company that have not previously been either distributed or capitalised, less its accumulated realised losses (see also **4.1.2**).

If the audit report is qualified by the auditors, a distribution cannot be made unless and until they have stated in writing that the subject matter of their qualification is not material in determining the legality of the proposed distribution. This additional report has to be laid before the company in general meeting (see also **2.4**). *s271(4)*

If no dividend is recommended this fact should be disclosed, whatever the results of the company. A suitable wording would be 'the directors recommend that no dividend should be paid'.

1.4 Post balance sheet events (PBSE)

The Act requires certain information concerning PBSE and future developments to be *6a, Sch 7* included in the directors' report. This is also covered by SSAP 17, but the standard distinguishes between events that require changes in the amounts shown in the accounts *SSAP 17,* (adjusting events) and events that only require disclosure (non-adjusting events). *22–23*

Adjusting events are post balance sheet events which provide additional evidence of *SSAP 17, 18–19* conditions existing at the balance sheet date. Non-adjusting events are post balance sheet events which concern conditions which do not exist at the balance sheet date.

The two requirements are not identical. SSAP 17 requires non-adjusting events to be disclosed in the accounts where they are of such materiality that their non-disclosure would affect the ability of users of the accounts to obtain a proper understanding of the financial position. The Act requires the directors' report to contain particulars of any important events affecting the company which have occurred since the year end. It could be argued that there is conflict between the two requirements because an event which might be thought sufficiently important to require disclosure in the directors' report, may not be necessary for a proper understanding of the financial position and therefore would not require disclosure under SSAP 17. Conversely, any event which needs to be disclosed in the notes under SSAP 17 is an important event which requires disclosure in the directors' report under CA 1985. *SSAP 17, 23–25*

Although the requirements of the Act and SSAP 17 are not identical, this difference is unlikely to give rise to any practical difficulties. If a matter is not disclosed in both the directors' report and the notes, then the directors' report will be the most appropriate place for disclosing non-adjusting post balance sheet events.

1.5 Directors

1.5.1 General

The Companies Act 1985 requires the names of directors at any time during the year under review to be presented. Some companies prefer to give the list of directors separately on an officers' and advisers' page, or alternatively, at the head of the report. By convention, the list usually states only the directors serving at the date of the report. A full list of directors, covering those who served at any time during the year should be given in the body of the report. *s234(2)*

There is no requirement to disclose a foreign director's nationality in the report, although CA 1985 requires a company to disclose a director's nationality in the register of directors. It is common practice, however, to include this information in the report for the directors concerned. *s289(1)*

1.5.2 Appointment, retirement and re-election of directors

The Companies Act 1985 requires the report to state the names of persons who, at any time during the financial year, were directors of the company. It is therefore necessary to give information of all appointments, resignations or retirements within the financial year so as to comply with this section. This is the only statutory requirement to show the names of directors anywhere in the report and accounts. *s234(2)*

Because of the interval between the end of the financial year and the date of the directors' report, it is accepted practice to include all changes up to the date of the report. As a result, changes between the end of the financial year and the date of the directors' report will be repeated in the following year's directors' report.

In addition, it is accepted practice to give the information relating to the re-election of directors (at the forthcoming general meeting) although this is not a statutory requirement. The Companies (Tables A to F) Regulations 1985 require directors appointed during the year and one-third of the board, other than managing directors, to retire each year. Where a company's articles of association state that Table A shall apply, and do not then specifically exclude the operation of clause 73, retirement by rotation must apply. Table A also requires those directors appointed since the last annual general meeting to retire and seek re-election.

1.6   Directors' interests in shares and debentures

1.6.1   Disclosures

The Act requires disclosure in either the directors' report or notes to the financial statements of directors' interests in the shares and debentures of the company or any other group companies at the beginning and end of the financial year, in accordance with the information in the register required to be kept by the company under s325. There is no requirement to show any of this information in respect of a director who retired during the year; but where a director is appointed during the year it is necessary to give his shareholding at the date of his appointment. *2(1), Sch 7*

A director's interest includes the shareholdings (if any) of his wife and infant children who are not themselves directors. Particulars of any duplication of holdings (e.g., joint holdings) should be given as interests of each of the holders. It is therefore quite possible for the notional aggregate of holdings stated in the directors' report to exceed the issued share capital. *2A/B, Sch 7* *s328*

The Companies Act 1985 requires a company to disclose arrangements for the benefit of directors for them to acquire shares or debentures in any company (including the company itself) in its directors' report, provided the company is a party to the arrangement. This disclosure is mandatory and is not at the discretion of the directors. The fact that no such arrangements existed at the year end does not exempt disclosure. The section refers to 'during the financial year' and matters confined to and completed within the year under review must, therefore, be disclosed. *2B, Sch 7* *2B, Sch 7*

1.6.2   Exemptions

The Companies (Disclosure of Directors' Interests) (Exceptions) Regulations 1985 make certain exemptions as to what constitutes an interest required to be notified to the company by a director under s324.

(a)   A director of a company which is the *wholly owned* subsidiary of a company incorporated outside Great Britain is not required to notify the company of his interests in the parent company. The effect is to dispense with the requirements to give the information under CA 1985 in respect of any director's interests in an overseas parent company. *SI 1985/802(3)*

(b)   A director of a company which is the *wholly owned* subsidiary of a company required to keep the register of interests under the Companies Act (i.e., a parent company incorporated in Great Britain and therefore subject to the requirements of the Act) is not required to notify the company of any interests in either itself or the parent company, provided that he is also a director of the parent company. The effect is to dispense with the requirements to give the information under CA 1985 in respect of such directors; the information regarding their interests in *SI 1985/802(3)* *s325* either the company or the parent company being given in the directors' report of the latter. It is common practice in these circumstances for it to be stated that the interests of parent company directors are disclosed in the financial statements of the parent company.

(c)   Certain trustee holdings.

In addition, nominee holdings in 100 per cent subsidiary companies are also exempt from disclosure.   *s324(6)*

1.6.3   Definition of interest

The Act elaborates on what constitutes an interest and is designed so as not to exclude   *Part I, Sch 13*
an interest by virtue of remoteness, restraint or restriction. In particular, it states that a
director is interested where the director:

(a)   is a beneficiary under a trust, unless the trust is discretionary;
(b)   is in a position to exercise control over, or possesses one-third of the voting power of, a company which holds shares or debentures in the company;
(c)   has rights to call for delivery of shares or debentures or to enforce an uncompleted contract for his purchase of them;
(d)   has a joint interest with another person;
(e)   is a trustee, unless he is just a bare or custodian trustee.

A *bare trustee* is a trustee with no duties except to convey the assets to or by the direction of the beneficiaries. He should have no beneficial interests in the context of these rules (e.g., a nominee).

A *custodian trustee* is a trustee in whose name assets have been vested but who has no powers of administration. He is bound to act in accordance with the directions of the managing trustees as long as there is no breach of trust.

A director's interest has to be disclosed under the Act however small it might be and if   *2A(1), Sch 7*
it is nil, this should be stated.

Although the Act does not require the information disclosed to distinguish between   *2, Sch 7*
beneficial and non-beneficial interests, it is a requirement of the Stock Exchange that   *SE 12.43(k)*
such information be given in the directors' reports of listed companies. It is good
practice for non-listed companies to distinguish between beneficial and non-beneficial
holdings.

Where no interest is required to be disclosed it should be stated that 'there are no directors' interests requiring disclosure under the Companies Act 1985'.

The directors' report should also disclose details of where the auditors act as trustees   *ICAEW Ethics*
for a trust which holds in aggregate 1 per cent or more of the shares in the company.   *guide*

1.7   Market value of interests in land

The Act requires the directors to disclose the difference between the market value of   *1(2), Sch 7*
interests in land and the value included in the balance sheet where, in the opinion of
the directors, the difference is of such significance that the attention of members and
debenture holders should be drawn thereto. Although the Act is silent on the point, it is
customary to include buildings in the valuation.

'Going concern' valuations are (normally) inappropriate since basic accounting concepts postulate that the accounts are already prepared on such a basis. The 'existing use' basis is generally the appropriate method of valuation because the 'alternative use' basis also has no relevance in the context of going concern. However, a value on the latter basis may be relevant to an overall appraisal of the company's situation and, where significant, should be disclosed in the directors' report, as envisaged by the Act.

Where the potential surplus or deficit on a valuation of a company's property is material in relation to net assets, the directors should consider the advisability of having independent valuations carried out regularly, preferably at intervals of three to five years. Such valuations, if not incorporated in the accounts, should be disclosed in the directors' report in compliance with the Act. In the intervening years, the latest valuation should be referred to in the directors' report, with an expression of opinion by the directors whether there has been a material increase or decrease in value since the date of that valuation. Valuations of company property assets should include all leasehold interests whether or not a premium was paid on their acquisition. The general principles apply equally to property companies, but the need for more frequent and class-analysed valuations is discussed in SSAP 19 (see also **6.5**).

The attention of the board of directors should be drawn to the points raised in the above paragraphs and, where the information is material and readily available, or may be obtained without involving disproportionate expense, the appropriate valuation should be either incorporated in the accounts or the difference between the valuation and book value disclosed in compliance with the Act. It is also considered that where the report shows a surplus on valuation in the directors' report then an indication should be given of the potential capital gains tax liability. *SSAP 15, 42*

1.8   Research and development activities

The directors are required to present an indication of the activities (if any) of the company in the field of research and development. Although the requirement is vague, it envisages a narrative statement that will supplement the details already required by SSAP 13 or provide an indication of the R&D activities of companies not subject to the requirements of the SSAP. The standard requires certain companies to disclose separately details of deferred development expenditure at the beginning and end of the year, movements during the year and the accounting policy. *6c, Sch 7* *SSAP 13*

1.9   Employee involvement

The Companies Act 1985 requires a description of the action taken to introduce, maintain or develop the provision of information to and consultation with employees. This applies to companies with more than 250 employees excluding those working mainly outside the UK. No disclosure is required in the financial statements of an individual company if there are more than 250 employees in a *group* but no one *company* within the group employs more than 250. *11(3), Sch 7*

1.10   Disabled employees

For companies with more than 250 employees working wholly or mainly in the UK, the directors' report must contain a note on the company's policy on the employment of disabled persons. The note should indicate the company's policy in relation to: *9(3), Sch 7*

(a)   applications for employment from disabled persons;
(b)   employees who become disabled;
(c)   the training, career development and promotion of disabled persons employed by the company.

This disclosure applies to *companies*. No disclosure is required if there are more than 250 employees in the *group* but no one company within the group employs in excess of 250. That stated, it may well be that the parent company's directors may wish to include a policy statement voluntarily. The figure of 250 relates to the average number of persons employed under contracts of service per month during the financial year, excluding persons who work wholly or mainly outside the UK.

1.11   Political and charitable donations

If political or charitable contributions severally or together exceed £200, the directors' report must give the total spent on each of the purposes. Disclosure is not required where the company is a wholly owned subsidiary of a company incorporated in Great Britain, as the ultimate parent company (if incorporated in Great Britain) is required to give the information on a group basis. It should be noted, therefore, that the exemption in respect of wholly owned subsidiaries will not apply if their immediate parent company is incorporated abroad.

3(2), Sch 7

4, Sch 7

Where an individual political contribution exceeds £200, the report must specify the amount and the recipient and/or the organisation supported. This information is not required for charitable donations which may be given in total.

3(2), Sch 7

Except as regards Scotland, where the Act prescribes that 'charitable' shall be construed in the way contained in the Income Tax Acts, it is considered that charities include those organisations registered with the Charity Commission, and not those organisations that the company supports for business reasons unless donations are made without expecting a return.

5(4), Sch 7

The disclosure requirement embraces all political contributions, including those in respect of overseas organisations, but the Act exempts contributions to overseas charities from being taken into account.

5(2)b. Sch 7
5(3), Sch 7

1.12   Auditors

It is customary, although not a statutory requirement, to indicate in the report the position regarding the auditors' forthcoming reappointment or otherwise, especially where the company has taken advantage of the dispensation not to appoint auditors annually.

SE 12.43(m)

If a company is exempt from audit, there is also no statutory requirement for a paragraph to be given concerning the reappointment of the reporting accountants. However, a paragraph may be given stating that the reporting accountant will be reappointed.

1.13 The company's acquisition of its own shares

The disclosure requirements are detailed and are fully set out in CA 1985. A synopsis of the information required is as follows: *s234(4) 7&8, Sch 7*

(a) Where shares are purchased by the company during the year:
    (i)   number;
    (ii)   nominal value;
    (iii)   percentage of called-up share capital of that class;
    (iv)   aggregate consideration;
    (v)   reasons for their purchase.

(b) Where shares are acquired during the year by the company, or the company's nominee, or with financial assistance from the company where the company has a beneficial interest in the shares:
    (i)   number;
    (ii)   nominal value;
    (iii)   percentage of called-up share capital of that class;
    (iv)   the amount of the charge in each case (where applicable).

(c) Maximum number, nominal value, and percentage of called-up share capital of each class held during the year by the company, or the company's nominee, or by another person where they provided financial assistance for the original purchase and the company has a beneficial interest in the shares.

(d) On disposal or cancellation of such shares during the year, including shares subject to a charge (see (b) above):
    (i)   number;
    (ii)   nominal value;
    (iii)   percentage of called-up share capital of each class;
    (iv)   the amount or value of any consideration.

(e) Where a public company's own shares are made subject to a lien, or a charge taken by the company itself.
    (i)   number;
    (ii)   nominal value;
    (iii)   percentage of called-up share capital of each class;
    (iv)   the amount of the charge.

1.14 Authorisation and signature

The directors' report must be approved by the board of directors and signed by either a director or, more customarily, the secretary. The name of the signatory must also be given. *s234A(1)/(2)/ (3)*

2 Auditors' report

2.1 General statutory requirements

An audit report is required to be attached to every set of accounts prepared for every accounting period with the exception of dormant companies which no longer need to reappoint auditors, and companies with a turnover of £350,000 or less – subject to certain provisions.

s235, s250

s249A

The report should state whether, in the opinion of the auditors, the balance sheet and profit and loss account have been properly prepared in accordance with the Companies Act 1985 and give a true and fair view.

s235(2)

If the auditor is of the opinion that any of the following apply:

s237, 1, 2 & 3

(a)   proper accounting records have not been kept;
(b)   the accounts are not in agreement with the accounting records and returns;
(c)   proper returns have not been obtained from branches not visited by him;
(d)   all the information and explanations considered necessary for the audit have not been obtained;

he must state that fact in the audit report.

If the auditor is of the opinion that the information relating to the year given in the directors' report is not consistent with the accounts, he must state that fact in the audit report.

s235(3)

Where the required particulars of any of the following:

(a)   emoluments of directors;
(b)   loans, quasi-loans and other dealings in favour of directors;
(c)   other transactions, arrangements and agreements;

Part I, Sch 6
Part II, Sch 6
Part III, Sch 6

are not disclosed in the notes to the accounts, the auditor must include in his report, so far as he is reasonably able to do so, a statement giving the required particulars.

s237(4)

2.2 SAS 600

The audit report format set out in SAS 600 attempts to explain more clearly to users of financial statements the respective roles of directors (see **1.1(b)**) and auditors in the preparation of the accounts and to explain the basis of the auditor's opinion.

SAS 600

Where, in the auditor's opinion, there is a fundamental inherent uncertainty which is *SAS 600, 54*
adequately accounted for and disclosed in the financial statements, the section
explaining the basis of opinion should include an explanatory paragraph and should
clearly indicate that the opinion is not qualified in this respect; in other words the onus
is very much in favour of clarity and fullness of disclosure.

2.3   Practical considerations

Care should be taken over the page numbers upon which the audit report is based. *SAS 600, 19*
These should not include the directors' report nor any appendices containing the
detailed profit and loss account or other management information.

The audit report should always be dated on or after the directors' report and approval *SAS 600, 76*
of accounts and strictly as the date of actual signature, having updated the post balance
sheet review appropriately. A minor delay may be acceptable depending on the
circumstances and nature of the client. Under no circumstances should the audit
report be signed and dated before the directors' report as, legally, the directors'
report and balance sheet and accounts do not exist until they have been signed.

The mandatory formats for the profit and loss account in the Act contain the item
'profit or loss for the financial year'. The audit report should refer to the profit or loss
by reference to this line in the profit and loss account even if a distribution is made
which exceeds the profit. Should neither profit nor loss be shown, the audit report
should refer to the results for the year.

Following the regulations introduced by CA 1989, the audit report must state the name *s236(3)*
of the auditors and be signed by them. Auditors should record their status as
'registered auditors'.

2.4   Section 271(4) reports

If the audit report is qualified and the company proposes to make a distribution, the *s271(4)*
auditors must state whether, in their opinion, the matter in respect of which their report
is qualified is material for determining whether the distribution would contravene the
Companies Act provisions. This may form part of the normal audit report or be given
separately in writing – the important point is that it must be placed before the
members.

The form of words to be used is prescribed by Practice Note 8, issued by the APB and
is illustrated below:

Auditors' statement to the shareholders of Russell Square Enterprises Limited pursuant to section 271(4) of the Companies Act 1985

PN 8, Example 7

We have audited the financial statements of Russell Square Enterprises Limited for the
year ended 30 September 1999 in accordance with Auditing Standards issued by the
Auditing Practices Board and have expressed a qualified opinion thereon in our report
dated 29 November 1999.

Basis of opinion

We have carried out such procedures as we considered necessary to evaluate the effect of the qualified opinion for the determination of profits available for distribution.

Opinion

In our opinion the subject matter of that qualification is not material for determining, by reference to those financial statements, whether the distribution (interim dividend for the year ended .... 19....) of £43,800 proposed by the company is permitted under section 263 of the Companies Act 1985.

BURLINGTON & GREENSLADE
Chartered Accountants
Registered Auditors
Date

Notes:

(1)   As an alternative the auditors' statement could be expressed in terms of the company's ability to make potential distributions up to a specific level. This may be particularly appropriate where the amount of dividend has not yet been determined. The opinion paragraph will be worded as follows:

> 'In our opinion the subject matter of that qualification is not material for determining, by reference to those financial statements, whether a distribution of not more than £....... by the company would be permitted under section 263 of the Companies Act 1985.'

(2)   This example assumes that a separate report is given regarding the company's ability to make a distribution. This matter is sometimes referred to in the statutory audit report by adding a separate paragraph. That paragraph might be worded as follows:

> 'In our opinion the subject matter of the foregoing qualification is not material for determining whether the distribution of £....... proposed by the company is permitted under section 263 of the Act.'

If abbreviated accounts are filed, the statement in respect of the distribution should not be reproduced with the text of the audit report on the full financial statements.

(3)   The reference to section 263 above should be extended to cover also section 264 in the case of a public company.

2.5   Exemptions for small and medium-sized groups

A parent company need not prepare group accounts for a financial year if the group qualifies as a small or medium-sized group (and is not an ineligible group). Accordingly, in the case of a small or medium group, the parent company is only required to prepare and deliver to the Registrar individual accounts. There is no provision for small or medium-sized group accounts: the parent company must prepare either individual accounts or full group accounts.

s248(1)
s248(2)

If the directors of a parent company propose to take advantage of the exemption in section 248 and in the auditors' opinion they are not entitled to do so, the auditors should state this fact in their report. *s237(4A)*

The requirement for the auditors to report that the directors were entitled to the exemption was repealed by the Companies Act 1985 (Miscellaneous Accounting Amendments) Regulations 1996. *SI 1996/189*

Reference should also be made in the accounting policy note to indicate the company has taken advantage of the exemption and that, consequently, the accounts present information about the company as a single undertaking.

2.6 Other statutory reports required from auditors

Practice Note 8, issued by the Auditing Practices Board, deals with a number of reports which auditors are required to provide from time to time. Apart from the auditors' report on abbreviated accounts which is dealt with separately in this book (see **15.5**), examples are provided of reports concerning the following which are those most likely to be encountered in practice: *PN 8*

- company's ability to make a distribution (see **2.4** above);
- revised financial statements or revised directors' report;
- summary financial statements;
- re-registration of a private company as a public company;
- purchase of own shares out of capital;
- financial assistance for purchase of shares;
- allotment by a public company of shares otherwise than for cash;
- transfer of non-cash assets to a public company by members;
- report on initial accounts when a public company wishes to make a distribution.

3 General matters relating to the presentation of accounts

3.1 True and fair view

There is a fundamental requirement for full accounts to show a true and fair view. This overriding requirement must be followed when determining accounting policies or the presentation and disclosure of information. *ss226 & 227*

Compliance with accounting standards is normally required for accounts to show a true and fair view. The Accounting Standards Board's *Foreword to accounting standards* states that

> 'Accounting Standards are authoritative statements of how particular types of transaction and other events should be reflected in financial statements and accordingly compliance with accounting standards will normally be necessary for financial statements to give a true and fair view. Accounting standards need not be applied to immaterial items.'

The Companies Act 1985 contains provisions that permit directors to depart from complying with the provisions of the Act and accounting standards if, in special circumstances, compliance is inconsistent with the requirement to give a true and fair view. The Act requires that 'particulars of any such departure, the reasons for it and its effect should be given in a note to the accounts'. *ss226(5) & 227(6)*

Cases when the true and fair override is invoked should be stated clearly and unambiguously. The statutory disclosure required should be interpreted as follows: *UITF 7, 4*

(a) 'particulars of any such departure' – a statement of the treatment which would normally be needed in the circumstances and a description of the treatment actually adopted;
(b) 'the reasons for it' – a statement as to why the treatment prescribed would not give a true and fair view;
(c) 'its effect' – a description of how the position shown in the accounts is different as a result of the departure, normally with quantification except:
   (i)   when quantification is already evident in the accounts themselves (for example, a presentation matter involving adaptation of the headings in the Act's format requirements); or
   (ii) whenever the effect cannot reasonably be quantified, in which case the directors should explain the circumstances.

Where a departure continues in subsequent financial statements, the disclosure should be made in all subsequent statements, and should include corresponding amounts for the previous year. *UITF 7, 5*

Where a departure affects only the corresponding amounts, the disclosures should be given for those corresponding amounts.   *UITF 7, 6*

3.2   Formats

3.2.1   Prescribed formats

The Companies Act 1985 prescribes formats for a company's accounts. The Act sets out in Part I of Schedule 4 two alternative formats for the balance sheet and four alternative formats for the profit and loss account. The Act leaves the choice of particular format to the company's directors. However, once a company has adopted a particular format, that format may not be changed in subsequent years unless there are special reasons, in which case these must be disclosed.   *8, Sch 4*

    2, Sch 4

Appendix I contains the full balance sheet format 1 and profit and loss account formats 1 & 2. Balance sheet format 2 and profit and loss account formats 3 & 4 are not illustrated as they are rarely used in practice.

Within the prescribed formats, each of the headings and the sub-headings is preceded in the Act by either a letter of the alphabet or a Roman or Arabic numeral. This is for identification purposes only. There is no requirement for accounts to include these letters or numbers. Whichever one of the balance sheet and profit and loss account formats a company chooses, the company must show the items in the fixed order and under the headings and sub-headings that the adopted format sets out.   *1(2), Sch 4*

    1(1), Sch 4

3.2.2   Exceptions

There are, however, certain exceptions to the rules on prescribed formats:

(a)   Departure is allowed if made to show a true and fair view. In this regard reference should be made to UITF 7 (see **3.1** above).   *s226(5)*
(b)   An item may be shown in greater detail than the prescribed formats require.   *s227(6)*
(c)   An item which is not covered in any of the prescribed formats may be shown separately. However, the following items may not be shown as assets in the balance sheet: *3(1), Sch 4*
    3(2), Sch 4
    (i)   preliminary expenses;
    (ii)   expenses of, and commission on, any issue of shares or debentures;
    (iii)   costs of research.
(d)   The arrangement, the headings and the sub-headings set out in the formats and preceded by Arabic numerals must be adapted if the special nature of the company's business requires this.   *3(3), Sch 4*
(e)   Items that are preceded by Arabic numerals in the Act may be combined where either:
    (i)   individual amounts are not material; or   *3(4a), Sch 4*
    (ii)   the combination facilitates the assessment of the company's affairs. In this case, however, the detailed breakdown of the combined items must be given in the notes.   *3(4b), Sch 4*
    4, 3(4), Sch 4
(f)   A heading or sub-heading need not be shown where there is no amount to be included for both the year in question and the immediately preceding year.   *3(5), Sch 4*

In addition, group accounts must follow the requirements of Schedule 4A and there are modifications for simplified and abbreviated accounts provided by Schedule 8.

3.2.3 Example

The sample accounts, Russell Square Enterprises Limited, have been prepared in accordance with Format 1 for the profit and loss account and balance sheet, but also include the profit and loss account prepared in accordance with Format 2.

3.3 Material items

Difficulties of interpretation and application of the provisions of the Companies Acts arise particularly where disclosure is required only if an item is 'material', 'significant' or 'substantial' as no definition of these terms is given. It should be noted that, except where the Acts give such an exemption, the information should be given even if considered unimportant or immaterial by the directors. As mentioned above, many of the reporting requirements emanate from Schedule 4 to CA 1985 and in the individual sub-sections there is often no reference to 'material' or 'substantial' as there is in the all-encompassing sub-section 86 which states that: *86, Sch 4*

> 'Amounts which in the particular context of any provision of this Schedule
> are not material may be disregarded for the purposes of that provision.'

Disclosures required exclusively by accounting standards are not required for immaterial items.

Guidance published by the Institute of Chartered Accountants in England and Wales *AR 2.401* regards a matter as being material if knowledge of that matter would be likely to influence the users of the financial statements. Interpretation of the term 'material' is a matter for the exercise of professional judgement based on experience and the requirements of the accounts. Materiality has to be considered in relation to context and although quantitative measures must be considered, materiality cannot be defined by financial quanta or percentages.

When applying the term 'material' to an individual item, the following matters should *AR 2.401* be considered:

(a) the amount itself, in relation to:
    (i) the overall view of the accounts;
    (ii) the total of which it forms or should form part;
    (iii) associated items (whether in the profit and loss account or in the balance sheet);
    (iv) the corresponding amount in previous years;
(b) the description, including questions of emphasis;
(c) the presentation and context of any statutory requirements for disclosure.

4 Profit and loss account and other primary statements

4.1 General requirements

4.1.1 Formats

A profit and loss account (with comparative figures) must be prepared, for the defined accounting reference period, in one of the four formats laid down in the CA 1985. The example in Russell Square Enterprises Limited has been prepared in accordance with Format 1. On page 6A of the accounts there is an illustration of the profit and loss account prepared in accordance with Format 2. It should be noted that once the directors have selected a particular format it should not be changed in subsequent years unless there are special reasons. *s226*

2, Sch 4

The Companies Act 1985 and FRS 3 require certain items to be shown on the face of the profit and loss account, these being:

(a)   turnover;
(b)   profit or loss before and after taxation;
(c)   exceptional and extraordinary items;
(d)   profit for the financial year;
(e)   transfers to/from reserves;
(f)   dividends.

FRS 3 further requires a layered format to highlight, where applicable, the results of continuing and discontinued operations, specific classes of exceptional items and in very rare circumstances extraordinary items. Illustrative examples are appended to the FRS. *FRS 3, Summary*

Since all the remaining items in the profit and loss formats are denoted by Arabic numerals they may be disclosed by way of note. They may also be combined if their individual amounts are not material to assessing the profit or loss of the company for the year or they may be adapted to meet the special nature of the company's business. *3(3) & (4), Sch 4*

4.1.2 Realised profits

The Companies Act 1985 requires that only profits realised at the balance sheet date should be included in the profit and loss account. This means that profits may not be anticipated and therefore they should be included only when they are earned and their amount ascertained. For this purpose, realised profits are defined as 'such profits or losses of the company as fall to be treated in accordance with principles generally accepted at the time when those accounts are prepared with respect to the determination for accounting purposes of realised profits or losses'. This definition may at first sight be rather too general to be useful. However, the purpose is to ensure that the term 'realised profits' is not construed as having the rather restricted meaning that it has for *12, Sch 4*

s262(3)

67

tax purposes, while at the same time not to impose a different, but equally rigid, statutory definition. Consequently, the determination of whether a profit or a loss is realised or unrealised must be made in the light of best accounting practice at the time. In effect, 'realised' means (in accordance with SSAP 2) realised in the form either of cash or of other assets, the ultimate cash realisation of which can be assessed with reasonable certainty.

AR 2.402, 4–11

4.1.3 Netting off

Amounts in respect of items representing income may not be set off against amounts representing expenditure, and vice versa.

5 & 14, Sch 4

4.1.4 Income and expenditure account

The Companies Act 1985 permits, in the case of a company not trading for a profit, the profit and loss account to be referred to as the income and expenditure account.

s262(2)

4.1.5 Changes in the business

If a company acquires an operation or disposes of part of its business during the year, FRS 3 requires the aggregate results of each of the continuing operations, acquisitions and discontinued operations to be disclosed separately.

FRS 3, 14
FRS 3, 15

The minimum disclosure required by FRS 3 is for turnover and operating profit to be analysed between continuing operations, acquisitions and discontinued activities. This analysis must be presented on the face of the profit and loss account. In addition, the statutory categories falling between turnover and operating profit must be analysed between continuing activities, acquisitions and discontinued operations. This analysis may be presented either on the face of the profit and loss account or in the notes to the financial statements.

FRS 3, 14

Examples are attached to FRS 3 to illustrate the analysis between continuing operations, acquisitions and discontinued activities. Example 2 illustrates the full analysis of all categories, from turnover to operating profit inclusive, on the face of the profit and loss account in separate columns for each of continuing operations, acquisitions and discontinued operations. Example 1 illustrates the minimum disclosure requirement of the standard where the traditional 'horizontal' format of the profit and loss account is retained and only the analysis of turnover and operating profit between categories of continuing operations, acquisition and discontinued activities is given on the face of the profit and loss account. The analysis of the section between turnover and operating profit would be given in the notes to the financial statements.

FRS 3,
Examples

Where it is not practicable to determine the post-acquisition results of an operation to the end of the period being reported upon, an indication should be given of the contribution of the acquisition to the turnover and operating profit of the continuing operations. This situation may have arisen if the operation acquired was integrated with the existing operation of the business and it has ceased to be possible to identify separately the results. If it is not possible to give an indication of the contribution of an acquisition to the results of the period, this fact and the reason should be explained.

FRS 3, 16

Discontinued operations are activities which are sold or terminated. For the *FRS 3, 4* · discontinuance of an activity to be separately disclosed all of the following conditions must be satisfied:

(a)   the sale or termination is completed either in the current accounting period or before the earlier of three months after the commencement of the subsequent period and the date on which the financial statements are approved;

(b)   if a termination, the former activities have ceased permanently;

(c)   the sale or termination has a material effect on the nature and focus of the company's operation and represents a material reduction in its operating facilities resulting either from its withdrawal from a particular market (whether class of business or geographical) or from a material reduction in turnover in the reporting entity's continuing markets;

(d)   the assets, liabilities, results of operations and activities are clearly distinguishable, physically, operationally and for financial reporting purposes.

If an operation fails to meet any of these criteria, it is classified as part of continuing operations.

Only income and costs which relate directly to discontinued operations should appear *FRS 3, 17* under this heading. Reorganisations and restructuring of continuing operations resulting from a sale or termination should be treated as part of continuing operations.

If a decision has been made to sell or terminate an operation, the write-down of any *FRS 3, 18* assets and any provisions which result from the plans should appear in the continuing operations category in the period unless the operation qualifies as a discontinued activity. In a subsequent period when the operation does qualify as discontinued, the provisions should be used to offset the results of the operation in the discontinued category. The utilisation of the provisions should be analysed as necessary between the operating loss and the loss on sale or termination of the discontinued operation and disclosed on the face of the balance sheet immediately below the relevant items.

For the majority of companies, where there has been no change in the operations during the reporting and comparative period, a footnote to the profit and loss account should state:

> 'None of the company's activities was acquired or discontinued during the above two financial periods.'

If a company's only trading activity commences or ceases in its entirety during the two years the above wording can be varied to deal with this and to amplify that the trading period may be in respect of a shorter timescale than the full accounting reference period.

4.1.6   Comparative figures

Comparative figures should be given for all items in the profit and loss account, related *4(1), Sch 4* notes and the primary statements introduced by FRS 3 (see also **4.29(b)**). *FRS 3, 30*

4.1.7   Operating profit

The term 'operating profit or loss' is frequently used to describe the results for the year after operating expenses and before interest and investment income. There is no statutory requirement for this term but its use adds to the clarity of presentation in the profit and loss account and also facilitates the identification of information required where a cash flow statement is included.

4.2 Turnover

4.2.1 Definition

The four alternative profit and loss accounts prescribed in CA 1985 each require the disclosure of turnover. The Act defines turnover as the amounts derived from the provision of goods and services that fall within the company's ordinary activities after deducting trade discounts, VAT and any other taxes that are based on the amounts so derived. The method by which turnover is arrived at no longer has to be disclosed but current practice indicates that the method of computing turnover should be disclosed either as an accounting policy or in a note to the accounts.

s262(1)

Turnover should exclude value added tax on taxable outputs, but if it is desired to show the gross turnover, the VAT should be shown as a deduction in arriving at the turnover exclusive of VAT in a note to the accounts.

SSAP 5, 8

Whilst the Act defines turnover, problems can arise in certain businesses, such as contractors engaged in long-term contracts, computer software supplies and agents buying and selling on behalf of principals. The company should indicate clearly the basis on which turnover is calculated so that the reader of the accounts may establish how this is computed and whether this includes, for example, amounts unbilled but recoverable on contracts. Similarly, an agency business should clearly indicate that it has included sales only where it acted as principal.

IAS 18 *Turnover* provides, in the absence of a UK standard, some guidance on the recognition of turnover.

Sale of goods

Revenue from the resale of goods should be recognised when all the following conditions have been satisfied:

IAS 18, 14

(a) the enterprise has transferred to the buyer the significant risks and rewards of ownership of the goods;

(b) the enterprise retains neither continuing managerial involvement to the degree usually associated with ownership nor effective control over the goods sold;

(c) the amount of revenue can be measured reliably;

(d) it is probable that the economic benefits associated with the transaction will flow to the enterprise;

(e) the costs incurred or to be incurred in respect of the transaction can be measured reliably.

Rendering of services

When the outcome of a transaction involving the rendering of services can be estimated reliably, revenue associated with the transaction should be recognised by reference to the stage of completion of the transaction at the balance sheet date.

IAS 18, 20

The outcome of a transaction can be estimated reliably when all of the following conditions are satisfied:

(a)   the amount of revenue can be measured reliably;
(b)   it is probable that the economic benefits associated with the transaction will flow to the enterprise;
(c)   the stage of completion of the transaction at the balance sheet date can be measured reliably;
(d)   the costs incurred for the transaction and the cost to complete the transaction can be measured reliably.

When the outcome of the transaction involving the rendering of services cannot be estimated reliably, revenue should be recognised only to the extent of expenses recognised that are recoverable.   *IAS 18, 26*

4.2.2   Segmental disclosures

The Act requires the notes to the accounts to include certain information analysed by class of business and by geographical market.

Firstly, where a company has carried on two or more classes of business during the financial year in question, the notes must, if in the directors' opinion the classes differ substantially, give in respect of each class the amount of turnover that is attributable to each class.   *55(1), Sch 4*

Secondly, where a company has supplied goods or services to two or more markets during the financial year in question, the turnover must be split between markets if, in the directors' opinion, the markets differ substantially. For this purpose, 'market' means a market delimited by geographical bounds.   *55(2), Sch 4*

The Act states that, in determining the source of turnover, the directors must have regard to the way in which the company's activities are organised.   *55(3), Sch 4*

Where classes of business do not, in the opinion of the directors, differ substantially, they are to be treated as one class. Similarly, markets that do not, in the opinion of the directors, differ substantially, are to be treated as one market.   *55(4), Sch 4*

Only those classes which contributed materially to turnover and profits need be disclosed and a useful guide is to consider as material a class of business with turnover or profits comprising 10 per cent or more of the total.

The information above need not be disclosed if, in the opinion of the directors, it would be seriously prejudicial to the company's interests. In such cases, however, the fact that, but not the reason why, any such information has been omitted must be stated.   *55(5), Sch 4*

SSAP 25 prescribes additional segmental disclosure for plcs, private subsidiaries of plcs and substantial private companies (those exceeding the definition of medium-sized by a factor of 10), although all companies are encouraged to apply the provisions of the standard. In practice, it is rare for these disclosures to be given by companies which are not mandatorily required to comply with SSAP 25. The standard requires that where substantially different classes of business or geographical markets have   *SSAP 25, 34* been operated, in addition to the statutory requirements, the following information should be given:

(a)   nature of each class of business and market;
(b)   turnover by class of business and market distinguishing external customers and other segments;
(c)   result by class of business and geographical segment, before accounting for taxation, minority interests and extraordinary items;
(d)   net assets by class of business and geographical segment.

The geographical segmentation of turnover should be disclosed by origin. The turnover to these parties should also be disclosed by destination or it should be stated that this amount is not materially different from turnover to third parties by origin. *SSAP 25, 34*

The SSAP also requires reconciliations to be made to the related total in the accounts where appropriate and a note of any changes in definition of segments or accounting policies for segmental information. Comparative figures should also be provided. *SSAP 25, 37–39*

4.3   Cost of sales

Only Formats 1 and 3 of the prescribed profit and loss accounts in CA 1985 require the disclosure of the cost of sales as a single figure. The other two formats require greater detail to be disclosed. The Act does not define cost of sales nor, for that matter, distribution costs and administrative expenses, but note 14 to the profit and loss account formats states that each of the expense classifications should be stated after taking into account any necessary provisions for depreciation or diminution in value of assets. When expenses are so classified the amount of any provision for depreciation must be disclosed separately in the notes to the accounts (note 17 on the profit and loss account formats). Provision is made in Formats 2 and 4 for depreciation to be shown on the face of the profit and loss account, in which case separate disclosure in the notes would be unnecessary.

In view of the absence of any precise definitions there can be a fairly wide interpretation of cost of sales, distribution costs and administrative expenses. The directors may be motivated to minimise the administrative expense figure or to distort the gross profit figure to maintain competitive advantage. The auditor will need to ensure that whatever view is taken by the directors is reasonable in the circumstances. The allocations adopted by an individual company should be applied consistently from one year to another. Only genuine head office overhead expenditure should be included in administrative expenses and, for example, the salary costs of the marketing and production directors may well be allocated to distribution and cost of sales respectively. The company's management accounts may give an indication as to the classification of expenditure.

Items that might comprise cost of sales include:

• opening stocks and work in progress;
• direct materials and other external charges relating to production or manufacture;
• direct labour;

- fixed and variable production overheads including depreciation of productive assets;
- research and development costs;
- factory costs;
- variances from standard where a standard costing system is used;
- less: closing stocks and work in progress and own work capitalised.

4.4 The Format 2 alternative to cost of sales

Format 2 to CA 1985 allows a company to adopt a different categorisation of items in its profit and loss account. By its nature this is very much aimed at manufacturing companies but this does not preclude other companies from using it. The principal headings are:

(a) *Changes in stocks of finished goods and work in progress.* The difference between opening and closing stocks of finished goods and work in progress is to be shown under this heading. Finished goods would include bought-in components as well as items manufactured by the company. Progress payments, which would be deducted from the valuation of stocks for balance sheet purposes, are not to be taken into account.

(b) *Own work capitalised.* This caption will include the value of direct materials and labour and appropriate interest and other overhead costs capitalised in connection with the company's own construction of tangible fixed assets. The cost elements shown under the other profit and loss headings will be shown at their gross amount.

(c) *Raw materials and consumables.* The difference between the opening and closing stocks of raw materials and consumables will be deducted from or added to the total cost of purchases of these items in arriving at the amount to be shown under this heading. Purchases of components should be included as forming part of raw materials.

Companies in the retail or wholesale trade which adopt this profit and loss account format should use more appropriate wording for headings (a) and (c) above such as 'change in stocks of goods for resale' and 'goods for resale'.

4.5 Net operating expenses (including other operating income)

Format 1 of the profit and loss account requires the disclosure of distribution costs, administrative expenses and other operating income. The information may be given on the face of the profit and loss account or in a note to the accounts. As stated in **4.3** above these items are not defined in the Act and accordingly it is for the directors to allocate expenditure to these headings. The allocation must be consistent from one year to another and the company's detailed management accounts may give an indication of the most appropriate classification. The above comment also applies to expenditure items specified in Format 2.

The separate headings within net operating expenses should include the following types of expenditure.

4.5.1 Distribution costs

Distribution costs should include all expenses related to the holding of goods for resale, selling costs, and the transfer of goods to customers, such as:

- salaries, commissions and related National Insurance and pension costs;
- advertising and trade shows/exhibitions;
- warehousing costs of finished products;
- travelling and motor vehicle running expenses;
- outward transportation costs including depreciation of vehicles;
- rent, rates, insurance, utilities, depreciation and maintenance of sales outlets and warehouses.

4.5.2 Administrative expenses

Administrative expenses includes all operating costs except those associated with production and distribution of products, and services and distribution costs which are required to be shown under separate headings. The following expenditure is normally included in administrative expenses:

- salary and related costs of administrative personnel (such as accounting department, directors and general managers) to the extent that they cannot be attributed elsewhere;
- rent, rates, insurance, utilities, depreciation and maintenance of administrative buildings;
- professional fees;
- bad debts;
- general overhead expenses.

4.5.3 Other operating income

For most companies, the amount of such income will not be considered material, in which case it may be included in turnover. This category should, however, include all other sources of income, if material, associated with the ordinary activities of the business except income from investments and interest receivable which are required to be shown under separate headings, if material. Examples of other operating income include:

- royalties;
- commissions;
- rental income from surplus facilities.

4.5.4 Other external charges and other operating charges

No guidance is provided by the Companies Act as to what items should be included in 'other external charges' as opposed to 'other operating charges'. Since it is linked in the formats with raw materials and consumables, it is suggested that as a minimum 'other external charges' must include those production costs from external sources which are not included as raw materials and overheads. 'Other operating charges' would then include selling and administrative costs which were not shown under the other headings. However, it is impossible to refute the argument that any charge which is neither a staff cost nor depreciation must be an external charge; on this basis everything that was not specifically included elsewhere would be included in 'other external charges', and 'other operating charges' would become redundant.

Companies should adopt whatever reasonable division is most convenient to them. The important point is that whatever division is adopted must be adhered to consistently from year to year.

4.6   Profit on ordinary activities before taxation

As all items in the profit and loss account formats are preceded by an Arabic numeral they may be relegated to the notes to the accounts, but whichever format is used the company's profit and loss account must show the profit or loss on ordinary activities before taxation.

3(6), Sch 4

4.7   Income from investments

Incoming dividends from UK companies should be included at the amount of cash received or receivable plus the tax credit and disclosure in the taxation charge of the contra tax credit as 'tax attributable to franked investment income'.

SSAP 8, 25

SSAP 8, 22

The profit and loss account formats require income from fixed asset investments to be shown separately from other investment income, for example interest receivable.

4.8   Grants

SSAP 4 *Accounting for grants* requires that grants relating to fixed assets should be credited to revenue over the expected useful life of the assets. This may be achieved by either reducing the cost of the asset by the amount of the grant or treating the grant as a deferred credit and transferring a proportion to revenue each year. However, the Companies Act prohibits companies from deducting the amount of the grant from the purchase cost of the asset since this has the effect of contravening rules relating to the definition of 'purchase price'. Where the amount of the deferred credit is material it should be shown separately in the balance sheet under the heading of 'creditors: amounts falling due after more than one year'.

SSAP 4, 23

17 & 26(1), Sch 4

SSAP 4 requires the accounting policy for grants to be stated together with the effects of government grants on the results for the period and/or the financial position together with details of any material effect on the results for the year of government assistance, other than grants.

SSAP 4, 28

Other grants relating to immediate financial assistance or support should be recognised in the period they become receivable, unless they relate to future periods in which case they should be recognised accordingly.

SSAP 4, 23

4.9   Research and development expenditure

In SSAP 13 *Accounting for research and development expenditure* there is a requirement for plcs and substantial private companies (those exceeding the definition of medium-sized by a factor of 10) to disclose the amount of research and development

SSAP 13, 22

expenditure written off. The amount to be disclosed is the current year's expenditure, the amount amortised from deferred expenditure and the total charge.

The Companies Act 1985 permits any company to capitalise development costs (but not research costs) in 'special circumstances'. This treatment is not mandatory and a company may choose a policy of either capitalisation or direct write-off. Research costs must be written off through the profit and loss account as they are incurred.

20, Sch 4

The reviewing of 'special circumstances' is clarified by SSAP 13 which goes considerably further than CA 1985 in that it defines all the specific circumstances that must exist before development costs may be capitalised.

SSAP 13, 25

Where these specific conditions are satisfied, SSAP 13 requires that the deferred expenditure be amortised on the commencement of commercial production of the product or process. Where development costs are shown as an asset the notes must disclose the period over which the amount of those costs originally capitalised is being, or is to be, written off and the reasons for capitalising the development costs. This note, if the unamortised costs are not to be treated as a realised loss for purposes of calculating distributable profits in accordance with s263 CA 1985, should also state that the unamortised development expenditure is not to be treated as a realised loss for the purpose of calculating distributable profits and the circumstances that the directors relied upon to justify their decision.

SSAP 13, 28

20(2), Sch 4

s269

4.10 Repairs and maintenance

Subsequent expenditure to ensure that the asset maintains its originally assessed standard of performance should be recognised in the profit and loss account as it is incurred.

FRS 15, 34

This type of expenditure is often referred to as 'repairs and maintenance expenditure'. In calculating the useful life of an asset it is assumed that such expenditure will be carried out. Examples are the cost of servicing or the routine overhauling of plant and equipment and repainting a building. Without such expenditure the depreciation expense would be increased because the useful life and/or residual value of the asset would be reduced.

FRS 15, 35

Subsequent expenditure should be capitalised in three circumstances:

FRS 15, 36

(a) where the subsequent expenditure provides an enhancement of economic benefits of the tangible fixed asset in excess of the orignally assessed standard of performance;
(b) where a component of the tangible fixed asset that has been treated separately for depreciation purposes and depreciated over its individual useful economic life, is replaced or restored;
(c) where the subsequent expenditure relates to a major inspection or overhaul of a tangible fixed asset that restores the economic benefits of the asset that have been consumed by the entity and have been reflected in depreciation.

Subsequent expenditure on a tangible fixed asset is recognised as an addition to the asset to the extent that the expenditure improves the condition of the asset beyond its

FRS 15, 37

previously assessed standard of performance. Examples of subsequent expenditure that results in and enhancement of economic benefits include:

- modification of an item of plant to extend its useful economic life or increase its capacity
- upgrading machine parts to achive a substantial improvement in the quality of output.

Some tangible fixed assets require, in addition to routine repairs and maintenance, substantial expenditure every few years for major refits or refurbishment or the replacement or restoration of major components. For example, a furnace may require relining every five years. For depreciation purposes the entity should account separately for major components (eg the furnace lining) that have substantially different useful economic lives from the rest of the asset. In such a case, each component is deprecitated over its individual useful economic life, so that the depreciation profile of the whole asset more accurately reflects the actual consumption of the asset's economic benefits. Subsequent expenditure incurred in replacing or renewing the component is accounted for as an addition to the tangible fixed asset and the carrying amount of the replaced component is removed from the balance sheet and treated as a disposal. *FRS 15, 38*

The same approach may also be applied to major inspections and overhauls of tangible fixed assets. For example, an aircraft may be required by law to be overhauled once every three years. Unless the overhaul is undertaken the aircraft cannot continue to be flown. The entity reflects the need to undertake the overhaul or inspection by depreciating an amount of the asset that is equivalent to the expected inspection or overhaul costs over the period until the next inspection or overhaul. In such a case, the cost of the inspection or overhaul is capitalised when incurred because it restores the economic benefits of the tangible fixed asset and the carrying amount representing the cost of the benefits consumed is removed from the balance sheet and also treated as a disposal. *FRS 15, 39*

The accounting treatment for subsequent expenditure should reflect the circumstances that were taken into account on the initial recognition of the asset and the depreciation profile adopted (or subsequent revisions thereof). Therefore, when the carrying amount of the asset already takes into account a consumption of economic benefits, eg by depreciating components of the asset at a faster rate than the asset as a whole (or by a previous impairment of the asset or component), the subsequent expenditure to restore those economic benefits is capitalised. The decision whether to identify separate components or future expenditures on overhauls or inspections for depreciation over a shorter useful economic life than the rest of the tangible fixed asset is likely to reflect: *FRS 15, 40*

- whether the useful economic lives of the components are, or the period until the next inspection or overhaul is, substantially different from the useful economic life of the remainder of the asset;
- the degree of irregularity in the level of expenditures required to restate the component or asset in different accounting periods; and
- their materiality in the context of the financial statements.

Where it has been determined not to account for each tangible fixed asset as several different asset components or to depreciate part of the asset over a different timescale *FRS 15, 41* from the rest of the asset, the cost of replacing, restoring, overhauling or inspecting the asset or components of the asset is not capitalised, but instead is recognised in the profit and loss account as incurred.

4.11   Depreciation

4.11.1   Background

Where a fixed asset has a limited useful economic life, its purchase price, its production cost (or its revalued amount) must be written off systematically over the period of that life. Accordingly the non-depreciation of an asset or full write-off on acquisition to profit and loss account are technically prohibited, unless the asset cost is immaterial. In determining the amount to be written off each year, CA 1985 specifically requires that account be taken of the asset's estimated residual value at the end of its useful economic life. *18, Sch 4 FRS 15, 77* *18(b), Sch 4*

4.11.2   Additional depreciation

The Companies Act 1985 provides in two circumstances for additional depreciation. Firstly, where a fixed asset investment that falls to be disclosed in the balance sheet formats has diminished in value, the Act permits the directors to make provisions in respect of this diminution in value. Any such provisions must, if not shown in the profit and loss account, be disclosed either separately or in aggregate in the notes to the accounts. Secondly, additional depreciation must be provided if a fixed asset (including a fixed asset investment) has diminished in value and the reduction is expected to be permanent. Where additional depreciation had been provided, but the factors that gave rise to it no longer apply to any extent, then the provision must be written back to that extent. The amounts must be disclosed either separately or in aggregate in the notes to the accounts if not shown in the profit and loss account. *19(1), Sch 4* *19(2), Sch 4* *19(3), Sch 4*

4.11.3   Disclosure requirements

In respect of the provision for depreciation for each item shown as a fixed asset there must be disclosed: *42(3), Sch 4*

(a)   accumulated depreciation at the beginning of the period and at the balance sheet date;
(b)   charge for the period and provisions for diminution;
(c)   adjustments for disposals;
(d)   other adjustments.

It should be noted that where the value of any fixed asset has been determined according to the alternative accounting rules (see **5.4.3**), CA 1985 permits the amount of any provision for depreciation charged in the profit and loss account to be based on the valuation or the historical cost of the asset. However, where the amount so charged is based on historical cost, the difference between that charge and the charge based on the asset's valuation must be disclosed separately. It must be disclosed either on the face of the profit or loss account or in the notes. The Act therefore allows the *32(3), Sch 4* difference to be either debited or credited (as appropriate) directly to the revaluation reserve. However, FRS 15 *Tangible fixed assets* clarifies the position in that depreciation must be based on cost or revalued amount and the resultant charge included in the profit and loss account. No part should be set directly against reserves, although its effect may be dealt with by a transfer between profit and loss account and revaluation reserves (see also **4.29**).

SSAP 15, 79

In addition to the statutory disclosures, FRS 15 requires the disclosure of the following in respect of each major class of depreciable assets:

SSAP 15, 100
36, Sch 4

(a)   the depreciation methods used;

(b)   the useful economic lives or the depreciation rates used;

(c)   total depreciation charged for the period;

(d)   where material, the financial effect of a change in either the estimate of useful economic lives or the estimate of residual values;

(e)   the cost or revalued amount at the beginning of the financial period and at the balance sheet date;

(f)   the cumulative amount of provisions for depreciation or impairment at the beginning of the financial period and at the balance sheet date;

(g)   a reconciliation of the movements, separately disclosing additions, disposals, revaluations, transfers, depreciation, impairment losses, and reversals of past impairment losses written back in the financial period;

(h)   the net carrying amount at the beginning of the financial period and at the balance sheet date.

Where there has been a change in the depreciation method used, the effect, if material, should be disclosed in the year of change. The reason for the change should also be disclosed.

FRS 15, 102

When a tangible fixed asset is revalued, any accumulated depreciation at the date of revaluation is eliminated and the cost or revalued amount of the asset is restated at its revalued amount.

FRS 15, 101

4.11.4 Depreciation policies

FRS 15 only permits a change from one method of providing depreciation to another on the grounds that the new method will give a fairer presentation of the results and of the financial position. Such a change does not, however, constitute a change of accounting policy; the net book amount is written off over the remaining useful economic life, commencing in the period in which the change is made.

FRS 15, 82

Where the tangible fixed asset comprises two or more major components with substantially different useful economic lives, each component should be accounted for as a separate asset and depreciated over its individual useful economic life.

FRS 15, 83

The FRS comments that a variety of methods can be used to depreciate a tangible fixed asset on a systematic basis over its useful economic life. It suggests that where the pattern of consumption of an asset's economic benefits is uncertain, a straight-line method of depreciation should usually be adopted.

FRS 15, 81

In the case of leasehold property, any improvements during the period of the lease should be written off in equal instalments over the remaining period of the lease or to the next review date depending on the circumstances. Amortisation of leasehold property should be provided over a period no longer than the period of the lease. This includes long leases irrespective of the fact that market value may be greater than book value.

Depreciation considerations will also arise where the remaining life of any leasehold investment properties is 20 years or less.   *SSAP 19, 10*

Abnormal depreciation or material losses or profits on disposal of fixed assets due, for example, to the closure of a factory should be shown separately (see **4.15**). Care should be taken, particularly as a result of the separate disclosure requirements, that the total depreciation charge agrees with the fixed asset note to the balance sheet where the movement of depreciation is disclosed.   *FRS 3, 20*

4.11.5   Requirement for depreciation

Land and buildings

The FRS addresses the issue of the non-depreciation of land and buildings and firmly states that buildings should be depreciated. It considers that land and buildings are separable assets and are dealt with separately for accounting purposes, even when they are acquired together. Land normally has an unlimited life and therefore is not depreciated. Buildings have a limited life and therefore are depreciated. An increase in the existing use value of the land on which a building stands does not affect the determination of the useful life or residual value of the building. Another example of separable assets that may have substantially different useful economic lives is the structure of a building and items within the structure such as general fittings.   *FRS 15, 84*

Previously buildings have not, in some cases, been depreciated on the grounds that the high standard of regular maintenance meant that the building had an indefinite life. FRS 15 refutes this by stating that subsequent expenditure on a tangible fixed asset that maintains or enhances the previously assessed standard of performance of the asset does not negate the need to charge depreciation.   *FRS 15, 86*

The FRS goes on to comment that in calculating the useful economic life of an asset it is assumed that subsequent expenditure will be undertaken to maintain the originally assessed standard of performance of the asset (for example the cost of servicing or overhauling plant and equipment). Without such expenditure the depreciation expense would be increased because the useful life and/or residual value of the asset would be reduced. This type of expenditure is recognised as an expense.   *FRS 15, 87*

In addition, subsequent expenditure may be undertaken that results in a restoration or replacement of a component of the asset that has been depreciated or an enhancement of economic benefits of the asset in excess of the originally assessed standard of performance. This type of expenditure may result in an extension of the useful economic life of the asset. However, such expenditure does not negate the need to charge depreciation. The subsequent expenditure should be capitalised as it is incurred and depreciated over the asset's (or, where the expenditure relates to a component, the component's) useful economic life, or the period to the next major overhaul or inspection, as appropriate.   *FRS 15, 88*

The only grounds for not charging depreciation, other than for non-depreciable land, are that the depreciation charge and accumulated depreciation are immaterial. The   *FRS 15, 90* depreciation charge and accumulated depreciation are immaterial if they would not reasonably influence a user of the accounts.

An entity must be able to justify that the uncharged depreciation is not material in aggregate as well as for each tangible fixed asset. Depreciation may be immaterial because of very long useful economic lives or high residual values (or both). A high residual value will reflect the remaining economic value of the asset at the end of its useful economic life to the entity. These conditions may occur when: *FRS 15, 91*

(a)   the entity has a policy and practice of regular maintenance and repair (charges for which are recognised in the profit and loss account) such that the asset is kept to its previously assessed standard of performance; and

(b)   the asset is unlikely to suffer from economic or technological obsolescence (e.g., due to potential changes in demand in the market following changes in fashion); and where estimated residual values are material:

   (i)   the entity has a policy and practice of disposing of similar assets well before the end of their economic lives; and

   (ii)   the disposal proceeds of similar assets (after excluding the effect of price changes since the date of acquisition or last revaluation) have not been materially less than their carrying amounts.

Where it is not reasonably practicable to perform impairment reviews on an individual asset basis, they should be performed for groups of assets, as part of income-generating units, in accordance with FRS 11. After the first period the reviews need only be updated. If expectations of future cash flows and discount rates have not changed significantly, the updating procedure will be relatively quick to perform. If there have been no adverse changes in the key assumptions and variables, or if the estimated recoverable amount was previously substantially in excess of the carrying amount, it may even be possible to ascertain immediately that the asset or income-generating unit is not impaired. *FRS 15, 92*

4.11.6   Disposals

Profits or losses on the disposal of an asset should be disclosed separately in the statutory profit and loss account if material and not included in the depreciation charge. *FRS 3, 20*

The profit or loss on disposal of an asset should be accounted for in the profit and loss account of the period in which the disposal occurs and be calculated as the difference between the net sale proceeds and the net carrying amount (whether carried out historical cost less depreciation) or at a valuation. *FRS 3, 21* *FRS 15, 72*

Where an asset (or a component of an asset) is replaced, its carrying amount is removed from the balance sheet (by eliminating its cost (or revalued amount) and related accumulated depreciation) and the resulting gain or loss on disposal is recorded as described above. For example, a new tangible fixed asset may be acquired from insurance proceeds when a previously held tangible fixed asset has been lost or destroyed. In such cases the lost or destroyed asset is removed from the balance sheet and the resulting gain or loss on disposal (being the difference between the carrying amount and the insurance proceeds) is recognised. The replacement asset is recorded at its cost. *FRS 15, 73*

4.12 Rental expenses

The total of operating lease rentals charged as an expense in the profit and loss account should be disclosed, analysed between amounts payable in respect of hire of plant and machinery and in respect of other operating leases. *SSAP 21, 55*

4.13 Directors' remuneration

4.13.1 Background to disclosures

The disclosures of directors' remuneration were significantly revised by SI 1997/570 which took effect from 31 March 1997. The revised disclosures are intended to be simpler to understand and, for smaller companies, the level of disclosure is reduced. A number of anomalies such as the chairman/highest paid director distinction have been eliminated.

4.13.2 Directors' emoluments

The following disclosures shall be given by companies which are not listed: *1(1) & 1(2), Sch 6*

(a)   the aggregate amount of emoluments paid to or receivable by directors in respect of qualifying services;

(b)   the aggregate of the following:
    (i)   the amount of money paid to or receivable by directors under long-term incentive schemes in respect of qualifying services; and
    (ii)   the net value of assets received or receivable by directors under such schemes in respect of such services;

(c)   the aggregate value of any company contributions paid, or treated as paid, to a money purchase pension scheme in respect of directors' qualifying services; and

(d)   in the case of each of money purchase pension schemes and defined benefit pension schemes, the number of directors (if any) to whom retirement benefits are accruing.

(e)   the directors who exercised share options; and

(f)   the directors in respect of whose qualifying services shares were received or receivable under long-term incentive schemes.

Emoluments

The emoluments of a director are defined as including:

1(3), Sch 6

(a)   salaries, fees and bonuses;

(b)   sums paid by way of expenses allowance (so far as they are chargeable to United Kingdom income tax); and

(c)   the estimated money value of any other non-cash benefits received by the director.

Emoluments do not include:

(a) the value of any share options granted to the director or the amount of any gains made on the exercise of any such options;
(b) any company contributions paid, or treated as paid, in respect of the director under any pension scheme or any benefits to which he is entitled under any such scheme; or
(c) any money or other assets paid to or received or receivable by the director under any long-term incentive scheme.

Qualifying services means services as a director of the company, and services as a director of any of its subsidiary undertakings. The definition also includes activities connected with the management of the affairs of the company or any of its subsidiary undertakings. *1(5), Sch 6*

Long-term incentive scheme means any agreement or arrangement under which money or other assets may become receivable by a director where there are qualifying conditions with respect to service or performance which cannot be fulfilled within a single financial year. Bonuses which are determined by reference to service or performance within a single financial year are excluded from this definition. *1(4), Sch 6*

Emoluments paid or receivable or share options granted in respect of a person's accepting office as a director shall be treated as emoluments paid or receivable or share options granted in respect of his services as a director. *1(6), Sch 6*

4.13.3 Details of highest paid director's emoluments

Where: *2, Sch 6*

(a) the aggregate of emoluments paid to or receivable by directors in respect of qualifying services, and
(b) the amount of money paid to or receivable by directors under long-term incentive schemes in respect of qualifying services; and
(c) the net value of assets received or receivable by directors under such schemes in respect of such services,

has a shown total £200,000 or more, the following shall be disclosed in respect of the highest paid director:

(a) the total emoluments attributable to the highest paid director; and
(b) the value of company contributions paid to a money purchase pension scheme in respect of the highest paid director.

In addition, in respect of the highest paid director, the following details should be given in respect of rights under defined benefit pension schemes:

(a) the amount at the end of the year of the director's accrued pension; and
(b) where applicable, the amount at the end of the year of the director's accrued lump sum.

4.13.4   Excess retirement benefits of directors and past directors

Disclosure should be made of the aggregate amount of:

(a)   the retirement benefits paid to or receivable by directors under pension schemes; and

(b)   the retirement benefits paid to or receivable by past directors under such schemes,

which are (in each case) in excess of the retirement benefits to which they were respectively entitled on the later of the date when the benefits first became payable and 31 March 1997.

Amounts paid or receivable under a pension scheme need not be included in the aggregate amount if:

(a)   the funding of the scheme was such that the amounts were or, as the case may be, could have been paid without recourse to additional contributions; and

(b)   amounts were paid to or receivable by all pensioner members of the scheme on the same basis.

References to retirement benefits include benefits otherwise than in cash. The estimated money value of the benefit and the nature of any such benefit should be disclosed.

4.13.5   Compensation to directors for loss of office

The aggregate amount of any compensation to directors or past directors in respect of loss of office should be disclosed.

This amount includes compensation received or receivable by a director or past director for the following:

(a)   loss of office as director of the company, or

(b)   loss, while director of the company or on or in connection with his ceasing to be a director of it, of:
   (i)   any other office in connection with the management of the company's affairs, or
   (ii)   any office as director or otherwise in connection with the management of the affairs of any subsidiary undertaking of the company.

References to compensation include non-cash benefits. In respect of non-cash benefits, the estimated money value of the benefit should be included in the aggregate. The nature of any non-cash compensation shall be disclosed.

References to compensation for loss of office include the following:

(a)   compensation in consideration for, or in connection with, a person's retirement from office; and

(b)   where such a retirement is occasioned by a breach of the person's contract with the company or with a subsidiary undertaking of the company:
   (i)   payments made by way of damages for the breach; or

(ii)   payments made by way of settlement or compromise of any claim in respect of the breach.

4.13.6   Sums paid to third parties in respect of directors' services
9, Sch 6

Disclosure should be made of the aggregate amount of any consideration paid to or receivable by third parties for making available the services of any person:

(a)   as a director of the company, or
(b)   while director of the company:
    (i)   as director of any of its subsidiary undertakings, or
    (ii)   otherwise in connection with the management of the affairs of the company or any of its subsidiary undertakings.

The reference to consideration includes benefits otherwise than in cash. The estimated money value of the benefit should be included in the aggregate. The nature of any non-cash consideration shall be disclosed.

The reference to third parties is to persons other than the following:

(a)   the director himself or a person connected with him or body corporate controlled by him, and
(b)   the company or any of its subsidiary undertakings.

For all directors' remuneration disclosures, references to amounts paid to or receivable by a person include amounts paid to or receivable by a person connected with him or a body corporate controlled by the person.

This disclosure will be most typically found where the director is also a partner in a professional practice such as a firm of solicitors or surveyors and the practice is in receipt of fees for his services.

4.13.7   Directors' share options

The UITF has concluded that the grant of an option in the company's shares to a director should be treated as giving rise to a benefit which should be included in the aggregate of directors' remuneration. However, it also accepts that there is currently no practicable way of specifying an appropriate valuation method for options as a benefit in kind. However, the UITF has identified a series of disclosures which should be presented by all companies in respect of individual directors to reflect their belief that options are a benefit. These disclosures are: *UITF 10, 9* *UITF 10, 10*

UITF 10, Appendix

(a)   the number of shares under option at the beginning and end of the year;
(b)   the number of options granted, exercised and lapsed unexercised during the year;
(c)   the exercise prices;
(d)   the dates from which the options may be exercised;
(e)   the expiry dates;
(f)   the cost of the options (if any);
(g)   for any options exercised during the year, the market price of the shares at the date of exercise;

(h)   a concise summary of any performance criteria conditional upon which the options are exercisable.

In addition, where directors have options which are exercisable at different prices and/ or different dates then separate figures are required for each exercise price and/or date combination.

The disclosure of the number of options granted or exercised during the year is a legal requirement. The other disclosures are recommended by the UITF, although they are not mandatory.

4.13.8   Responsibility of the auditors

If the requirements for disclosure of the requisite information are not complied with by the company then, under CA 1985, the auditors are required to include in their report on the accounts, so far as they are reasonably able, a statement giving the required particulars.   *s237(4)*

4.14   Auditors' remuneration

This should be the sum of the audit fee and related expenses, including benefits in kind and after adjusting for any previous year under/over-provision. Companies defined as 'large' must also state the amount of fees and benefits derived from non-audit work.   *s390A* *s390B*

Fees paid to reporting accountants do not need to be disclosed.

4.15   Exceptional items

The provisions of CA 1985 require disclosure of the effect of any transaction that is exceptional by virtue of size or incidence even though it falls within the ordinary activities of the company.   *57(3), Sch 4*

FRS 3 includes a definition of exceptional items being those material items which derive from events or transactions that fall within the ordinary activities of the reporting entity and which individually or, if of a similar type, in aggregate, need to be disclosed separately by virtue of their size or incidence if the financial statements are to give a true and fair view.   *FRS 3, 5*

Generally, exceptional items should be included as part of the statutory format heading to which they relate in arriving at the profit on ordinary activities before taxation and should be attributed to continuing or discontinued operations. Additional information should be in a separate note detailing the amount of each exceptional item, either individually, or as an aggregate of items of a similar type. Alternatively the items should be disclosed on the face of the profit and loss account if required to show a true and fair view. Whichever treatment is adopted, an adequate description of each exceptional item should be given to enable its nature to be understood.   *FRS 3, 19*

The following items, including provisions in respect of such items, should be shown separately on the face of the profit and loss account after operating profit and before interest, and included under the appropriate heading of continuing or discontinued operations:

FRS 3, 20

(a) profits or losses on the sale or termination of an operation;
(b) costs of a fundamental reorganisation or restructuring having a material effect on the nature and focus of the reporting entity's operation; and
(c) profits or losses on the disposal of fixed assets.

In calculating the profit or loss in respect of the above items, consideration should only be given to revenue and costs directly related to the items in question.

When the net amount of (a) or (c) above is not material, but the gross profits or losses are material, the relevant heading should still appear on the face of the profit and loss account with a reference to a related note analysing the profits and losses.

FRS 3, 20

Relevant information regarding the effect of these items on the taxation charge should be shown in a note to the profit and loss account. As a minimum, the related tax and the minority interest should be shown in aggregate, but if the effect of the tax and minority interest differs for the various categories of items, further information should be given, where applicable, to assist users in assessing the impact of the different items on the net profit or loss attributable to shareholders.

FRS 3, 20

In addition, SSAP 6 (now withdrawn) suggested that research and development expenditure could give rise to separate disclosure if its size and incidence would result in a true and fair view not being given if disclosure were not made. However, if there is a continuous annual policy of writing off such expenditure, then it should not be regarded as 'exceptional'.

Similar considerations may arise in relation to advertising or promotional expenditure where it is normal practice to incur such large amounts on a regular basis.

4.16 Interest payable and similar charges

The Companies Act 1985 requires the disclosure of separate totals for interest on the following loans made to the company:

53(2), Sch 4

(a) bank loans and overdrafts; and
(b) loans of any other kind made to the company.

The provisions of CA 1985 do not apply to interest or charges on loans to a company from other group companies, but, with that exception, they apply to interest or charges on all loans, whether made on the security of debentures or not. Note 16 to the profit and loss account formats in CA 1985 states that the amount of interest payable should be disclosed separately and therefore whilst any such interest should not be included in either of the amount at (a) and (b) above it should nevertheless be disclosed.

53(2), Sch 4

8(16), Sch 4

SSAP 21 also requires that the interest element of finance lease payments be disclosed (see chapter **9**).

SSAP 21, 53

Where interest is capitalised and included in the production cost of any asset, for example a property under development, the amount should be stated. This is best achieved by stating the gross amount of the interest charge in the profit and loss account note and deducting amounts capitalised in that year. The relevant balance sheet note should then also disclose the cumulative amount of interest capitalised.

26(3), Sch 4

4.17 Employee information

4.17.1 Staff numbers

The following must be disclosed in the notes to the accounts:

56(1a), Sch 4

(a) The average number of employees in the financial year (including executive directors). This is to be calculated by ascertaining the number of persons employed under a contract of service, whether full-time or part-time, for each month of the year; adding together all the monthly numbers and dividing by the number of months in the financial period.

(b) The average number of employees by category. This number is to be calculated in the same manner as in (a) above. For this purpose, the categories of persons employed are to be such categories as the directors select, having regard to the way in which the company's activities are organised.

56(1b&5), Sch 4

This rather vague guideline as to how categories are to be selected results in a variety of different categories being chosen by directors of different companies, for example between hourly paid, weekly paid and salaried staff, or between production, sales and administrative staff.

4.17.2 Staff costs

The Companies Act 1985 also requires particulars of certain costs relating to all persons employed by the company (including executive directors). In particular, the notes must disclose in aggregate each of the following amounts:

56(4), Sch 4

56(4a), Sch 4
94(3), Sch 4

(a) The wages and salaries that were paid or payable. To ensure consistency with directors' remuneration disclosure, this should include an estimate of benefits in kind to the extent that they are material and ascertainable. P11Ds provide a useful source of reference.

94(1), Sch 4

(b) Social security costs that the company has incurred. This means any contributions by the company to any social security or pension scheme fund, or arrangement run by the state.

(c) Other pension costs. These should be split between defined benefit and defined contribution schemes (see **4.18** below). This includes costs incurred by the company in respect of pension schemes established for the purpose of providing pensions for current or former employees and sums set aside for the future payment of pensions directly by the company to current or former employees. Any pensions paid directly to present or former employees which have not been previously set aside should also be included. Contributions by the company to any state social security or pension scheme, fund or arrangement should be included under (b) above.

94(2), Sch 4

4.18 Pension costs

4.18.1 Background

SSAP 24 deals with the recognition of pension costs in company accounts and does not have any direct effect on the funding policy adopted for the scheme.

The standard applies where the employer has a legal or contractual obligation (or a commitment implied by the employers' actions) to provide pensions for his employees, and the same principles apply irrespective of whether the scheme is funded or unfunded. *SSAP 24, 73*

SSAP 24 does not apply to state social security contributions or redundancy payments. *SSAP 24, 76*

The basic objective of SSAP 24 is that the cost of pensions should be charged against profit on a systematic and rational basis over the period during which the employer derives benefit from the employees' service. Consequently, the pensions cost is accounted for on an accruals basis with pension prepayments or accruals arising as a result. *SSAP 24, 77*

Pension costs can be split into 'regular costs' and 'variations' therefrom. Regular costs is the consistent ongoing cost recognised under the actuarial methods used. Variations from the regular cost will typically arise through experience surpluses or deficiencies, changes in the actuarial assumptions or method, benefit changes or increases in pensions' payments not previously provided for. The cost of such variations will normally be allocated over the employees' average remaining service lives. *SSAP 24, 20 & 21*

As a result of applying SSAP 24, the pension expense figure will in many cases be different from the amount actually contributed to a scheme (or paid out under an unfunded arrangement). Since there is no intention to place any restrictions on an employer's funding policy any differences should be shown in the company balance sheet as a provision for pension liabilities or a prepayment of pension costs, as appropriate. *SSAP 24, 16*

SSAP 24, 86

Tax relief is normally only granted on contributions actually paid and therefore if a pension provision or a prepayment is set up, the deferred tax implications should be considered. SSAP 15 permits either the full provision basis or the partial provision basis to be used when accounting for the deferred tax implications of pensions and other post-retirement benefits. The policy adopted should be disclosed. *SSAP 15, 32A*

If SSAP 24 is being implemented for the first time, a cumulative adjustment will normally arise as a result of previous year's pension costs not having been calculated in accordance with SSAP 24. There are two options for dealing with this: *SSAP 24, 92*

(a) The estimated surplus or deficiency is spread at the implementation date over the average expected remaining service life of current employees.

(b) The actuarial surplus or deficiency at the date of implementation of SSAP 24 should be treated as a prior year adjustment. That is, the surplus or deficiency will be recognised in full by making adjustment to retained profits and creating a corresponding provision or prepayment.

4.18.2 Disclosure requirements

Defined contribution schemes: *SSAP 24, 87*

(a)   nature of scheme (i.e., defined contribution);
(b)   accounting policy;
(c)   the pension cost charge for the period;
(d)   any outstanding or prepaid contributions at the balance sheet date.

Defined benefit schemes: *SSAP 24, 88*

(a)   nature of scheme (i.e., defined benefit);
(b)   whether funded or unfunded;
(c)   the accounting policy and, if different, the funding policy;
(d)   whether pension costs have been assessed in accordance with the advice of a professionally qualified actuary and, if so, the date of the most recent formal actuarial valuation. If the actuary is an officer or employee of the company or group of which the company is a member, this fact should be disclosed;
(e)   the pension cost charge for the period together with explanations of significant changes in the charge compared to that in the previous accounting period;
(f)   any pension provision or prepayments in the balance sheet;
(g)   the amount of any deficiency on a current funding level basis, indicating the action, if any, being taken to deal with it in current and future accounting periods;
(h)   an outline of the results of the most recent formal actuarial valuation or later formal review of the scheme on an ongoing basis. This should include disclosure of:
   (i)   the actuarial method used and a brief description of the main actuarial assumptions;
   (ii)   the market value of the scheme assets at the date of their valuation or review;
   (iii) the level of funding, expressed in percentage terms;
   (iv)   comments on any material actuarial surplus or deficiency indicated by (iii) above;
(i)   any commitment to make additional payments over a limited number of years;
(j)   the accounting treatment adopted in respect of a refund made in accordance with the provisions of para 83 of SSAP 24 where a credit appears in the financial statements in relation to it;
(k)   details of the expected effects on future costs of any material changes in the group's and/or company's pension arrangements.

If a company or a group has more than one scheme then disclosure should be on a   *SSAP 24, 89*
combined basis. For a subsidiary company included in a group scheme, details in (g)   *SSAP 24, 90*
and (h) above are not required providing reference is given to the parent company
whose accounts provide reference to the group scheme. Details should also be given of
the nature of the group scheme and whether contributions are based on pension costs
across the group as a whole.

The above details can be disclosed by way of a single note or alternatively different   *SSAP 24,*
elements of the disclosure may be given in different places. SSAP 24 gives examples   *Appendix*
in appendix 1 of disclosure by way of a single note.

4.18.3 Accounting for post-retirement benefits other than pensions

As well as providing pensions for their employees, some employers also provide post-retirement healthcare or other benefits. These costs are liabilities and should be recognised in financial statements.
UITF 6, 5

Disclosures in relation to post-retirement benefits must be given which are equivalent to those required in respect of pension schemes under SSAP 24. These include details of any important assumptions which are specific to the measurement of such benefits, such as the assumed rate of inflation in the cost of providing the benefits. Material post balance sheet provisions for post-retirement benefits other than pensions should be distinguished from other provisions in the notes to the financial statements.
UITF 6, 9

4.19   Tax on profit on ordinary activities

4.19.1   Statutory requirements

The Companies Act 1985 requires disclosure of the charge to revenue for UK corporation tax, before and after double taxation relief, the amount of the charge for taxation imposed outside the UK on profits, income and (so far as charged to revenue) capital gains.
54(3), Sch 4

The Companies Act 1985 requires that any special circumstances affecting the tax liability in respect of profits, income or capital gains for the current or succeeding financial years should be noted. 'Special circumstances' could include for example, the effect, if material, on the tax charge of losses utilised or losses carried forward.
54(2), Sch 4

It is good practice to show any adjustment to provisions of previous years as a separate item as para 57(1), Sch 4 states that, where any amount relating to any preceding financial year is included in any item in the profit and loss account, the effect should be stated.
57(1), Sch 4

In addition, where a company has incurred an extraordinary profit or loss, the notes must disclose separately taxation on the profit or loss on ordinary activities and taxation on the extraordinary profit or loss.
FRS 3, 22
SSAP 15, 34
54(3), Sch 4

4.19.2   Standard accounting practice

Any special circumstances affecting the overall tax charge or credit for the period, or that may effect those of future periods, should be described by way of note to the profit and loss account and their effects quantified.
FRS 3, 23

This will include any special circumstances affecting the tax attributable to exceptional items (see **4.15** above). The amount of tax attributed to such items should be calculated by comparing the results of tax computations including and excluding the particular items and determining the difference.
FRS 3, 23

FRS 3, 24

Any effects of a fundamental change in the basis of taxation should be included in the tax charge and separately disclosed on the face of the profit and loss account.
FRS 3,23

The tax attributed to the share of profits of associated companies and joint ventures should be disclosed separately within the group tax charge in consolidated accounts.
FRS 9, 21, 27

Accounting standards require that the following items should be included in the taxation charge in the profit and loss account and, where material, should be separately disclosed:

(a)   The amount of UK corporation tax specifying: *SSAP 8, 22*
    (i)   the charge for corporation tax on the income of the year (where such corporation tax includes transfers between the deferred taxation account and the profit and loss account these also should be separately disclosed where material);
    (ii) tax attributable to franked investment income;
    (iii) irrecoverable ACT; and
    (iv) the relief for overseas taxation.

(b)   The total overseas taxation relieved and unrelieved, specifying that part of the   *SSAP 8, 22*
unrelieved overseas taxation which arises from the payment or proposed payment of dividends.

(c)   If the rate of corporation tax is not known for the whole or part of the period   *SSAP 8, 23*
covered by the accounts, the latest known rate should be used and disclosed.

(d)   Outgoing dividends should not include either the related ACT or the attributable   *SSAP 8, 24*
tax credit.

(e)   Incoming dividends from UK resident companies should be included at the   *SSAP 8, 25*
amount of cash received or receivable plus the tax credit.

(f)   Adjustments in respect of a prior year charge are included (normally) in the   *SSAP 8, 28*
charge for the year, but disclosed separately if material.

SSAP 15 *Accounting for deferred tax* requires that deferred tax should be accounted for on timing differences only to the extent that it is probable that a liability or asset will crystallise. Deferred tax should not be accounted for to the extent that it is probable that a liability will not crystallise. The standard lays down the criteria for determining this and it is the responsibility of the directors to assess whether a tax   *SSAP 15, 28* liability will or will not crystallise.

There should be disclosed in the profit and loss account or the notes to the profit and loss account:

(a)   the amount of deferred tax included within the overall tax charge or credit;   *SSAP 15, 33*
(b)   the amount of deferred tax relating to extraordinary items;   *SSAP 15, 34*
(c)   the amount of any unprovided deferred tax in respect of the period, analysed
    into its major components;   *SSAP 15, 35*
(d)   adjustments to the deferred tax account which result from changes in the rate of   *SSAP 15, 36*
    corporation tax or tax allowances should be disclosed separately. If the change
    in rate is associated with a fundamental change in basis of taxation the
    adjustment, if material, should be treated as an extraordinary item;
(e)   assumptions made as to the availability of, and any payment for, group relief.   *SSAP 15, 43*

4.20   Extraordinary items

4.20.1   Statutory requirements

The notes must disclose particulars of any transactions that are extraordinary. In this connection, either the profit and loss account or the notes must disclose both the gross amount of, and the charge relating to, extraordinary items.   *57(2), Sch 4*

4.20.2 Definition of extraordinary items

FRS 3 defines extraordinary items as material items possessing a high degree of abnormality which arise from events or transactions that fall outside the ordinary activities of the reporting entity and which are not expected to recur. They do not include prior period items merely because they relate to a prior period. *FRS 3, 6*

This definition is drawn very tightly and it is highly unlikely that any such items will arise. Accordingly the FRS gives no illustrative examples although it does indicate that their presentation should be following profit after tax and if appropriate, minority interests, disclosing the amount of tax attributable to the extraordinary items separately. *FRS 3, 22 & 48*

4.21 Profit for the financial year

All four profit and loss account formats in CA 1985 include as the last item to be disclosed the 'profit or loss for the financial year'. The formats do not include reference to appropriations of profit but CA 1985 requires that every profit and loss account must show separately the allocation of profit or treatment of loss and in particular: *3(7), Sch 4*

(a) any amount that has been set aside, or that it is proposed to set aside, to reserves;
(b) any amount that has been withdrawn, or that it is proposed to withdraw, from reserves;
(c) the aggregate amount of any dividends that have been paid and proposed.

4.22 Dividends

The Companies Act 1985 requires the profit and loss account to show separately the aggregate of dividends paid and proposed. Dividends paid should not include either the related ACT or the attributable tax credit. Where both equity and non-equity shares are in issue, the profit and loss caption for dividends should include references to the class of shares on which they arise. *3(7), Sch 4* *SSAP 8, 24* *FRS 4, 58*

If a material illegal dividend was paid during the year, for example, where there were insufficient realised profits, this fact should be disclosed and the possibility that it may be repayable by the shareholders. *s226(4)* *SAS 120, 23*

4.23 Statement of retained profits and accumulated losses

A statement of movement on the profit and loss account balance should follow the profit and loss account for the year or be given in a note to the accounts. *46, Sch 4*

This statement is required in addition to the reconciliation of movement on shareholders' funds (see **10.2**). If the statement does not immediately follow the profit and loss account then a reference to where it can be found should be given on the face of the profit and loss account.

4.24   Prior year adjustments

FRS 3 defines prior year adjustments as being limited to items arising from changes in *FRS 3, 7*
accounting policies or from the correction of fundamental errors. The majority of prior
year items, however, arise mainly from the corrections and adjustments which are the
natural result of estimates inherent in accounting, and should be dealt with through the
current year's profit and loss account in the normal way and only disclosed separately
if material. Prior year items are not exceptional merely because they relate to a prior
year; their nature will determine their classification.

Prior period adjustments should be accounted for by restating the comparative figures *FRS 3, 29*
for the preceding period in the primary statements and notes and adjusting the opening
balance of reserves for the cumulative effect. The cumulative adjustments should also *FRS 3, 7*
be noted at the foot of the statement of total recognised gains and losses of the current
period and included in the reconciliation of movements in shareholders' funds of the
corresponding period in order to highlight for users the effect of the adjustment. The
effect of prior period adjustments on the results for the preceding period should be
disclosed where practicable.

4.25   Changes in accounting policy

It is a fundamental accounting concept that there is consistency of accounting
treatment within each accounting period and from one period to the next. A change *FRS 3, 62*
in accounting policy therefore can only be made if it can be justified on the grounds
that the new policy is preferable to the one that it replaces because it will give a fairer
presentation of the results and of the financial position of the company.

Following a change in accounting policy, the amounts for the current and corresponding *FRS 3, 62*
periods should be restated on the basis of the new policies. If the change is material, it
should be reported as a prior period adjustment.

An indication should also be given of the effect on the current year's results of the *UITF 14, 3*
change in accounting policy. If the effect is either immaterial or similar to the effect
on prior years, a single statement in the notes saying this will be sufficient disclosure.
Where it is not practicable to give the effect on the current year, that fact, together
with the reasons should be stated.

4.26   Exchange adjustments

4.26.1   Statutory requirements

The Companies Act 1985 specifically requires that the method of translating foreign *58(1), Sch 4*
currency amounts into sterling should be disclosed in the notes to the accounts, but it
does not deal with the treatment of exchange gains and losses except indirectly in that
only realised profits may be included in the profit and loss account (see **4.1.2** above).

4.26.2 Standard accounting practice

SSAP 20 *Foreign currency translation* distinguishes between accounting for foreign currency in the accounts of individual companies and in consolidated accounts for groups of companies. Generally, exchange movements in the accounts of individual companies should be taken to profit and loss account, whereas in consolidated accounts exchange movements arising on the annual retranslation of net investment in subsidiaries should be dealt with through reserves. This treatment should normally be applied to the exchange movement in the accounts of an individual company when translating the investment in an overseas branch.

SSAP 20, 46–51
SSAP 20, 52–58

SSAP 20, 58

The standard requires the following disclosures to be made in the accounts:

(a) the methods used in the translation of the amounts of foreign currencies and the treatment of exchange differences; *SSAP 20, 59*

(b) the net amount of exchange gains and losses on foreign currency borrowings less deposits, identifying separately: *SSAP 20, 60*
  (i)   the amount set off in reserves;
  (ii) the amount included in the profit and loss account;

(c) the net movement on reserves arising from exchange differences. *SSAP 20, 60*

The standard also details the circumstances when amounts may be offset in reserves. *SSAP 20,5 1, 57–58*

4.27 Statement of total recognised gains and losses

This statement brings together all gains and losses which are recognised in an accounting period. *FRS 3, 27 & 56*

Gains and losses may only be excluded from the profit and loss account if they are specifically permitted or required to be taken directly to reserves by law or accounting standards. In the majority of circumstances there will be no gains and losses other than the profit or loss for the period – in which case a simple statement to this effect will satisfy the requirements of the Standard. *FRS 3, 57*

The most likely additional item to be included is a surplus or deficit arising an a revaluation of fixed assets during the period. In this case it is important not to double count the unrealised gain when the asset is subsequently sold.

Other items featuring in this statement might include unrealised gains on investments, either from revaluation or currency translation differences, and also the effect of prior year adjustments not previously dealt with.

4.28 Note of historical cost profits and losses

The note of historical cost profits and losses is a memorandum item, the primary purpose of which is to present the profits or losses of reporting entities that have revalued assets on a more comparable basis with those of entities that have not. It is an abbreviated restatement of the profit and loss account which adjusts the reported profit *FRS 3, 26 54–55* or loss, if necessary, so as to show it as if no asset revaluation has been made. Unless the historical cost information is unavailable, the note is required whenever there is a *material* difference between the result as disclosed in the profit and loss account and the result on an unmodified historical cost basis; it should be presented immediately following the profit and loss account or the statement of total recognised gains and losses.

The note should include a reconciliation of the reported profit before taxation to the equivalent historical cost amount and also show the retained profit for the year on a historical cost basis.

FRS 3, 26

Typically this note will include details of gains recognised in previous periods which are now realised (e.g., difference between profit on disposal of an asset calculated on depreciated historical cost and that calculated on a revalued amount) and details of the difference between a depreciation charge based on historic cost as opposed to based on a revalued amount. This is frequently dealt with by a transfer between revaluation reserve and profit and loss account, the amount reflecting the depreciation 'realised'.

4.29   Other matters

The notes above do not deal with the following matters:

(a)   The Companies Act 1985 requires that there shall be disclosure, if material, of the amount set aside to provisions other than provisions for depreciation, renewals or diminution in the value of assets or, if material, withdrawals from such provisions.

46, Sch 4

(b)   The Companies Act 1985 requires comparative figures to be shown for the immediate preceding financial year for all items shown in the profit and loss account and related notes. Where the comparative figure is not comparable with the amount shown for the item in question of the financial year to which the profit and loss account (or balance sheet) relates, the former amount shall be adjusted and particulars of the adjustment and reasons for it must be disclosed in a note to the accounts.

4(1) & 4(2), Sch 4

58(2), Sch 4

(c)   The Companies Act 1985 requires that where any amount relating to any preceding financial year is included in any item in the profit and loss account, the effect shall be stated if material. This provision also relates to material adjustments to provisions made in previous years, e.g., adjustments to prior year tax provisions.

57(1), Sch 4

86, Sch 4

5   Balance sheet general matters

5.1   Format requirements

A balance sheet (with comparative figures) must be prepared as at the date to which *s226(1a)*
any profit and loss account prepared under s226(1b) CA 1985 is made up. It must be
drawn up in one of the formats laid down in CA 1985. Russell Square Enterprises
Limited has been prepared in accordance with Format 1. It should be noted that once
the directors have selected a particular format it should not be changed in subsequent   *2, Sch 4*
years unless there are special reasons.

In Format 1, net assets can be equated with the aggregate of share capital and reserves.
This method of presentation represents the most common existing practice of UK
companies. The Act does not, however, prescribe where the totals should be struck,
and thus it would be possible in this format to equate total assets less current liabilities
with creditors falling due after more than one year, provisions for liabilities and
charges, and capital and reserves. In Russell Square Enterprises Limited net assets
have been equated with the aggregate of share capital and reserves.

Both the balance sheet formats laid down in the Act include headings preceded by:
letters of the alphabet, Roman numerals and Arabic numerals.

Any item required to be shown in a company's balance sheet may be presented in   *3(1), Sch 4*
greater detail than required by the format adopted. The balance sheet may include an
item representing or covering the amount of any asset or liability not otherwise   *3(2), Sch 4*
covered by any of the items listed in the format adopted, but preliminary expenses,
expenses of and commission on any issue of shares or debentures, or costs of research
may not be treated as assets. The directors may adapt the arrangement and headings
and sub-headings in the formats, if they are preceded by an Arabic numeral, where the
special nature of the company's business requires such adaptation. Items preceded by   *3(3), Sch 4*
Arabic numerals may also be combined if the individual amounts are not material or
the combination facilitates the assessment of the state of affairs. In the latter case the
individual amounts combined must be shown in the notes. This means that, where   *3(4), Sch 4*
applicable, the items preceded by letters of the alphabet and Roman numerals must be
shown on the face of the balance sheet and cannot be combined. The detail may be
shown in the notes.

5.2   Comparative figures

In respect of every item shown in the company's balance sheet and related notes the   *4(1) & (2),*
corresponding amount for the preceding year must be shown. Where that corresponding   *Sch 4*
amount is not comparable with the current year's figure, the former should be adjusted
and particulars of the adjustment and reasons for it must be disclosed in a note.   *58(2), Sch 4*

The requirement to state comparatives does not apply to certain balance sheet notes which require the movement in the year to be given, e.g., fixed assets, reserves, provisions for liabilities and charges and directors' interest disclosures.

58(3), Sch 4

5.3   Netting off

Assets and liabilities may not be set off against each other. Consequently companies may not, for example, show hire-purchase liabilities or government grants as a deduction from the related asset. An exception to this rule is that payments received on account must be shown under creditors unless they are shown as a deduction from stocks, unless they exceed the amount of the specific asset in which case they should be included within creditors.

5, Sch 4

8(8), Sch 4

5.4   Valuation rules and adjustments

Some years ago the EEC Fourth Directive introduced two new terms into UK accounting: valuation rules and value adjustments. Valuation rules basically comprise fundamental accounting concepts, accounting bases and specific accounting principles. Value adjustments comprise depreciation and amounts necessary to write down cost to a lower net realisable value.

Part II of Schedule 4, CA 1985 deals with the following three concepts:

(a)   accounting principles;
(b)   historical cost accounting rules;
(c)   alternative accounting rules.

5.4.1   Accounting principles

These are the fundamental accounting concepts of 'going concern', 'consistency', 'prudence' and 'accruals'. These are set out in the Act and are effectively a reproduction of SSAP 2. The overriding consideration in preparing accounts is that they must give a true and fair view. Thus in common with other areas of CA 1985 the directors are permitted to depart from any of the accounting concepts where there are special reasons for doing so. If they do so, the notes to the accounts must give particulars of the departure, the directors' reason for it and its effect.

SSAP 2, 14

15, Sch 4

The Act has added a dimension to the concept of prudence in that only realised profits at the balance sheet date may be included in the profit and loss account (see **4.1.2**), and liabilities and losses which have arisen or are likely to arise in respect of the financial year to which the accounts relate or a previous financial year shall be taken into account, including those which only become apparent after the end of the year but prior to the date on which the directors sign the accounts. This treatment equates to that recommended in SSAP 17 (see **1.4**).

12(a), Sch 4

12(b), Sch 4

It should be noted that CA 1985 requires that each constituent item of assets and liabilities has to be valued separately. Although this rule is not described in SSAP 2 as a fundamental accounting concept, it has always been inherent in good accounting practice. Its effect is to ensure, for example, that if there are, say, six different lines of

14, Sch 4

stock, each line must be valued separately at the lower of cost and net realisable value, rather than be valued on a global basis.

5.4.2 Historical cost accounting rules

The basic rules are that fixed assets must be shown at either their purchase price or production cost. Where a fixed asset has a limited useful economic life, its purchase price or its production cost must be written off over the period of that life.   *17 & 18, Sch 4*

Current assets must be shown at the lower of purchase price or production cost and net *22 & 23, Sch 4* realisable value. It is this requirement for current assets which has given rise to problems of including an element of profit in the valuation of long-term contracts as profit is not at cost. SSAP 9 addresses this problem by recommending that attributable profit should be included in turnover together with an appropriate proportion of attributable costs in cost of sales. The debit is reflected in debtors in the balance sheet, if not paid, as amounts recoverable on contracts. Long-term contract work in progress would then be shown in the balance sheet at net cost less foreseeable losses and payments on account.

Where certain conditions are satisfied, tangible fixed assets and raw materials can be *25, Sch 4* shown at a fixed quantity and at a fixed value. These conditions (all of which must be satisfied) are that:

(a)   they must be assets of a kind that are constantly being replaced;
(b)   their overall value must not be material to the assessment of the company's state of affairs;
(c)   their quantity, value and composition must not be subject to material valuation.

Where this provision applies, all subsequent purchases of the assets in question will be charged directly against profit. The basis is best suited to low value, short-life assets, such as tools and moulds.

5.4.3 Alternative accounting rules

The EEC Fourth Directive was based on the historical cost convention. It was only at a relatively late stage that it was amended to permit some form of accounting designed to take account of inflation and of other changes in the value of assets. Companies may adopt any of the alternative accounting rules set out in the Act, provided that they comply with certain conditions. However, companies are not forced to adopt any of the alternative accounting rules.

The alternative accounting rules that the Act permits are as follows: *31, Sch 4*

(a)   Intangible fixed assets may be stated at their current cost. This does not apply to goodwill, which must be shown at the value of the consideration for which it was acquired, less amortisation.
(b)   Tangible fixed assets may be stated either at their market value as at the date of the last valuation or at their current cost.
(c)   Fixed asset investments may be shown at their market value or at a value determined on any basis that the directors think appropriate in the circumstances of the company.

(d)   Current asset investments may be stated at their current cost.

(e)   Stocks may be stated at their current cost.

The effect of these provisions is to permit accounts to be prepared in any of the following ways:

(a)   according to the historical cost convention;

(b)   according to the historical cost convention, modified to take account of selective revaluations, the most common example being in respect of property;

(c)   according to current cost principles.

Should advantage be taken of the alternative accounting rules, any difference (irrespective of when it arises) between the amount of any item determined according to one of the alternative accounting rules and the amount that would have been disclosed if the historical cost convention had been adhered to, must be credited/debited to 'revaluation reserve'. This reserve must be shown on the face of the balance sheet as a separate amount but need not be shown in that name (see **10.6**).   *34(1), Sch 4*

34(2), Sch 4

Where any of the alternative accounting rules have been applied, the notes to the accounts must state the items affected and the basis of valuation. In addition, for each item affected (except stock) one of the following amounts must be disclosed: *33(2), Sch 4*

33(3), Sch 4

(a)   the comparable amounts (for cost and depreciation) determined according to the historical cost convention; or

(b)   the differences between those comparable amounts and the actual amounts shown in the balance sheet.

For this purpose, 'comparable amounts' means the aggregate amount that would have been shown if the historical cost convention had been applied, and the aggregate amount of the cumulative provisions for depreciation that would have been permitted according to that convention.   *33(4), Sch 4*

6 Fixed assets

6.1 Definition

A fixed asset is defined as any asset that is intended for use on a continuing basis in the company's activities. Any assets not intended for such use should be treated as current assets.

s262(1)

6.2 Statutory disclosure

The Companies Act 1985 requires, in both the permitted formats, that fixed assets be designated as intangible assets, tangible assets or investments, and that the net book value of each be shown on the balance sheet. In respect of either the cost or the valuation of each item included under these headings the notes to the accounts must disclose:

*42(1) & (2),
Sch 4*

(a)   the appropriate aggregate amounts in respect of that item at both the beginning and end of the financial year, disclosing whether it be 'cost' or 'cost or valuation';
(b)   the effect of any application of the alternative accounting rules during the financial year (see **5.4.3**);
(c)   the amount of any acquisitions, and the amount of any disposals, during the financial year;
(d)   the amount of any transfers of assets to or from that item during the financial year.

It is emphasised that the above requirements apply to all categories of fixed assets, whether intangible assets, tangible assets or investments. Moreover, it is required that the information be split between each of the sub-headings in the formats.

6.2.1 Cost of assets

The Companies Act 1985 sets out detailed definitions of the purchase price and the production cost of an asset which both equate to cost for purposes of disclosing fixed assets.

Purchase price is defined as the actual price paid plus any expenses that are incidental to acquisition. Whilst the Act makes no specific reference to capital grants received, it is considered that they should not be deducted from the purchase price of the asset to arrive at cost but should be included as a deferred credit in the balance sheet.

26(1), Sch 4

Fixed assets

Production cost includes:

(a)   the cost of raw materials;

26(2) & (3),

(b)   direct costs of production;
    Sch 4

(c)   certain other costs which may be included such as a reasonable proportion of indirect overheads and interest on any capital borrowed.   *26(3)(a), Sch 4*

If interest is included in the production cost the amount must be disclosed.   *26(3)(b), Sch 4*

Where there is no record of the purchase price or production cost of any asset the earliest recorded value may be substituted for original cost if the latter is not known or cannot be ascertained without unreasonable expense or delay.   *28, Sch 4*

Irrecoverable VAT attributable to fixed assets (and to other items) disclosed separately in published accounts should be included in their cost where practicable and material.   *SSAP 5, 9*

6.2.2 Provisions

The Companies Act 1985 requires details to be disclosed of any provisions made in respect of each fixed asset item. In particular, the notes must disclose: *42(3), Sch 4*

(a)   the cumulative amount of provisions for depreciation or the diminution in value of assets at both the beginning and the end of the financial year;

(b)   the amount of any such provisions that have been made during the financial year;

(c)   the amount of such provisions that had been eliminated on the disposal of the fixed assets to which they related during the financial year;

(d)   the amount of any other adjustments made in respect of any such provisions during the financial year.

It should be noted that if the value of a fixed asset has diminished below that of its book value and this is expected to be permanent, then provision shall be made for this diminution and the amount disclosed. If such a provision has to be written back this must also be disclosed.   *19(2), Sch 4*   *19(3), Sch 4*

6.2.3 Revaluation

For all fixed assets included at a valuation details of the valuation must be disclosed (i.e., year, amount, names or qualifications of valuer and basis of valuation) and either the comparable amounts determined on the historical cost basis or the difference between the amount shown in the balance sheet and the amount which would have been shown on an historical cost basis. In respect of fixed assets the amounts referred to include gross cost and accumulated depreciation, not the net book value.   *43 & 33, Sch 4*

In addition to the statutory disclosure requirements the tax on any potential capital gain on disposal at the valuation date does not have to be provided in the accounts where it can be demonstrated that no liability is expected to arise, but the amount must nevertheless be disclosed in the notes.   *SSAP 15, 42*

When any asset is revalued in accordance with the alternative accounting rules (see **5.4.3**) any profit or loss arising (after allowing for any provisions for depreciation) must be credited or debited to a separate revaluation reserve. The amount of the reserve must be shown on the balance sheet and it shall be reduced where the directors are of the opinion that the amount standing to the credit of the reserve is no longer   *34(1), Sch 4*   *34(2), Sch 4* necessary for the purpose of the accounting policy adopted. The amount so transferred must be disclosed and may only pass through the profit and loss account if: *34(3), Sch 4*

(a)   it had previously been charged in that account; or
(b)   it represents a realised profit.

Where any amount has been either credited or debited to the revaluation reserve its treatment for taxation purposes must be disclosed. *34(4), Sch 4*

For purposes of distributable profits as defined in CA 1985, the increase in depreciation charge arising from revaluing assets may be treated as a realised profit and hence it is permissible to transfer from revaluation reserve to accumulated profits and losses (but not through the profit and loss account) an amount equal to the excess of the depreciation charged based on the valuation compared to the charge based on historical cost (see **10.6**). *s263(3)*

s275(2)

Comparative figures must be shown for net values, but it is not necessary to show comparative figures for movements. *58(3), Sch 4*

6.3   Intangible assets

The Companies Act 1985 requires that intangible assets be shown under the headings of: *8, Sch 4*

- development costs;
- concessions, patents, licences, trade marks and similar rights and assets;
- goodwill;
- payments on account.

These headings may be added to so as to show intangible assets in greater detail. *3(1), Sch 4*

The Companies Act 1985 prohibits the capitalisation of preliminary expenses, share or debenture issue expenses and commission, and costs of research which must be written off to the profit and loss account. *3(2), Sch 4*

6.3.1   Development costs (refer also to 4.9)

The Companies Act 1985 permits only development costs (not research costs) to be capitalised. When such costs are capitalised the notes must disclose the period over which the amount is being, or is to be, written off and the reasons for capitalising the costs. *3(2c), Sch 4* *20(2), Sch 4*

In practice this treatment must be read in conjunction with SSAP 13 *Accounting for research and development*. This goes considerably further than the Act in that it defines all the specific circumstances that must exist before development costs may be capitalised. Development expenditure may be deferred under the SSAP only where all of the following conditions are satisfied: *SSAP 13, 25*

(a)   there is a clearly defined project;
(b)   the related expenditure is separately identifiable;

(c)   the outcome of the project has been assessed with reasonable certainty as to both its technical feasibility and its ultimate commercial viability;

(d)   all costs (including future costs to be incurred) are reasonably expected to be more than covered by related future revenues;

(e)   adequate resources exist, or are reasonably expected to be available, to enable the project to be completed, and to provide any consequential increases in working capital.

The expenditure must be amortised from the commencement of commercial production of the product or process. Such amortisation must be allocated to each accounting period on a systematic basis. This can be done by reference to the sale or the use of the product or the process, or by reference to the period over which the product or process is expected to be sold or used.   *SSAP 13, 28*

Development expenditure written off in previous periods should not be reinstated even though the uncertainties which led to it being written off no longer apply.

Where development expenditure is deferred and the unamortised development expenditure is not treated as a realised loss the note must also state: *20(2), Sch 4 s269(2b)*

(a)   that the amount of unamortised development expenditure is not to be treated as a realised loss for the purpose of calculating distributable profits;

(b)   the circumstances that the directors relied upon to justify their decision not to treat the unamortised development expenditure as a realised loss.

The movement on deferred development expenditure and the amounts brought forward and carried forward should be stated, as should the accounting policy.   *SSAP 13, 30 & 32*

6.3.2   Concessions, patents, licences, trade marks and similar rights and assets

These may be included as amounts in the balance sheet only when they were acquired for valuable consideration in circumstances that do not require them to be shown as goodwill or were created by the company itself.   *8(2), Sch 4*

The economic useful life over which these intangibles should be amortised should be the shorter of the anticipated period of profitable exploitation and the period to the expiry of the right. Renewal periods should be included if the holder has an option to renew which he is likely to exercise and any additional costs are small in relation to the costs carried forward.   *19(1), Sch 4*

6.4   Goodwill and intangible assets

The Companies Act 1985 requires that the original amount at which goodwill is shown in a company's balance sheet must be written off systematically. The period over which it is to be written off is to be chosen by the directors or the company, but it may not exceed the useful economic life of the goodwill in question. Moreover, the period the directors choose, and their reasons for choosing that particular period, must be disclosed in the notes to the financial statements.   *21, Sch 4*

6.4.1 Definition

Goodwill is the difference between the cost of an acquired entity and the aggregate of the entity's identifiable assets and liblities.   *FRS 10, 2*

Positive goodwill arises when the acquisition cost exceeds the aggregate fair values of the identifiable assets and liabilities.

Negative goodwill arises when the aggregate fair values of the identifiable assets and liabilities exceed the acquisition cost.

6.4.2 Initial recognition

Initial recognition of goodwill

Positive goodwill should be capitalised and classified as an asset on the balance sheet.   *FRS 10, 7*

Initial recognition of intangible assets

An intangible asset which is acquired as part of the acquisition of a business should be capitalised separately from goodwill if its value an be measured reliably on initial recognition.   *FRS 10, 10*

The intangible asset should be initially recorded at fair value, subject to the constraint that, unless the asset has a reasonably ascertainable market value, the fair value should be limited to an amount that does not create or increase any negative goodwill arising on the acquisition.   *FRS 10, 10*

If the value of an intangible purchased as part of a business acquisition cannot be measured reliably, it should be subsumed within the amount of the purchase price attributed to goodwill.   *FRS 10, 13*

6.4.3 Amortisation

Where goodwill and intangible assets are regarded as having limited useful economic lives they should be systematically amortised over those lives.   *FRS 10, 15*

In exceptional circumstances, where goodwill and intangible assets are regarded as having indefinite useful economic lives, they should not be amortised.

Determining useful economic lives   *FRS 10, 19*

There is a rebuttable presumption that the useful economic lives of purchased goodwill and intangible assets are limited to periods of 20 years or less.

This presumption may be rebutted and a useful economic life regarded as a longer period or indefinite only if:

(a) the durability of the acquired business or intangible asset can be demonstrated and justifies estimating the useful economic life to exceed 20 years; and
(b) the goodwill or intangible asset is capable of continued measurement (so that annual impairment reviews will be feasible).

The presumption that goodwill has a limited useful life arises because the normal *FRS 10, 20* nature of business makes it unlikely that any premium paid for an acquisition can be maintained indefinitely. In some cases, it might not be possible to recognise any goodwill in the balance sheet, because of the high cost of continued measurement. For example, this could arise when the acquired businesses are merged with existing businesses to such an extent that the goodwill associated with the acquired business cannot readily be tracked.

FRS 10 stresses that uncertainty cannot be used as a default for treating a useful *FRS 10, 22* economic life as indefinite or for adopting a 20-year period. If the useful economic life is expected to be less than 20 years, the FRS requires an estimate of the useful economic life to be made. However, although prudence should influence the determination of useful life, it does not form the grounds for choosing a life that is unrealistically short.

Residual value

No residual value may be assigned to goodwill. *FRS 10, 28*

Method of amortisation

The method of amortisation should be chosen to reflect the expected pattern of *FRS 10, 30* depletion of the goodwill or intangible asset. A straight-line method should be chosen unless another method can be demonstrated to be more appropriate.

6.4.4 Review of useful economic lives

The useful economic lives of goodwill and intangible assets should be reviewed at the *FRS 10, 33* end of each reporting period and revised if necessary.

If the useful economic life is revised, the carrying value of the goodwill or intangible asset at the date of revision should be amortised over the revised remaining useful economic life.

6.4.5 Impairment

Requirement for impairment reviews

Goodwill and intangible assets that are amortised over a finite period not exceeding 20 *FRS 10, 34* years from the date of acquisition should be reviewed for impairment:

(a)   at the end of the first full final year following the acquisition; and
(b)   in other periods if events or changes in circumstances indicate that the carrying values may not be recoverable.

If an impairment is identified at the end of the first full year after acquisition, this *FRS 10, 35* impairment reflects:

(a)   an overpayment;
(b)   an event that occurred between the acquisition and the first-year review; or
(c)   depletion of the acquired goodwill or intangible asset between the acquisition and the first-year review that exceeds the amount recognised through amortisation.

Goodwill and intangible assets that are amortised over a priod exceeding 20 years from the date of acquisition or are not amortised should be reviewed for impairment at the end of each reporting period.

FRs 10, 37

After the first period, reviews need only to be updated if the expectations of future cash flows and discount rates change significantly.

FRS 10, 38

A re-performance of the review may not be required if the key assumptions and variables in the first review are unchanged, or the underlying assumptions are unchanged and the first review indicates that the recoverable amount was substantially in excess of the carrying value.

Application to FRS 10

The first-year impairment review may be performed in two stages:

FRED 10, 40

(a) initially identifying any possible impairment by comparing post-acquisition performance in the first year with pre-acquisition forecasts used to support the purchase price; and

(b) performing a full impairment review in accordance with the requirements of the FRS on impairment of fixed assets and goodwill only if the initial review indicates that the post-acquisition performance has failed to meet pre-acquisition expectations or if any other previously unforeseen events or changes in circumstances indicate that the carrying values may not be recoverable.

If an impairment loss is recognised the revised carrying value, if being amortised, should be amortised over the current estimate of the remaining useful economic life.

FRS 10, 41

If goodwill arising on consolidation is found to be impaired, the carring amount of the investment held in the financial statements of the parent undertaking should also be reviewed from impairment.

FRS 10, 42

6.4.6 Revaluation and restoration of past losses

FRS 10 permits an intangible asset, which has a readily ascertainable market value, to be revalued to its market value. The standard requires a policy of revaluation to be applied to all intangible assets of the share class, and not just to single 'flagships' which are known to have risen in value from their original cost. Once intangible assets have been revalued, further revaluation should be performed sufficiently often to ensure that the carrying value does not differ materially from the market value at the balance sheet date.

FRS 10, 43

Goodwill and intangible assets may also be revalued to correct past losses arising from the identification of an impairment in the carrying amount. A reversal is permitted if subsequent events clearly and demonstrably reverse the effects of the events giving rise to the impairment in a way that was not foreseen in the original calculations. Such reversals should be recognised as a gain in the period in which they are identitied.

FRS 10, 44

6.4.7 Negative goodwill

Negative goodwill is a relatively rare concept which arises when the fair value of the separable net assets is greater than the consideration paid. The situation may arise in a situation where there are important unresolved contingencies or commitments, or where, despite a strong balance sheet position, financial weakness has occurred causing a 'forced' sale.

Negative goodwill should be recognised and separately disclosed on the face of the balance sheet, immediately below the goodwill heading and followed by a subtotal showing the net amount of the positive and negative goodwill. *FRS 10, 48*

Negative goodwill up to the fair values of the non-monetary assets acquired should be recognised in the profit and loss account in the periods in which the non-monetary assets are recovered, whether through depreciation or sale. *FRS 10, 49*

Any negative goodwill in excess of the fiar values of the non-monetary assets should be recognised in the profit and loss account in the periods expected to be benefited. *FRS 10, 50*

6.4.8 Disclosures

The following information should be disclosed separately for positive goodwill, negative goodwill and each class of intangible asset capitalised on the balance sheet: *FRS 10, 53*

(a) the cost or revaled amount at the beginning of the financial period and at the balance sheet date;
(b) the cumulative amount of provisions for amortisation or impairment at the beginning of the financial period and at the balance sheet date;
(c) a reconciliation of the movements, separately disclosing additions, disposal, revaluations, transfers, amortisation, impairment losses, reversals of past impairment losses and amounts of negative goodwill written back in the financial period; and
(d) the net carrying amount at the balance sheet date.

Amortisation of positive goodwill and intangible assets

The financial statements should disclose the methods and periods of amortisation of goodwill and intangible assets and the reasons for choosing these periods. *FRS 10, 55*

Where an amortisation period is shortened or extended following a review of the remaining useful economic lives of goodwill and intangible assets, the reasons and the effect, if material, should be disclosed in the year of change. *FRS 10, 56*

Where there has been a change in the amortisation method used, the reason and the effect, if material, should be disclosed in the year of change. *FRS 10, 57*

Where goodwill or an intangible asset is amortised over a period that exceeds 20 years from the date of acquisition or is not amortised, the grounds for rebutting the 20 year presumption should be given. This should be a reasoned explanation based on the specific factors contributing to the durability of the acquired business or intangible asset. *FRS 10, 58*

In addition, where goodwill in the financial statements of companies is not amortised, the financial statements should state that they depart from the specific requirement of companies legislation to amortise goodwill over a finite period for the overriding purpose of giving true and fair view. Particulars of the departure, the reasons for it *FRS 10, 59* and its effect should be given in sufficient detail to convey to the reader of the financial statements the circumstances justifying the use of the true and fair override. The reasons for the departure should incporate the explanation of the specific factors contributing to the durability of the acquired business or intangible asset as required above.

Revaluation

Where a class of assets has been revalued, the financial statements should disclose: *FRS 10, 61*

(a)   the year in which the assets were valued, the values and the bases of valuation; and

(b)   the original cost (or original fair value) of the assets ad the amount of any provision for amortisation that would have been recognised if the assets had been valued at their original cost or fair value.

Where any asset has been revalued during the year, the name and qualification of the   *FRS 10, 62*
person who valued it should be disclosed.

Negative goodwill

The financial statements should disclose the period(s) in which negative goodwill is   *FRS 10, 63*
being written back in the profit and loss account.

Where negative goodwill exceeds the fair values of the non-monetary assets, the   *FRS 10, 64*
amount and source of the 'excess' negative goodwill and the period(s) in which it
is being written back should be explained.

6.4.9   Transitional arrangements

FRS 10 comments that, ideally, all goodwill that had previously been eliminated   *FRS 10, 68*
against reserves, but would not have been fully written down under the requirements
of the FRS, would be reinstated by means of prior year adjustment on implementation
of the FRS. However, the ASB recognises that this will not be practicable in all
circumstances, and therefore does not require reinstatement.

Where all goodwill previously eliminated against reserves is not reinstated on   *FRS 10, 69*
implementation of FRS 10, the goodwill remaining eliminated against reserves
should comprise one of the following:

(a)   goodwill relating to acquisitions made before 23 December 1989 where the necessary information is unavailable or cannot be obtained without unreasonable expense of delay; or

(b)   all goodwill eliminated before the implementtion of FRS 7; or

(c)   all goodwill previously eliminated.

Where goodwill that was previously eliminated against reserves is reinstated on   *FRS 10, 70*
implementation of the FRS:

(a)   any impairment that is attributed to prior periods must be determined on the basis of impairment reviews performed in accordance with the FRS on impairment of fixed assets and goodwill;

(b)   the notes to the financial statements should disclose the original cost of the goodwill and the amounts attributed to prior period amortisation and, separately, prior period impairment; and

(c) it is not necessary to identify separately intagible assets that are subsumed within the goodwill.

If goodwill remains eliminated against reserves:

FRS 10, 71

(a) The financial statements should state:
    (i) the accounting policy followed in respect of that goodwill;
    (ii) the cumulative amounts of positive goodwill eliminated against reserves and negative goodwill added to reserves, net of any goodwill attributable to businesses disposed of before the balance sheet date; and
    (iii) the fact that this goodwill had been eliminated as a matter of accounting policy and would be charged or credited in the profit and loss account on subsequent disposal of the business to which it related.

(b) The eliminated goodwill should not be shown as a debit balance on a separate goodwill write-off reserve but should be offset against the profit and loss account on another appropriate reserve. The amount by which the reserve has been reduced by the elimination of goodwill (or increased by the addition of negative goodwill) should not be shown separately on the face of the balance sheet.

(c) In the reporting period in which the business with which the goodwill was acquired is disposed of or closed:
    (i) the amount included in the profit or loss account in respect of the profit or loss on disposal or closure should include attributable goodwill to the extent that it has not previously been charged in the profit and loss account; and
    (ii) the financial statements should disclose as a component of the profit or loss on disposal or closure the attributable amount of goodwill so included.

Where it is impractical or impossible to ascertain the goodwill attributable to a business that was acquired before 1 January 1989, this should be stated and the reasons given.

Any impairment loss relating to previously capitalised goodwill and intangible assets that is recognised on first implementing the FRS 10 should be charged as an expense in the period.

FRS 10, 74

6.5 Tangible fixed assets

The Companies Act 1985 requires that tangible fixed assets be shown under the headings of:

- land and buildings;
- plant and machinery;
- fixtures, fittings, tools and equipment;
- payments on account and assets in the course of construction.

Each item in the above classification is preceded by Arabic numerals (see **5.1**).

In addition to the statutory disclosure requirements referred to in **6.2** above, there are additional disclosure requirements for specific matters which are set out below.

6.5.1 Land and buildings

Analysis of interests in land and buildings is among: *44, Sch 4*

(i)   freeholds;
(ii)   long leaseholds (i.e., more than 50 years unexpired); and
(iii)   short leaseholds, being those of less than 50 years or with less than 50 years
        unexpired term.   *83, Sch 4*

FRS 15 was issued in February 1999 and sets out in detail practice for accounting for tangible fixed assets. In particular, extensive guidance is given on which initial costs should be capitalised. Standard practice is introduced on the basis for capitalising finance costs and for the conduct of revaluations. The accounting practices in the *FRS 15, 103* standard apply to accounting periods ending on or after 23 March 2000, although earlier adoption is encouraged.

6.5.2 Initial measurement

A tangible fixed asset should initially be measured at its cost. The costs that are *FRS 15, 6 & 7* included are only those that are directly attributable to bringing the asset into working condition for its intended use.

The cost of a tangible fixed asset (whether acquired or self-constructed) comprises its *FRS 15, 8* purchase price (after deducting any trade discounts and rebates) and any costs directly attributable to bringing it into working condition for its intended use.

Directly attributable costs include: *FRS 15, 9*

(a)   the labour costs of own employees such as site workers, in-house architects and
        surveyors which arise from the construction, or acquisition, of the specific
        tangible fixed asset; and
(b)   the incremental costs to the entity that would have been avoided only if the
        tangible fixed asset had not been constructed or acquired.

Administration and other general overhead costs should be excluded from the cost of a *FRS 15, 9* tangible fixed asset on the grounds that they are not directly attributable to bringing the asset into working condition for its intended use. Employee costs not related to the specific asset (such as site selection activities) are not directly attributable costs.

Examples of directly attributable costs include: *FRS 15, 10*

- acquisition costs (such as stamp duty);
- the cost of site preparation and clearance;
- initial delivery and handling costs;
- installation costs;
- professional fees (such as legal, architects' and engineers' fees);
- the estimated cost of dismantling and removing the asset and restoring the site, to
  the extent that it is recognised as a provision under FRS 12.

Abnormal costs (such as those relating to design errors, industrial disputes, idle *FRS 15, 11*
capacity, wasted materials, labour or other resources and production delays) and
costs such as operating losses that occur because a revenue activity has been
suspended during the construction of a tangible fixed asset are not regarded by the
FRS as being directly attributable to bringing the asset into working condition for its
intended use. Therefore such costs must not be capitalised.

Capitalisation of directly attributable costs should cease when substantially all the *FRS 15, 12*
activities that are necessary to get the tangible fixed asset ready for use are complete,
even if the asset has not yet been brought into use. The standard deems that a tangible
fixed asset is ready for use when its physical construction is complete.

6.5.3 Start-up costs

The FRS contains clear guidance on which start-up costs may be capitalised. It draws a *FRS 15, 14–15*
distinction between costs incurred in testing or commissioning an asset and costs
arising during a period when an asset is underused whilst it establishes its place in the
market.

The costs associated with a start-up or commissioning period should be included in the *FRS 15, 14*
cost of the tangible fixed asset only where the asset is available for use but incapable
of operating at normal levels without such a start-up or commissioning period.

The FRS's distinction is between: *FRS 15, 15*

(a)   the commissioning period for plant, in which it is impossible for it to operate at
       normal levels because of, for example, the need to run in machinery, to test
       equipment and generally to ensure the proper functioning of the plant; and
(b)   an initial operating period in which, although the plant is available for use and
       capable of running at normal levels, it is operated at below normal levels
       because demand has not yet built up.

The costs of an essential commissioning period are included as part of the cost of *FRS 15, 16*
bringing the asset up to its normal operating potential, and therefore as part of its cost.
However, there is no justification for regarding costs relating to other start-up periods,
where the asset is available for use but not yet operating at normal levels, for example
because of a lack of demand, as part of the cost of the asset. An example is the start-up
period of a new hotel or shop, which could operate at normal levels almost
immediately, but for which experience teaches that demand will build up slowly
and full utilisation or sales levels will be achieved only over a period of several
months.

6.5.4 Capitalisation of finance costs

The FRS does not prescribe that finance costs have to be capitalised by reporting *FRS 15, 19*
entities. However, where an entity adopts a policy of capitalising finance costs, finance
costs that are directly attributable to the construction of tangible fixed assets should be
capitalised as part of the cost of those assets. The total amount of finance costs
capitalised during a period should not exceed the total amount of finance costs
incurred during that period. Once an entity has adopted a policy of capitalisation of *FRS 15, 20*
finance costs, then it should be applied consistently to all tangible fixed assets where
finance costs fall to be capitalised in accordance with the requirements of the FRS.

Only finance costs that are directly attributable to the construction of a tangible fixed asset, or the financing of progress payments in respect of the construction of a tangible fixed asset by others for the entity, should be capitalised. Directly attributable finance costs are those that would have been avoided (for example by avoiding additional borrowings or by using the funds expended for the asset to repay existing borrowings) if there had been no expenditure on the asset. Finance costs are capitalised on a gross basis i.e., before the deduction of any tax relief to which they give rise.   *FRS 15, 21*

Where funds specifically for the purpose of financing the construction of a tangible fixed asset have been borrowed, the amount of finance costs capitalised is limited to the actual costs incurred on the borrowings during the period in respect of expenditures to date on the tangible fixed asset. Finance costs in respect of leased tangible fixed assets should be accounted for in accordance with SSAP 21 *Accounting for leases and hire purchase contracts.*   *FRS 15, 22*

Where the funds used to finance the construction of a tangible fixed asset form part of the entity's general borrowings, the amount of finance costs capitalised is determined by applying a capitalisation rate to the expenditure on that asset. For this purpose the expenditure on the asset is the weighted average carrying amount of the asset during the period, including finance costs previously capitalised. The capitalisation rate used in an accounting period is based on the weighted average of rates applicable to the entity's general borrowings that are outstanding during the period. This excludes borrowings by the entity that are specifically for the purpose of constructing or acquiring other tangible fixed assets (e.g., obligations in respect of finance leases), or for other specific purposes, such as loans used to hedge foreign investments.   *FRS 15, 23*

In determining the borrowings to be included in the weighted average, the objective is a reasonable measure of the finance costs that are directly attributable to the construction of the asset. Accordingly, judgement will be required to make a selection of borrowings that best accomplishes the objective. In some circumstances, it is appropriate to include all borrowings by the parent and its subsidiaries when computing a weighted average of the finance costs; in other circumstances, it is appropriate for each subsidiary to use a weighted average of the finance costs applicable to its own borrowings.   *FRS 15, 24*

Where finance costs are capitalised, capitalisation should begin when: *FRS 15, 25*

(a) finance costs are being incurred; and
(b) expenditures for the asset are being incurred; and
(c) activities that are necessary to get the asset ready for use are in progress.

As an example, finance costs incurred while land is under development are capitalised during the period in which activities related to the development are being undertaken. However, finance costs incurred while land acquired for building purposes is held without any associated development activity do not qualify for capitalisation.   *FRS 15, 26*

Capitalisation of finance costs should be suspended during extended periods in which active development is interrupted. Such costs are costs of holding partially completed assets and do not qualify for capitalisation.   *FRS 15, 27*
FRS 15, 28

Capitalisation of finance costs should cease when substantially all the activities that are necessary to get the tangible fixed asset ready for use are complete. When construction of a tangible fixed asset is completed in parts and each part is capable   *FRS 15, 29* of being used while construction continues on other parts, capitalisation of finance costs relating to a part should cease when substantially all the activities that are necessary to get that part ready for use are completed. For example, where several buildings are being developed on a site, then each individual building may be used when completed. By contrast, a complex piece of plant may not be usable until each individual section is completed. *FRS 15, 30*

Disclosures – finance costs

Where a policy of capitalisation of finance costs is adopted, the financial statements should disclose: *FRS 15, 31*

(a)   the accounting policy adopted;
(b)   the aggregate amount of finance costs included in the cost of tangible fixed assets;
(c)   the amount of finance costs capitalised during the period;
(d)   the amount of finance costs recognised in the profit and loss account during the period; and
(e)   the capitalisation rate used to determine the amount of finance costs capitalised during the period.

6.5.5   Valuation

The FRS introduces extensive rules in respect of the revaluation of assets. Tangible fixed assets should be revalued only where the entity adopts a policy of revaluation. Where such a policy is adopted then it should be applied to individual classes of tangible fixed assets, but need not be applied to all classes of tangible fixed assets held by the entity. *FRS 15, 42*

6.5.6   Frequency

Where a tangible fixed asset is subject to a policy of revaluation its carrying amount should be its current value as at the balance sheet date. The FRS does not insist on annual revaluations, but it regards the objective of a revaluation policy to be to reflect current values as at the balance sheet date. Therefore it sets standards on the need for periodic valuations and for interim review of these valuations. As a result it is no longer possible to make a 'one-off' valuation and leave the valuation as a 'permanent' item in the accounts. *FRS 15, 43* *FRS 15, 44*

6.5.7   Properties

Where properties are revalued the requirements of the FRS will be met by a full valuation at least every five years and an interim valuation in year 3. Interim valuations in years 1, 2 and 4 should be carried out where it is likely that there has been a material change in value. *FRS 15, 45*

Alternatively, for portfolios of properties, a full valuation may be performed on a rolling basis designed to cover all the properties over a five-year cycle, together with an interim valuation on the remaining four-fifths of the portfolio where it is likely that there has been a material change in value. This approach is appropriate only where the property portfolio held by the entity either: *FRS 15, 46*

(a)   consists of a number of broadly similar properties whose characteristics are such that their values are likely to be affected by the same market factors; or

(b)   can be divided on a continuing basis into five groups of a broadly similar spread.

Examples would include chains of shops or branded public houses.

A full valuation of a property will normally involve, the following: *FRS 15, 47*

(a)   detailed inspection of the interior and exterior of the property (on an initial valuation this will involve detailed measurement of floor space etc., but this would need to be re-performed in future full valuations only if there was evidence of a physical change to the buildings);

(b)   inspection of the locality;

(c)   enquiries of the local planning and similar authorities;

(d)   enquiries of the entity or its solicitors; and

(e)   research into market transactions in similar properties, identification of market trends, and the application of these to determine the value of the property under consideration.

A full valuation of a property should be conducted by either: *FRS 15, 48*

(a)   a qualified external valuer; or

(b)   a qualified internal valuer, provided that the valuation has been subject to review by a qualified external valuer. The review involves the valuation of a sample of the entity's properties by the external valuer and comparison with the internal valuer's figures leading to expression of opinion on the overall accuracy of the valuation, based upon analysis of this sample. The external valuer must be satisfied that the sample represents a genuine cross-section of the entity's portfolio.

An interim valuation of a property is conducted by a qualified (external or internal)   *FRS 15, 49*
valuer and consists of:

(a)   research into market transactions in similar properties, identification of market trends, and the application of these to determine the value of the property under consideration (as in para 47(e));

(b)   confirmation that there have been no changes of significance to the physical buildings, the legal rights or local planning considerations; and

(c)   an inspection of the property or the locality by the valuer to the extent that this is regarded as professionally necessary, having regard to all the circumstances of the case, including recent changes to the property or the locality and the date on which the valuer previously inspected the property.

6.5.8   Other tangible fixed assets

For certain tangible fixed assets other than properties, for example company cars, there   *FRS 15, 50*
may be an active secondhand market for the asset, or appropriate indices may exist, such that the entity's directors can establish the asset's value with reasonable reliability. In such cases it may be unnecessary to use the services of a qualified valuer and the valuation should instead be updated annually by the directors. Otherwise, the valuation should be performed by a qualified valuer at least every five years, with an update in year 3, also performed by a qualified valuer. In addition,

the valuation should be updated in the intervening years where it is likely that there has been a material change in value. If a qualified internal valuer is used for the five-yearly valuation, the valuation should be subject to review by a qualified external valuer.

For an index to be appropriate for use by the directors in valuing a tangible fixed asset other than property, the index table will:

FRS 15, 51

(a) be appropriate to the class of asset to which it is to be applied, as well as to the asset's location and condition, and take into account technological change; and

(b) have a proven record of regular publication and use and be expected to be available in the foreseeable future.

6.5.9   Material change in value

Valuations need to be updated where it is likely that there has been a material change in value. A material change in value is a change in value that would reasonably influence the decisions of a user of the accounts. In assessing whether a material change in value is likely, the combined impact of all relevant factors (e.g., physical deterioration in the property, general movements in market prices in the area etc.) should be considered.

FRS 15, 52

6.5.10   Valuation basis

The following valuation bases should be used for revalued properties that are not impaired:

FRS 15, 53

(a) non-specialised properties should be valued on the basis of existing use value (EUV), with the addition of notional directly attributable acquisition costs where material. Where the open market value (OMV) is materially different from EUV, the OMV and the reasons for the difference should be disclosed in the notes to the accounts;

(b) specialised properties should be valued on the basis of depreciated replacement cost;

(c) properties surplus to an entity's requirements should be valued on the basis of OMV, with expected directly attributable selling costs deducted where material.

The definitions of 'specialised' and 'non-specialised' property and the various bases of valuation are taken from the Royal Institute of Chartered Surveyors *Appraisal and Valuation Manual*. To assist readers the following definitions have been reproduced with the permission of the Royal Institution of Chartered Surveyors:

FRS 15, Appendix 1

Specialised properties
'those which, due to their specialised nature, are rarely, if ever, sold on the open market for single occupation for a continuation of their existing use, except as part of a sale of the business in occupation. Their specialised nature may arise from the construction, arrangement, size or location of the property, or a combination of these factors, or may be due to the nature of the plant and machinery and items of equipment which the buildings are designed to house, or the function, or the purpose for which the buildings are provided. Examples of specialised properties, which are usually valued on the Depreciated Replacement Cost (DRC) basis, are:

(a) oil refineries and chemical works where, usually, the buildings are no more than housings or cladding for highly specialised plant;

(b) power stations and dock installations where the buildings and site engineering works are related directly to the business of the owner, it being highly unlikely that they would have a value to anyone other than a company acquiring the undertaking;

(c) properties of such construction, arrangement, size or specification that there would be no market (for a sale to a single owner occupier for the continuation of existing use) for those buildings;

(d) standard properties in particular geographical areas and remote from main business centres, located there for operational or business reasons, which are of such an abnormal size for that district, that there would be no market for such buildings there;

(e) schools, colleges, universities and research establishments where there is no competing market demand from other organisations using these types of property in the locality;

(f) hospitals, other specialised health care premises and leisure centres where there is no competing market demand from other organisations wishing to use these types of property in the locality; and

(g) museums, libraries, and other similar premises provided by the public sector.'

Non-specialised properties

'all properties except those coming within the definition of specialised properties. Hence they are those for which there is a general demand, with or without adaptation, and which are commonly bought, sold or leased on the open market for their existing or similar uses, either with vacant possession for single occupation, or (whether tenanted or vacant) as investments or for development. Residential properties, shops, offices, standard industrial and warehouse buildings, public houses, petrol filling stations, and many others, are usually non-specialised properties.'

Open market value

'An opinion of the best price at which the sale of an interest in property would have been completed unconditionally for cash consideration on the date of valuation, assuming:

(a) a willing seller;

(b) that, prior to the date of valuation, there had been a reasonable period (having regard to the nature of the property and the state of the market) for the proper marketing of the interest, for the agreement of the price and terms and for the completion of the sale;

(c) that the state of the market, level of values and other circumstances were, on any earlier assumed date of exchange of contracts, the same as on the date of valuation;

(d) that no account is taken of any additional bid by a prospective purchaser with a special interest; and

(e) that both parties to the transaction had acted knowledgeably, prudently and without compulsion.'

Existing use value
'An opinion of the best price at which the sale of an interest in property would have been completed unconditionally for cash consideration on the date of valuation, assuming:

(a)   a willing seller;

(b)   that, prior to the date of valuation, there had been a reasonable period (having regard to the nature of the property and the state of the market) for the proper marketing of the interest, for the agreement of the price and terms and for the completion of the sale;

(c)   that the state of the market, level of values and other circumstances were, on any earlier assumed date of exchange of contracts, the same as on the date of valuation;

(d)   that no account is taken of any additional bid by a prospective purchaser with a special interest;

(e)   that both parties to the transaction had acted knowledgeably, prudently and without compulsion;

(f)   that the property can be used for the foreseeable future only for the existing use; and

(g)   that vacant possession is provided on completion of the sale of all parts of the property occupied by the business.'

Depreciated replacement cost (of property)
'The aggregate amount of the value of the land for the existing use or a notional replacement site in the same locality, and the gross replacement cost of the buildings and other site works, from which appropriate deductions may then be made to allow for the age, condition, economic or functional obsolescence, environmental and other relevant factors; all of these might result in the existing property being worth less to the undertaking in occupation than would a new replacement.'

Value of plant and machinery to the business
'An opinion of the price at which an interest in the plant and machinery utilised in a business would have been transferred at the date of valuation assuming:

(a)   that the plant and machinery will continue in its present uses in the business;

(b)   adequate potential profitability of the business, or continuing viability of the undertaking, both having due regard to the value of the total assets employed and the nature of the operation; and

(c)   that the transfer is part of an arm's length sale of the business wherein both parties acted knowledgeably, prudently and without compulsion.'

Where the valuation results present an indication of impairment, an impairment review should be performed in accordance with FRS 11. The asset should be recorded at the lower of the revalued amount, determined in accordance with the valuation principles given above, and recoverable amount (which is the higher of net realisable value and value in use). *FRS 15, 54*

Notional directly attributable acquisition costs includes normal dealing costs, such as professional fees, non-recoverable taxes and duties. It does not include expenditure incurred with the objective of enhancing the site value, such as site improvements, costs involved in obtaining planning consent, the cost of site preparation and *FRS 15, 55* clearance, or other costs that would already be reflected in EUV. For practical purposes, where notional acquisition costs (or expected selling costs for properties surplus to requirements) are not material they may be ignored.

Certain types of non-specialised properties are bought and sold, and therefore valued, *FRS 15, 56* as businesses. The EUV of a property valued as an operational entity is determined by having regard to trading potential, but excludes personal goodwill that has been created in the business by the present owner or management and is not expected to remain with the business in the event of the property being sold.

Some entities make structural changes to their properties or include special fittings *FRS 15, 57* within their properties in order to meet the particular needs of their individual businesses (for example specialised shop fronts on a retail unit). These structural changes and specialised fittings are referred to as 'adaptation works' and have a low or nil market value owing to their specialised nature. In such cases, the adaptation works and shell of the property (i.e., the property in its state before adaptation) may be treated separately, with only the shell of the property revalued using EUV. In such a case, the adaptation works are held at depreciated replacement cost or depreciated historical cost.

Specialised properties, where a market value is not available, are valued using *FRS 15, 58* depreciated replacement cost. The objective of depreciated replacement cost is to make a realistic estimate of the current cost of constructing an asset that has the same service potential as the existing asset.

Tangible fixed assets other than properties should be valued using market value, where *FRS 15, 59* possible. Where market value is not obtainable, assets should be valued on the basis of depreciated replacement cost. For tangible fixed assets other than property that are *FRS 15, 60* used in the business, notional directly attributable acquisition costs should be added to market value where material. For other tangible fixed assets that are surplus to requirements, expected selling costs should be deducted if material. Where market value is not obtainable, depreciated replacement cost, which provides a realistic estimate of the value attributable to the remaining service potential of the total useful economic life of the asset, should be used, with the assistance of a qualified valuer.

6.5.11   Class of assets

Where a tangible fixed asset is revalued all tangible fixed assets of the same class *FRS 15, 61* should be revalued. In those rare cases where it is impossible to obtain a reliable valuation of an asset held outside the UK or the Republic of Ireland the asset may be excluded from the class of assets. However, the carrying amount of the tangible fixed asset and the fact that it has not been revalued must be stated.

For the purposes of valuation, entities may, within reason, adopt other, narrower *FRS 15, 62* classes that meet the definition of a class of tangible fixed assets than the categories given by the Companies Act 1985 and are appropriate to their business. For example, land and buildings may be split into specialised properties, non-specialised properties and short leasehold properties. The disclosures required by the FRS should be given for each class of asset adopted by an entity for revaluation purposes.

6.5.12 Disclosures

Where any class of tangible fixed assets of an entity has been revalued the following *FRS 15, 74* information should be disclosed in each reporting period:

For each class of revalued assets:

(a) the name and qualifications of the valuer(s) or the valuer's organisation and a description of its nature;
(b) the basis or bases of valuation (including whether notional directly attributable acquisition costs have been included or expected selling costs deducted);
(c) the date and amounts of the valuations;
(d) where historical cost records are available, the carrying amount that would have been included in the financial statements had the tangible fixed assets been carried at historical cost less depreciation;
(e) whether the person(s) carrying out the valuation is (are) internal or external to the entity;
(f) where the directors are not aware of any material change in value and therefore the valuation(s) have not been updated, a statement to that effect; and
(g) where the valuation has not been updated, or is not a full valuation, the date of the last full valuation.

In addition, for revalued properties:

(a) where properties have been valued as fully equipped operational entities having regard to their trading potential, a statement to that effect and the carrying amount of those properties; and
(b) the total amount of notional directly attributable acquisition costs (or the total amount of expected selling costs deducted), included in the carrying amount, where material.

Other professional bodies may require disclosures in the financial statements in *FRS 15, 75* addition to the above disclosures. For example, the RICS requires confirmation in a published document containing a reference to a valuation report that the valuation has been made in accordance with the RICS Appraisal and Valuation Manual or a (named) alternative pursuant to Practice Statement 1.2.2, or the extent of and reason(s) for departure therefrom.

In addition, CA1985 requires disclosure, in the directors' report, of the difference, *FRS 15, 76* with such precision as is practicable, between the carrying amount and market value of interests in land, where, in the opinion of the directors, it is of such significance that it needs to be drawn to the attention of the members of the entity.

6.5.13 Review of useful economic life and residual value

The useful economic life of a tangible fixed asset should be reviewed at the end of *FRS 15, 93* each reporting period and revised if expectations are significantly different from previous estimates. If a useful economic life is revised, the carrying amount of the tangible fixed asset at the date of revision should be depreciated over the revised remaining useful economic life.

If a tangible fixed asset is carried in the balance sheet at a revaluation (particularly if *FRS 15, 94* valued using depreciated replacement cost), a reassessment of useful economic life may necessitate a revaluation of the asset. The revalued amount should be depreciated over the revised useful economic life.

Where the residual value is material it should be reviewed at the end of each reporting period to take account of reasonably expected technological changes based on prices prevailing at the date of acquisition (or revaluation). A change in its estimated residual value should be accounted for prospectively over the asset's remaining useful economic life, except to the extent that the asset has been impaired at the balance sheet date.

FRS 15, 95

The reassessed residual value is, where practicable, restated in terms of the price level that existed when the asset was purchased (or revalued). Where such a restatement is not practicable, the residual value is restated in terms of current values only where the residual value at current prices is below the original estimate of residual value. Events or changes in circumstances that cause the residual value to fall may also be indicative of an impairment of the asset (i.e., when the asset's recoverable amount falls below its carrying amount), in which case an impairment review should be performed in accordance with FRS 11.

FRS 15, 96

6.5.14 Transitional arrangements

FRS 15 contains several transitional provisions which can be applied on its first implementation. These provisions are 'one-offs' and may not be used in subsequent periods as a means of changing accounting policy or avoiding the requirements of the FRS.

FRS 15, 103–108

Where, an entity does not adopt a policy of revaluation, but the carrying amount of its tangible fixed assets reflects previous revaluations, it may:

FRS 15, 104

(a)   retain the book amounts (subject to the requirement to test the assets for impairment in accordance with FRS 11 where there is an indication that an impairment may have occurred). In these circumstances the entity should disclose the fact that the transitional provisions of the FRS are being followed and that the valuation has not been updated and give the date of the last revaluation; or

(b)   restate the carrying amount of the tangible fixed assets to historical cost (less restated accumulated depreciation), as a change in accounting policy.

The adoption of the FRS may result in revisions to the useful economic lives or residual values of tangible fixed assets which gives rise to the depreciation of tangible fixed assets that were previously not depreciated on the grounds of immateriality. In such cases, the carrying amounts of the tangible fixed assets should be depreciated prospectively over the remaining useful economic lives of the assets.

FRS 15, 107

Where, on adoption of the FRS, entities separate tangible fixed assets into different components with significantly different useful economic lives for depreciation purposes, the changes should be dealt with as prior period adjustments, as a change in accounting policy. Other revisions to the useful economic lives and residual values of tangible fixed assets which are recognised on the adoption of the FRS are not the result of a change in accounting policy and should be not be treated as prior period adjustments.

FRS 15, 108

6.6   Investment properties

SSAP 19 requires investment properties to be included in the balance sheet at open   *SSAP 19, 11*
market value. The standard does not normally require the valuation to be made by
qualified or independent valuers. Disclosure is required of the names or qualifications   *SSAP 19, 12*
of the valuers, the bases used by them and whether the person making the valuation is
an employee or officer of the company. However, where investment properties   *SSAP 19, 6*
represent a substantial proportion of the total assets of a major enterprise (e.g., a
listed company) the valuation thereof would normally be carried out:

(a)   annually by persons holding a recognised professional qualifiction and having
      recent post-qualification experience in the location and category of the
      properties concerned; and
(b)   at least every five years by an external valuer.

Definition

An investment property is an interest in land and/or buildings: *SSAP 19, 7*

(a)   in respect of which construction work and development have been completed;
      and
(b)   which is held for its investment potential, any rental income being negotiated at
      arm's length.

The following are exceptions from the definition: *SSAP 19, 8*

(a)   a property which is owned and occupied by a company for its own purposes is
      not an investment property;
(b)   a property let to and occupied by another group company is not an investment
      property for the purposes of its own accounts or the group accounts.

Accounting

Changes in the market value of investment properties should not be taken to the profit   *SSAP 19, 13*
and loss account but should be taken to the statement of total recognised gains and
losses (being a movement on an investment revaluation reserve), unless a deficit (or its
reversal) on an individual investment property is expected to be permanent, in which
case it should be charged (or credited) in the profit and loss account of the period.

Investment properties should not be subject to periodic charges for depreciation except   *SSAP 19, 10*
for properties held on lease which should be depreciated on the basis set out in FRS 15
at least over the period when the unexpired term is 20 years or less.

SSAP 19 requires that the carrying value of investment properties and the investment   *SSAP 19, 15*
revaluation reserve should be displayed prominently in the financial statements.

The application of the standard will usually be a departure for the overriding purpose
of giving a true and fair view, from the otherwise specific requirement of the law to   *SSAP 19, 17*
provide depreciation on any fixed asset which has a limited useful economic life. In
this circumstance there will need to be given in the notes to the accounts particulars of
that departure, the reasons for it and its effect. An appropriate wording may be: *UITF 7, 4*

'In accordance with SSAP 19, investment properties are revalued annually and the aggregate surplus or deficit is transferred to the revaluation reserve. In the case of a permanent diminution the deficit is taken to the profit and loss account. No depreciation is provided in respect of freehold or leasehold investment properties with over 20 years to run.

The Companies Act 1985 requires all properties to be depreciated. However, this requirement conflicts with the generally accepted accounting principle set out in SSAP 19. The directors consider that, because these properties are not held for consumption but for their investment potential, to depreciate them would not give a true and fair view. Therefore it is necessary to adopt SSAP 19 in order to give a true and fair view.

If this departure from the Act had not been made, the profit for the financial year would have been reduced by depreciation. However, the amount of depreciation cannot reasonably be quantified because depreciation is only one of many factors reflected in the annual valuation and the amount which might otherwise have been shown cannot be separately identified or quantified.'

6.7   Impairment of fixed assets and goodwill

Pre FRS 11

The Companies Act 1985 has required that fixed assets should be written down to their recoverable amount where they have suffered permanent diminution in value.   *19(1), Sch 4*

The difficulty presented by this requirement was that the Act (and accounting standards) contained no definition of recoverable amount and did not identify when diminutions would be considered to be permanent.

FRS 11 objectives

The objective of this FRS is to ensure that: *FRS 11, 1*

(a)   fixed assets and goodwill are recorded in the financial statements at no more than their recoverable amount;

(b)   any resulting impairment loss is measured and recognised on a consistent basis; and

(c)   sufficient information is disclosed in the financial statements to enable users to understand the impact of the impairment on the financial position and performance of the reporting entity.

Impairment is defined as being a reduction in the recoverable amount of a fixed asset or goodwill below its carrying amount.   *FRS 11, 2*

Recoverable amount is the higher of net realisable value and value in use.   *FRS 11, 2*

The requirements of FRS 11 apply to purchased goodwill that is recognised in the balance sheet and all fixed assets, except: *FRS 11, 5*

(a) fixed assets within the scope of FRS 13 *Derivatives and other financial instruments: disclosures*;

(b) investment properties as defined in SSAP 19 *Accounting for investment properties*;

(c) an entity's own shares held by an ESOP and shown as a fixed asset in the entity's balance sheet under UITF Abstract 13 *Accounting for ESOP trusts*; and

(d) costs capitalised pending determination (i.e., costs capitalised while a field is still being appraised) under the Oil Industry Accounting Committee's SORP *Accounting for oil and gas exploration and development activities*.

Indications of impairment

FRS 11 requires that a review for impairment of a fixed asset or goodwill should be carried out if events or changes in circumstances indicate that the carrying amount of the fixed asset or goodwill may not be recoverable. *FRS 11, 8*

Impairment occurs because something has happened either to the fixed assets themselves or to the economic environment in which the fixed assets are operated. It is possible, therefore, to rely on the use of indicators of impairment to determine when a review for impairment is needed. *FRS 11, 9*

Examples of events and changes in circumstances that indicate an impairment may have occurred include: *FRS 11, 10*

- a current period operating loss in the business in which the fixed asset or goodwill is involved or net cash outflow from the operating activities of that business, combined with either past operating losses or net cash outflows from such operating activities or an expectation of continuing operating losses or net cash outflows from such operating activities;
- a significant decline in a fixed asset's market value during the period;
- evidence of obsolescence or physical damage to the fixed asset;
- a significant adverse change in:
    - either the business or the market in which the fixed asset or goodwill is involved, such as the entrance of a major competitor;
    - the statutory or other regulatory environment in which the business operates;
    - any 'indicator of value' (for example turnover) used to measure the fair value of a fixed asset on acquisition;
- a commitment by management to undertake a significant reorganisation;
- a major loss of key employees;
- a significant increase in market interest rates or other market rates of return that are likely to affect materially the fixed asset's recoverable amount.

Recognition and measurement of impairment losses

The impairment review should comprise a comparison of the carrying amount of the fixed asset or goodwill with its recoverable amount (the higher of net realisable value and value in use). To the extent that the carrying amount exceeds the recoverable amount, the fixed asset or goodwill is impaired and should be written down. The impairment loss should be recognised in the profit and loss account unless it arises on a previously revalued fixed asset, in which case it should be recognised as required by the paragraph below. *FRS 11, 14*

An impairment loss on a revalued fixed asset should be recognised in the profit and loss account if it is caused by a clear consumption of economic benefits. Other impairments of revalued fixed assets should be recognised in the statement of total recognised gains and losses until the carrying amount of the asset reaches its depreciated historical cost and thereafter in the profit and loss account.

FRS 11, 63

When an impairment loss on a fixed asset or goodwill is recognised, the remaining useful economic life and residual value should be reviewed and revised if necessary. The revised carrying amount should be depreciated over the revised estimate of the remaining useful economic life.

FRS 11, 21

A reversal of an impairment loss should be recognised in the profit and loss account to the extent that the original impairment loss (adjusted for subsequent depreciation) was recognised in the profit and loss account. Any remaining balance of the reversal of an impairment should be recognised in the statement of total recognised gains and losses.

FRS 11, 66

Calculation of recoverable amount

FRS 11 contains extensive guidance on the calculation of the recoverable amount of an asset which is thought to be impaired. This involves discounting the future cash flows associated directly with the asset or the income-generating unit in which the asset is located.

FRS 11, 22–46

Presentation and disclosure

Impairment losses recognised in the profit and loss account should be included within operating profit under the appropriate statutory heading, and disclosed as an exceptional item if appropriate. Impairment losses recognised in the statement of total recognised gains and losses should be disclosed separately on the face of that statement.

FRS 11, 67

In the notes to the financial statements in accounting periods after the impairment, the impairment loss should be treated as follows:

FRS 11, 68

(a) For assets held on a historical cost basis, the impairment loss should be included within cumulative depreciation: the cost of the asset should not be reduced.
(b) For revalued assets held at a market value (e.g., existing use value or open market value), the impairment loss should be included within the revalued carrying amount.
(c) For revalued assets held at depreciated replacement cost, an impairment loss charged to the profit and loss account should be included within cumulative depreciation: the carrying amount of the asset should not be reduced; an impairment loss charged to the statement of total recognised gains and losses should be deducted from the carrying amount of the asset.

If the impairment loss is measured by reference to value in use of a fixed asset or income-generating unit, the discount rate applied to the cash flows should be disclosed. If a risk-free discount rate is used, some indication of the risk adjustments made to the cash flows should be given.

FRS 11, 69

Where an impairment loss recognised in a previous period is reversed in the current period, the financial statements should disclose the reason for the reversal, including

FRS 11, 70

any changes in the assumptions upon which the calculation of recoverable amount is based.

There are also several very specific disclosures, which arise from the methodology used to calculate the recoverable amount of an asset:

(a)   Where an impairment loss would have been recognised in a previous period had the forecasts of future cash flows been more accurate but the impairment has reversed and the reversal of the loss is permitted to be recognised, the impairment now identified and its subsequent reversal should be disclosed.   *FRS 11, 71*

(b)   Where, in the measurement of value in use, the period before a steady or declining long-term growth rate has been assumed extends to more than five years, the financial statements should disclose the length of the longer period and the circumstances justifying it.   *FRS 11, 72*

(c)   Where, in the measurement of value in use, the long-term growth rate used has exceeded the long-term average growth rate for the country or countries in which the business operates, the financial statements should disclose the growth rate assumed and the circumstances justifying it.   *FRS 11, 73*

6.8   Investments

6.8.1   General

Investments may be included in the balance sheet as either fixed or current assets. Investments in the nature of trade investments or other investments held on a long-term basis should normally be treated as fixed, and investments of a temporary nature (e.g., investments representing the employment outside the business of temporarily surplus funds) should be treated as current assets.

The statutory disclosure requirements described in **6.2** above (including those relating to valuations) apply to fixed asset investments with the obvious exception that depreciation need not be provided. This said, it may be necessary, e.g., where the value of any investment has permanently diminished, for provision to be made for the diminution in value. Any such provision not shown in the profit and loss account must be disclosed in a note to the accounts.   *19(1), Sch 4*

Investments analysed as current asset investments should be analysed between own shares and other investments.   *8, Sch 4*

In addition, CA 1985 requires the notes to include certain information about any investments that a company holds (irrespective of whether these are shown as fixed assets or as current assets). In particular, the notes must disclose:

(a)   the amount that relates to listed investments;   *45(1), Sch 4*

(b)   the aggregate market value of those investments listed on a recognised stock exchange, where it differs from the amount at which they are stated in the balance sheet;   *45(2), Sch 4*

(c)   the stock exchange value of any investments shown at market value, where the latter is taken as being higher than their stock exchange value. This disclosure is required because the market value and the stock exchange value may differ according to the size of the investment and its marketability. For example, a   *45(2b), Sch 4* controlling stake would be worth more than a mere minority interest in shares of a company, but stock exchange prices traditionally reflect the values of small parcels of shares;

(d)   for investments which are included at a directors' valuation, which is not market value, the details of the valuation need to be given together with reasons for adopting it.

For this purpose, a 'listed investment' means any investment that is listed on an investment exchange other than an overseas investment exchange within the meaning of the Financial Services Act 1986 or on any other reputable stock exchange outside Great Britain. For guidance as to whether or not a stock exchange outside Great Britain is 'reputable', the Stock Exchange should be consulted.

All other investments, including those traded on the Alternative Investment Market, are to be regarded as unlisted. In this connection, there is no requirement to disclose either the directors' valuation or other information in respect of unlisted companies.

For investments included at valuation, or for which a valuation is given, the amount of tax payable, if disposed of at that value, should be disclosed.

6.8.2   Shareholdings above 20 per cent

Where a company holds more than 20 per cent of the nominal value of any class of shares of another company, or the amount of the holdings (as stated in the company's accounts) exceeds 20 per cent of the company's assets, and the holding is not treated as a subsidiary the following information should be disclosed: *ss7 & 8, Sch 5*

(a)   the name of the company;
(b)   either the country in which it is:
    (i)   incorporated (if outside Great Britain); or
    (ii)   the address of its principal place of business if it is unincorporated;
(c)   (i)   the identity of each class of share held by the company; and   *58(3)(b),*
    (ii)   the proportion of the nominal value of the shares of that class represented   *Sch 4*
        by those shares.

Corresponding information for the preceding year need not be given.

The Companies Act 1985 contains provisions which simplify the above requirements in respect of overseas shareholdings where disclosure would be seriously prejudicial   *s231(3)*
to the business of the company or the undertakings.

When the number of investments falling into the above category is large, only those   *s231(5) & (6)*
principally affecting the profit or assets need to be included. When advantage is taken of this section, the note dealing with the principal shareholdings must state that the note includes only the principal shareholdings and the first annual return of the investing company, after taking advantage of this section, must have annexed to it the above details of those investments omitted from the note to the accounts.

In addition, CA 1985 requires that for shareholdings in excess of 20 per cent the   *s9(1), Sch 5 &*
following information should be given: *s25(1), Sch 5*

Fixed assets

(a)   the aggregate amount of the capital and reserves of the company as at the end of its relevant financial year;

(b)   the profit or loss of that company for that financial year.

The relevant financial year of an undertaking is:

(a)   its financial year end if coterminous with the company;

(b)   if not, its last financial year end before the end of the company's financial year.

This information need not be disclosed if it is immaterial or when:

(a)   the investing company is included in the accounts of a larger group and need not prepare group accounts;   *ss9(2) &
25(3), Sch 5*

(b)   the investment is less than 50 per cent of the nominal value of the shares in the undertaking and the company does not have to publish accounts in Great Britain.   *s9(3), Sch 5
s25(2), Sch 5*

The note should also disclose the nature of the business of an associated company.   *FRS 9, 52*

Additional Companies Act 1985 requirements

In addition, to the disclosures required above, the nature of the business of the principal subsidiaries and the proportion of voting rights held by the parent and its subsidiary undertakings should be disclosed.   *s17(1), Sch 5
FRS2, 33*

The shares in group undertakings should be analysed between those relating to the parent undertaking and those attributable to other members of the group.   *s16(1), Sch 5*

It should be noted that under the Companies Act 1985 formats it is not permissible to combine, on the face of the balance sheet, the cost of the investment in subsidiaries with the net indebtedness on current account to/from subsidiaries. Amounts due to/from subsidiaries on current accounts must be disclosed in either current assets or creditors.

The Act does permit loans to subsidiaries, which are of a long-term nature, to be disclosed separately under this section of the balance sheet.

If the disclosures that are required would, in the opinion of the directors, be of excessive length then only information relating to those subsidiaries which principally affect the amount of the profit or loss or the assets of the company as well as those subsidiaries excluded from consolidation need be given. If this is done, the fact must be stated and the full particulars annexed to the next annual return.   *s231(5)*

With the consent of the Department of Trade and Industry, the information required to be given for subsidiaries need not be given in respect of subsidiaries, incorporated or carrying on business outside the United Kingdom if, in the opinion of the directors of the parent company, this would be harmful to the business of the parent company or of any other company in the group, or of the subsidiary.   *s231(3)*

In addition to the details required by the Act, FRS 2 also requires the disclosure of: *FRS 2, 31*

(a)   particulars of the balances between the excluded subsidiary undertakings and the rest of the group;

(b)	the nature and the extent of transactions of the excluded subsidiary undertakings with the rest of the group;

(c)	for an excluded subsidiary undertaking carried other than by the equity method, any amounts included in the consolidated financial statements in respect of:

   (i)	dividends received and receivable from that undertaking; and

   (ii)	any write-down in the period in respect of the investment in that undertaking;

(d)	for subsidiary undertaking excluded because of different activities, the separate financial statements of those undertakings. Summarised information may be provided for undertakings that individually, or in connection with those with similar operations, do not account for more than 20 per cent of any one or more of operating profits, turnover or net assets of the group. The group amounts should be measured by including all excluded subsidiary undertakings.

Where a subsidiary is excluded from consolidation, FRS 2 requires the disclosure of the name of:

(a)	the principal subsidiaries excluded;

(b)	the reasons why they had been excluded.

### 6.8.3	Group accounts exemptions

A parent undertaking need not prepare group accounts under certain circumstances. The circumstances, and the disclosures which are required are:

(a)	Small and medium-sized groups fulfilling the criteria for the production of abbreviated accounts are exempt from preparing group accounts providing a statement is made in the accounting policies to this effect.	*s248*

(b)	If the company is a wholly owned subsidiary it is exempt from preparing its own group accounts providing it is consolidated in the accounts of a larger group and this fact is stated together with details of the parent and its location.	*s228*

Exclusion of a particular subsidiary from consolidation may arise on the grounds of:	*s229*

(a)	immateriality;

(b)	severe long-term restrictions;

(c)	disproportionate expense or delay;

(d)	holding for resale, not previously consolidated;

(e)	activities so different that to consolidate would be incompatible with true and fair view.

In each case the reason should be stated separately for each subsidiary excluded.

### 6.8.4	FRS 2 disclosures

In addition to the details required by the Act, FRS 2 also requires the disclosure of:	*FRS 2, 31*

(a)	particulars of the balances between the excluded subsidiary undertakings and the rest of the group;

(b)	the nature and extent of transactions of the excluded subsidiary undertakings with the rest of the group;

(c)   for an excluded subsidiary undertaking carried other than by the equity method, any amounts included in the consolidated financial statements in respect of:
   (i)   dividends received and receivable from that undertaking; and
   (ii) any write-down in the period in respect of the investment in that undertaking or amounts due from that undertaking;

(d)   for subsidiary undertakings excluded because of different activities, the separate financial statements of those undertakings. Summarised information may be provided for undertakings that individually, or in combination with those with similar operations, do not account for more than 20 per cent of any one or more of operating profits, turnover or net assets of the group. The group amounts should be measured by including all excluded subsidiary undertakings.

Where a subsidiary is excluded from consolidation, FRS 2 requires the disclosure of: *FRS 2, 26*

(a)   the names of the principal subsidiaries excluded;
(b)   the reasons why they had been excluded.

A subsidiary should be excluded from consolidation where: *FRS 2, 25*
s229, 3 & 4

(a)   severe long-term restrictions substantially hinder the exercise of the rights of the parent undertaking over the assets or management of the subsidiary undertaking. The rights referred to are those by reason of which the parent undertaking is defined as such under s258 and in the absence of which it would not be the parent undertaking; or

(b)   the interest in the subsidiary undertaking is held exclusively with a view to subsequent resale and the subsidiary undertaking has not previously been consolidated in group accounts prepared by the parent undertaking; or

(c)   the subsidiary undertaking's activities are so different from those of other undertakings to be included in the consolidation that its inclusion would be incompatible with the obligation to give a true and fair view. It is exceptional for such circumstances to arise and it is not possible to identify any particular contrast of activities where the necessary incompatibility with the true and fair view generally occurs. The Act provides that exclusion on the grounds of different activities does not apply 'merely because some of the undertakings are industrial, some commercial and some provide services, or because they carry on industrial or commercial activities involving different products or provide different services'.

6.8.5   Accounting policies

Where uniform accounting policies are not adopted by group companies there should be shown: *4, Sch 4A*

(a)   the different accounting policies used and the reasons for different treatment;
(b)   an indication of the amounts of the assets and liabilities involved, and, where practicable, an indication of the effect on results and net assets of the adoption of different policies from those of the group.

6.8.6 Non-coterminous financial periods

Where the financial periods of any subsidiary are not coterminous with that of the parent company the following information should be shown:

4 & 19, Sch 5

(i)   the name of the subsidiary;
(ii)   its accounting date (last before the end of the financial year of the parent company);
(iii)   the reason for using a different accounting date

6.8.7 Acquisition of subsidiary undertakings

Disclosures in respect of the acquisition of subsidiary undertakings are set out in para 21–37 of FRS 6.

6.9 Associates and joint ventures

FRS 9 requires investors to report the effect on their financial position and performance of interests in associates and joint ventures and other joint arrangements which do not meet the FRS's definition of an associate and a joint venture.

6.9.1 Definitions

Associate

An entity in which an investor has a participating interest and over whose operating and financial position it exercises a significant influence.

FRS 9, 4

A participating interest is an interest held in the shares of another entity on a long-term basis for the purpose of securing a contribution to the investor's activities by the exercise of control or influence arising from or related to that interest. The investor's interest must, therefore, be a beneficial one and the benefits expected to arise must be limited to the exercise of its significant influence over the investee's operating and financial policies.

A participating interest is usually represented by a holding of equity shares. However, a participating interest may also be represented by an interest convertible into an interest in shares or an option to acquire shares.

Significant influence arises when an investor is actively involved and is influential in the direction of its investee through its participation in policy decisions covering aspects of policy relevant to the investor, including decisions on strategic issues such as the development of the business and dertmining the balance between dividend and reinvestment.

There is a statutory presumption that a holding of 20 per cent or more of the voting rights in another entity should be presumed to exercise a significant influence over the other entity unless the contrary is shown. The interest of 20 per cent is represented by the aggregate of shares held directly by the entity and by its subsidiaries.

Joint venture

FRS 9, 4

This is an entity in which the reporting entity holds an interest on a long-term basis and which is jointly controlled by the reporting entity and one or more other venturers under a contractual arrangement.

A joint venture is a situation where the controlling entities are unable to exercise control individually but are able to exercise control collectively and decisions regarding the development, management, performance and financial position of the venture require each venturer's consent.

6.9.2 Accounting for associates in individual financial statements

In the investor's own financial statements, its interest in associates should be treated as fixed asset investments and shown at cost, less any amount written off, or at valuation.

FRS 9, 26

6.9.3 Accounting for joint ventures

Joint ventures should be included in the primary statements of the consolidated financial statements using the gross equity method.

FRS 9, 20

In the investor's individual financial statements, investments in joint ventures should be treated as fixed asset investments and shown either at cost, less any amounts written off, or at valuation.

FRS 9, 20

6.9.4 Non-corporate associates and joint ventures

Where an investor has an interest in a non-corporate associate or joint venture, the investor should ensure that all its liabilities with respect to the entity are reflected appropriately in its financial statements.

FRS 9, 45

Such liabilities could arise from a joint and several liability in a partnership where the investor's share of the liability exceeds the amounts resulting from taking into account only the investor's share of net assets.

FRS 9, 46

If this arises, it may be necessary either to include an additional amount for that liability or to report it as a contingent liability.

FRS 9, 47

6.9.5 Investor does not prepare consolidated financial statements

Where an investor does not prepare consolidated financial statements, it should present the relevant amounts for associates and joint ventures, as appropriate, by preparing a separate set of financial statements or by showing the relevant amounts, together with the effects of including them, as additional information to its own financial statements.

FRS 9, 48

Investing entities that are exempt from preparing consolidated financial statements, or which would be exempt if they had subsidiaries, are exempt from this requirement.

6.9.6 Disclosures

For all associates and joint ventures

FRS 9, 52

The names of the principal associates and joint ventures should be disclosed in the financial statements of the investing group, showing for each associate and joint venture:

(a)   the proportion of the issued shares in each class held by the investing group, indicating any special rights or constraints attaching to them;
(b)   the accounting period or date of the financial statements used if they differ from those of the investing group; and
(c)   an indication of the nature of its business.

Any notes relating to the financial statements of associates and joint ventures, or matters that should have been noted had the investor's accounting policies been applied, that are material to understanding the effect on the investor of its investments should be disclosed, in particular noting the investor's share in contingent liabilities incurred jointly with other venturers or investors and its share of the capital commitments of the associates and joint ventures themselves.   *FRS 9, 53*

If there are significant statutory, contractual or exchange control restrictions on the ability of an associate or joint venture to distribute its reserves (other than those shown as non-distributable), the extent of the restrictions should be indicated.   *FRS 9, 54*

The amounts owing and owed between an investor and its associates or its joint ventures should be analysed into amounts relating to loans and amounts relating to trading balances. This disclosure may be combined with those required by FRS 8 *Related party disclosures*.   *FRS 9, 55*

A note should explain why the facts of any particular case rebut either the presumption that an investor holding 20 per cent or more of the voting rights of another entity exercises significant influence over the operating and financial policies of that entity or the presumption that an investor holding 20 per cent or more of the shares of another entity has a participating interest.   *FRS 9, 56*

Additional disclosure at 15 and 25 per cent thresholds

The disclosures required for all associates and joint ventures should be supplemented if certain thresholds are exceeded. The thresholds are applied by comparing the investor's share for either its associates in aggregate or its joint ventures in aggregate or its individual associates or joint ventures, as appropriate, of the following: *FRS 9, 57*

(a)   gross assets;
(b)   gross liabilities;
(c)   turnover;
(d)   operating results (on a three-year average),

with the corresponding amounts for the investor group (excluding any amount included by the equity method for associates and the gross equity method for joint ventures). If any of the relevant amounts for the investor's share exceeds the specified proportion of the same amounts for the investor group, the threshold has been exceeded and the additional disclosures required by the following paragraph should be made.

The following are the additional disclosures that should be made:

(a)   Where the aggregate of the investor's share in its associates exceeds a 15 per cent threshold with respect ot the investor group, a note should give the aggregate of the investor's share in its associates of the following:

Fixed assets

      (i)   turnover (unless it is already included as a memorandum item);

      (ii)   fixed assets;

      (iii)   current assets;

      (iv)   liabilities due within one year;

      (v)   liabilities due after one year or more.

(b) Where the aggregate of the investor's share in its joint ventures exceeds a 15 per cent threshold with respect to the investor group, a note should give the aggregate of the investor's share in its joint ventures of the following:

- fixed assets;
- current assets;
- liabilities due within one year;
- liabilities due after one year or more.

(c) Where the investor's share in any individual associate or joint venture exceeds a 25 per cent threshold with respect to the investor group, a note should name the associate or joint venture and give its share of each of the following:

- turnover;
- profit before tax;
- taxation;
- profit after tax;
- current assets;
- liabilities due within one year;
- liabilities due after one year or more.

If that individual associate or joint venture accounts for nearly all of the amounts included for that class of investment, only the aggregate, not the individual, information need be given, provided that this is explained and the associate or joint venture identified.

In addition to the disclosures in (a)–(c) above, further analysis should be given where this is necessary to understand the nature of the total amounts disclosed. In deciding into which balance sheet headings the amounts should be analysed, regard should be had to the nature of the businesses and, therefore, which are the most relevant and descriptive balance sheet amounts to disclose. It may be important to give an indication of the size and maturity profile of the liabilities held.

7 Current assets

7.1 Definition

The Companies Act 1985 defines a current asset as being any asset which is not intended for use on a continuing basis in the company's activities. All current assets must be included at the lower of purchase price or production cost and net realisable value. *s262(1)*

22 & 23, Sch 4

7.2 Stocks

Special rules may be applied to the determination of the purchase price or the production cost (see **6.2.1** for definition) of stocks. The following methods are permitted by CA 1985: *27(1) & (2), Sch 4*

(a)   the first-in, first-out (FIFO) method;
(b)   the last-in, first-out (LIFO) method;
(c)   a weighted average price;
(d)   any other similar method.

The Companies Act 1985 requires that the directors must choose from the above four methods the method that is most appropriate in the circumstances. When choosing a method, the directors must ensure that the method chosen provides the fairest practical approximation to actual cost. SSAP 9 considers that the LIFO method does not usually bear a reasonable relationship to actual cost. *27(1), Sch 4*

SSAP 9, 39

Whichever method the directors choose, the notes to the accounts must disclose any material differences between the purchase price/production cost and the relevant alternative amount of each category of stocks. This will normally be the current replacement cost but may instead be determined according to the most recent actual purchase price. The Act leaves it to the company's directors to form an opinion as to which gives the more appropriate comparison to cost. *27(3), Sch 4*

27(4), Sch 4

27(5), Sch 4

SSAP 9 includes guidance on the elements comprising the 'cost' of stocks and work in progress and deals with long-term contract work in progress (see **5.4.2**). *SSAP 9, 17*

The requirements of SSAP 9 are as follows:

(a)   The amount at which stocks and work in progress, other than long-term work in progress, is stated in periodic financial statements should be the total of the lower of cost and net realisable value of the separate items of stock and work in progress or of groups of similar items. *SSAP 9, 26*
(b)   Long-term contracts should be assessed on a contract by contract basis and *SSAP 9, 28*

reflected in the profit and loss account by recording turnover and related costs as contract activity progress. Turnover is ascertained in a manner appropriate to the stage of completion of the contract, the business and the industry in which it operates. Where it is considered that the outcome of a long-term contract can be assessed with reasonable certainty before its conclusion, the prudently calculated attributable profit should be recognised in the profit and loss account as the difference between the reported turnover and related costs for that contract.

SSAP 9, 29

(c)   The accounting policies which have been used in calculating cost, net realisable value, attributable profit and foreseeable losses (as appropriate) should be stated.

SSAP 9, 14 & 32

(d)   Stocks and work in progress should be sub-classified in balance sheets or in notes to the financial statements in a manner which is appropriate to the business and so as to indicate the amounts held in each of the main categories. This will often be achieved by giving the analysis required by the CA 1985 formats for the balance sheets.

SSAP 9, 27

(e)   Long-term contracts should be disclosed in the balance sheet as follows:

SSAP 9, 30

    (i)   the amount by which recorded turnover is in excess of payments on account should be classified as 'amounts recoverable on contracts' and separately disclosed within debtors;

    (ii)   the balance of payments on account, in excess of amounts:
- matched with turnover,
- offset against long-term contract balances,

should be classified as 'payments on account' and separately disclosed within creditors;

    (iii)   the amount of long-term contracts, at costs incurred, net of amounts transferred to cost of sales, after deducting foreseeable losses and payments on account not matched with turnover, should be classified as long-term contract balances and separately disclosed within the balance sheet heading 'stocks'. The balance sheet note should disclose separately the balances of:
- net cost less foreseeable losses,
- applicable payments on account;

    (iv)   the amount by which the provision or accrual for foreseeable losses exceeds the costs incurred (after transfers to cost of sales) should be included within either 'provisions for liabilities and charges' or 'creditors' as appropriate.

Appendix 3 to SSAP 9 gives several detailed examples of the treatment required for long-term contracts.

SSAP 9, Appendix

7.3   Debtors

A total figure for debtors must be disclosed on the face of the balance sheet as it is preceded by a Roman numeral in the balance sheet formats prescribed in CA 1985, but, either on the face of the balance sheet or more usually in the notes, it must be analysed among:

(a)   trade debtors;
(b)   amounts owed by group companies (see **7.4**);
(c)   amounts owed by associated companies (see **8.5**);
(d)   other debtors;

(e)   called-up share capital not paid;

(f)   prepayments and accrued income.

The amount of any pension costs prepaid should also be disclosed.

SSAP 24, 87d & 88f

If a company has granted financial assistance for the acquisition of its own shares (or those of its parent company) under the authority of CA 1985 and the amounts outstanding are included under any item shown in the company's balance sheet the aggregate of the following loans must be disclosed:

51(2), Sch 4
s153(4b) or (4c) or s155

(a)   loans under employee share schemes;

s153(4b)

(b)   loans to non-director employees;

s153(4c)

(c)   permissible loans by private companies.

s155

The amount falling due after more than one year must be shown separately for each item included in debtors. For this purpose, a balance is considered to be receivable on the earliest date on which payment is due, rather than on the earliest date on which payment is expected. If material, debtors falling due after more than one year should be shown on the face of the balance sheet.

8(5), Sch 4

UITF 4, 3

7.4   Amounts owed by (or to) group undertakings

The balance sheet or the notes to the balance sheet must, where the company is a parent company or a subsidiary undertaking, show the aggregate of indebtedness with:

(a)   its parent undertaking and any fellow subsidiary undertakings;

(b)   its subsidiary undertakings.

59, Sch 4

It is not permitted to set off amounts due from one group undertaking with amounts due to another. Hence, the amounts to be shown under (a) and (b) above represent the gross amounts due to and from group undertakings with the exception that loans to subsidiaries which are of a long-term nature may be shown separately under fixed asset investments (refer to **6.7** above).

The term 'undertakings' encompasses listed companies and unincorporated bodies which fall within group ownership.

7.5   Loans to and transactions with directors

The provisions of CA 1985 in this area are complex. In general, a company is, with certain specific exceptions, prohibited from making loans or providing security for loans to directors. Nevertheless, details of such transactions together with details of substantial contracts with directors must be disclosed. Corresponding figures for the previous year are not required. Where the company fails to make adequate disclosure the auditors must include the relevant information in their report.

s330
s317
s232
58(3), Sch 4

s237(4)

7.5.1   Requirements to disclose

Subject to certain specific exemptions below, the requirements to disclose apply to all transactions or arrangements whether or not:

19, Sch 6

(a)   they are unlawful;

(b)   the director with whom they were made was a director or connected person at the time the transactions were made:

(c)   a company was a subsidiary of a company other than its current parent company when the transactions were made.

The transactions or arrangements concerned include principally: *15 & 16, Sch 6*

(a)   loans;

(b)   guarantees;

(c)   provision of security;

(d)   quasi-loans;

(e)   credit transactions;

(f)   any other transaction or arrangement in which a person who was a director at any time during the period, had, either directly or indirectly, a material interest   *15(c), 16(c) &* in that transaction. 'Material' is not defined in the legislation, but it appears to   *17(1), Sch 6* apply primarily to the extent of the director's interest rather than to the size of the contract.

The transactions or arrangements to be disclosed include those between the company or its subsidiary, and a director or connected person of the company or its parent   *17(1), Sch 6* company.

Transactions and arrangements are deemed to include a 'shadow director', defined as a person in accordance with whose instructions the directors are accustomed to act, unless such instructions merely represent advice given in a professional capacity.   *s741(2) & (3)*

A connected person is a director's spouse, or child or stepchild under 18 years of age, a body corporate with which the director is associated, a trustee of a trust of which a director is a beneficiary, or a partner of the director or of any person connected with the director.   *s346(2) & (3)*

A quasi-loan is defined as a transaction under which one party (the 'creditor') defrays   *s331(3)* or agrees to defray the expenditure of another ('the borrower') either:

(a)   on terms that the borrower will reimburse the creditor; or

(b)   in circumstances where the borrower becomes liable to reimburse the creditor.

A credit transaction is a transaction under which one party, the 'creditor':   *s331(7)*

(a)   supplies any goods or sells any land under a hire-purchase agreement or conditional sale agreement; or

(b)   leases or hires any land or goods in return for periodic payments; or

(c)   otherwise disposes of land or supplies goods or services on the understanding that payment (whether in a lump sum or instalments or by way of periodic payments or otherwise) is to be deferred.

7.5.2   Disclosures

The following particulars must be given in the notes to the accounts for any transaction, arrangement or agreement required to be disclosed in respect of items   *22, Sch 6* referred to above:

(a) a statement that it was made or subsisted during the year;   *22(2)(a), Sch 6*

(b) names of directors (and, where relevant, connected persons) concerned and, for   *22(2)(b), Sch 6*
transactions to which paras 15c & 16c, Sch 6 of CA 1985 apply (see above), the   *22(2)(c), Sch 6*
nature of the directors' interests;

(c) principal terms (including those relating to repayment, interest and security);   *22(1), Sch 6*

(d) for loans or agreements for or arrangements relating to loans: *22(2)(d), Sch 6*

   (i)   the amount of the liability (principal and interest) at the beginning and
end of the year;

   (ii) the maximum amount of liability during the year;

   (iii) the amount of any arrears of interest;

   (iv) any provision against non-repayment of the whole or any part of the
principal or interest.

Although loans by a company (and its subsidiaries) totalling a maximum of
£5,000 and made to one of its directors (or to a parent company director) are   *s334*
legal, full disclosure must still be made irrespective of how small the amount   *15, Sch 6*
might be;

(e) for guarantees or the provision of security, or agreements or arrangements   *22(e), Sch 6*
relating thereto:

   (i)   the amount for which the company (or its subsidiary) was liable at the
beginning and end of the year;

   (ii) the maximum amount for which the company (or its subsidiary) may
become so liable;

   (iii) any amount paid or liability incurred in fulfilling the guarantee or
discharging the security;

(f) for any other transactions, arrangements or agreements, the value of the   *22(2)(f), Sch 6*
transaction or arrangement. For a quasi-loan, value is the maximum amount
liable to be repaid, and for a credit transaction, value is the arm's length value of
the goods or services concerned.   *s340(3) & (6)*

7.5.3 Exemptions

The following are exempted from the disclosure requirements set out above:

(a) transactions, arrangements or agreements between two companies where a
director is interested only by virtue of being a director of both companies;   *18(a), Sch 6*

(b) service contracts between a company and its directors or directors of its parent   *18(b), Sch 6*
company;

(c) transactions, arrangements or agreements with a director which, in aggregate,
did not exceed £5,000 and which are credit transactions or related to credit   *24, Sch 6*
transactions;

(d) transactions or arrangements (of the type envisaged by paras 15(c) and 16(c),
Sch 6) in which the director had a material interest if the value of each such
transaction did not at any time in the year exceed in the aggregate: *25, Sch 6*

   (i)   £1,000; or if greater than £1,000

   (ii) the lower of £5,000 or 1 per cent of the company's net assets at the year
end;

(e) transactions, arrangements or agreements which were not entered into during
the relevant period and did not subsist at any time during the period;   *18c, Sch 6*

(f) material interest transactions also need not be disclosed if any other group
company involved in the transaction entered into it in the ordinary course of
business, and the terms of the transaction are no less favourable to that company
than if they were on an arm's-length basis.   *20, Sch 6*

7.5.4   Transactions with officers other than directors

In respect of each of the following categories (which include related guarantees, *28, Sch 6* securities, arrangements and agreements to enter into such transactions):

(a)   loans,
(b)   quasi-loans, and
(c)   credit transactions

made between the company (and, in the case of a parent company, its subsidiaries) and persons who were officers of the company at any time during the year, there must be shown: *29(1), Sch 6*

(a)   the aggregate amounts outstanding at the end of the year;
(b)   the numbers of officers with whom such transactions or agreements were made.

However, no corresponding amounts need be shown for the previous year and *58(3), Sch 4* consolidated accounts need only include the information relating to parent company *63 & 68, Sch 4* officers.

Where the aggregate amount due to the company (or group) from an officer at the year *29(2), Sch 6* end under all transactions of the types mentioned above is less than £2,500, the information relating to that officer is not required to be included in the totals disclosed.

The Companies Act 1985 defines an officer as including a director, manager or *s744* secretary. This is not a precise definition and it appears that an officer is a person acting in a decision-making capacity, rather than one who merely implements the decisions of others. All persons named in the accounts as officers should be regarded as officers for the purpose of these disclosures. If the company fails to make the necessary disclosure, the auditor should include the information in his report. *s237(4)*

There are special rules, outside the scope of these explanatory notes, dealing with *s338* arrangements by recognised banks for their officers or their parent company's officers.

7.6   Cash at bank and in hand

The balance sheet formats in CA 1985 prescribe that funds at bank and in hand shall be classified as 'cash at bank and in hand'. Bank loans and overdrafts must be included under creditors. Note that 'funds' should not be offset against overdrafts unless there is a legal right of set-off. In a consolidated balance sheet the balances of all group companies with the same bank may be set off only if there is a legal right to do so.

Consideration should be given to the classification of surplus cash held on deposit as 'current asset investments'.

7.7   Transfers from current assets to fixed assets

Where assets are transferred from current to fixed, the current asset accounting rules should be applied up to the effective date of transfer, which is the date of *UITF 5, 5* management's change of intent. Consequently the transfer should be made at the lower of cost and net realisable value. Therefore an assessment should be made of the net realisable value at the date of transfer and if this is less than its previous carrying value, the diminution should be charged in the profit and loss account, reflecting the loss to the company while the asset was held as a current asset.

Subsequent to the date of transfer, fixed asset accounting rules will apply to the assets. In cases where the transfer is at net realisable value, the asset should be accounted for as a fixed asset at a valuation (under the alternative accounting rules of the Act) as at the date of transfer; at subsequent balance sheet date it may or may not be revalued, but in either event the disclosure requirements appropriate to a valuation should be given.

UITF 5, 6

8 Creditors including long-term liabilities

8.1 General disclosures

Whichever format of the balance sheets prescribed in CA 1985 is adopted, there must be separate disclosure of:

(a)   amounts falling due within one year,
(b)   amounts falling due after more than one year,

showing, under each of these two main headings, the amount of each item and the aggregate. For this purpose a creditor is considered to be payable on the earliest date on which payment falls due, rather than on the earliest date on which payment is expected to be made.

8.1.1 Amounts falling due within one year

Amounts falling due within one year must be analysed among:

(a)   debenture loans (i.e., that part which falls due within one year). The amount of any convertible loans must be shown separately (see also **8.2**);   *8(7), Sch 4*
(b)   bank loans and overdrafts (see **7.6**);
(c)   payments received on account (see **8.3**);
(d)   trade creditors. This category should include liabilities for services performed and goods received which have been invoiced by the balance sheet date. Where they are immaterial, bills of exchange payable and accruals (see below) should be included within this category;
(e)   bills of exchange payable;
(f)   amounts owed to group companies (see **7.4**);
(g)   amounts owed to associated companies (see **8.5**);
(h)   other creditors including taxation and social security. The amounts for creditors in respect of taxation and social security should be shown separately from the amount for other creditors. If the amount for taxation and social security is combined it is still necessary to show by way of an additional note   *8(9), Sch 4* the amount of any provision for current and deferred taxation. It is therefore recommended that in the notes this category is sub-divided into the following three headings: *47, Sch 4*
   (i)   corporation tax (including ACT payable);
   (ii)   other taxes and social security costs;
   (iii) other creditors;
(i)   accruals and deferred income. There are two positions given for this item in Format 1; in creditors due within one year and after one year which are an

alternative to showing one amount at position J (see Format 1). However, if the   *8(10), Sch 4*
item is not shown in a position corresponding to that at 'J' it may be shown in
either or both of the other positions as the case may require. The two positions
given for this item in Format 2 are alternatives.

   Accruals should include estimates of liabilities for which services have been
performed or goods received but the invoice has not been received by the year
end (see also **8.6**);

(j)   proposed dividends (see **8.7**);   *SSAP 8, 32*

(k)   convertible debt. If relegated to a note, the face of the balance sheet must   *FRS 4, 25*
specify that creditors include convertibles.

8.1.2   Amounts falling due after more than one year

In Format 1 the analysis of amounts falling due after more than one year is the same as
that noted above.

8.1.3   Repayment analysis

For each item shown under creditors, there must be stated the aggregate amount of any   *48(1), Sch 4*
debts which:

(a)   are payable (otherwise than by instalments) and fall due for repayment after the
end of a five-year period. The five years are deemed to commence with the first
day after the balance sheet date;

(b)   are payable by instalments any of which fall due for payment after the end of the
five-year period.

The amounts to be shown under (a) and (b) above may not be combined. In the Format
1 presentation this disclosure will be restricted to items falling due after more than one
year.

For each item included under (a) and (b) above the terms of repayment and the
applicable rate of interest must be disclosed. Where the number of items is such   *48(2), Sch 4*
that, in the opinion of the directors, this requirement would result in a statement of
excessive length, this information need be given only in general terms.   *48(3), Sch 4*

For the purposes of determining the date on which a loan falls due for repayment (or
an instalment) it should be taken as the earliest date on which the lender could require   *85, Sch 4*
repayment if he were to exercise all options and rights available to him.

The maturity of debt is further discussed in **8.2.1**.

8.1.4   Secured creditors

For each item under creditors for which security has been given, an indication of the
nature of the security given and the aggregate amount of the debts included under that
item covered by the security must be stated. In giving an indication of the nature of the   *48(4), Sch 4*
security it is acceptable to describe the charge in general terms, referring, for example,
to 'mortgages on freehold land and buildings' rather than specifying the particular
buildings involved. The disclosure of the security does not apply to the situation where
an unpaid supplier has supplied stock that is subject to reservation of title. This is

because in such a case, the person who reserves title does not pass ownership in the goods and, therefore, his rights are not in the nature of security. However, good accounting practice would require the disclosure, if material, of the existence of such a reservation of title providing the legal aspects are clear.

8.2 Debentures and other borrowings

There is no precise definition of a debenture, either in law or in practice. It is essentially a formal acknowledgement of a debt, although the term is often applied to the debt itself. Debentures are usually (but do not need to be) secured; and there may or may not be a trust deed to set out the respective rights of the company and the debenture holders. If the company has issued any debentures during the financial year *41(1), Sch 4* there must be stated in the accounts:

(a)   the reason for making the issue;
(b)   the classes of debentures issued; and
(c)   for each class, the amount issued and the consideration received for the issue.

The notes must also disclose, in respect of debentures, the nominal amount and the *41(3), Sch 4* book value of any debentures that are held by either a nominee or a trustee of the company.

If a company's subsidiary (or its nominee) beneficially holds the company's debentures, *6, Sch 5* the number, description and amount so held should be disclosed in a note to the *40, Sch 4* accounts. If the company has issued convertible loan stock the terms of conversion should be disclosed.

8.2.1   Analysis of the maturity of debt

An analysis of the maturity of debt should be presented showing amounts falling due: *FRS 4, 33*

(a)   in one year or less, or on demand;
(b)   between one and two years;
(c)   between two and five years;
(d)   in five years or more.

The maturity of debt should be determined by reference to the earliest date on which *FRS 4, 34* the lender can require repayment.

Where committed facilities are in existence at the balance sheet date that permit the *FRS 4, 35* refinancing of debt for a period beyond its maturity, the earliest date at which the lender can require repayment should be taken to be the maturity date of the longest refinancing permitted by a facility in respect of which all the following conditions are met:

(a)   the debt and the facility are under a single agreement or course of dealing with the same lender or group of lenders;
(b)   the finance costs for the new debt are on a basis that is not significantly higher than that of the existing debt;
(c)   the obligations of the lender (or group of lenders) are firm: the lender is not able legally to refrain from providing funds except in circumstances the possibility of which can be demonstrated to be remote;

(d)   the lender (or group of lenders) is expected to be able to fulfil its obligations under the facility.

In these situations, the amounts of the debt so treated, analysed by the earliest date on which the lender could demand repayment in the absence of the facilities, should be disclosed.   *FRS 4, 36*

8.2.2   Convertible debt

The conversion of convertible debt should not be anticipated. Convertible debt should be reported within liabilities and the finance cost should be calculated on the assumption that the debt will never be converted. The amount attributable to convertible debt should be stated separately from that of other liabilities.   *FRS 4, 25*

8(7), Sch 4

When convertible debt is converted, the amount recognised in shareholders' funds in respect of the shares issued should be the amount at which the liability for the debt is stated as at the date of conversion. No gain or loss should be recognised on conversion.   *FRS 4, 26*

Details of the dates of redemption and the amount payable on redemption should be disclosed.   *FRS 4, 62*

The following conversion details should be stated: *FRS 4, 62*

(a)   whether conversion is at the option of issuer or holder;
(b)   dates or periods of possible conversion;
(c)   class of share it may convert to;
(d)   numbers of share it may convert to.

If further information is required to understand the commercial effect of the convertible debt, details must be given of where that information can be obtained.   *FRS 4, 65*

8.2.3   Application notes

FRS 4 contains application notes explaining the features and accounting treatments of a range of capital instruments which can be collectively described as 'unusual debt'.

8.2.4   Other disclosures

A brief description should be given of the legal nature of any instrument included in debt where it is different from that normally associated with debt. Unusual features might include substantial debt, a conditional obligation to repay or the existence of limited recourse debt.   *FRS 4, 63*

The amount payable on winding-up of convertible debt should be stated if it is different from the book value.   *FRS 4, 63*

If further information is required to understand the commercial effect of the unusual debt, details must be given of where that information can be found.   *FRS 4, 65*

8.3 Derivatives and other financial instruments: disclosures

8.3.1 Scope

FRS 13 applies to all entities, other than insurance companies, that have one or more *FRS 13, 3* of their capital instruments listed or publicly traded on a stock exchange or market and to all banks and similar institutions. There may be occasions when other entities may consider it appropriate to make such disclosures. This may arise because of the materiality of the financial instruments held, or as a way of explaining how the directors' are managing the financial risks facing the business.

The FRS requires disclosure of certain information on the financial instruments held *FRS 13, 1* by the reporting entity. The objective of these disclosures is to provide information about the impact of financial instruments on the entity's risk profile, how the risks arising from financial instruments might affect the entity's performance and financial condition, and how these risks are being managed.

8.3.2 The approach adopted in the FRS

The FRS requires both narrative and numerical disclosures. The narrative disclosures *FRS 13c* describe the role that financial instruments have in creating or changing the risk that the entity faces, including its objectives and policies in using financial instruments to manage these risks. The numerical disclosures show how these objectives and policies were implemented in the period and provide supplementary information for evaluating significant or potentially significant exposures. Together these disclosures provide a broad overview of the entity's financial instruments and of the risk positions created by them, focusing on those risks and instruments that are of greatest significance.

8.3.3 Narrative disclosures

The FRS requires an explanation to be provided of the role that financial instruments *FRS 13d* play in creating or changing the risks that the entity faces in its activities. The entity should also explain the directors' approach to managing each of those risks, including a description of the objectives, policies and strategies for holding and issuing financial instruments. Where the directors decide, before the balance sheet date, to change these objectives, policies or strategies, that change should also be explained.

The narrative disclosures are mandatory, although the FRS permits them to be given in *FRS 13e* a statement accompanying the financial statements (such as the operating and financial review or the directors' report) provided that they are incorporated into the financial statements by a suitable cross-reference.

8.3.4 Numerical disclosures

Although all entities within the scope of the FRS are required to provide the same type *FRS 13f* of narrative disclosures, the FRS requires different numerical disclosures for each of:

(a)   entities that are not financial institutions;
(b)   banks and similar institutions;

(c)   other types of financial institution.

These different disclosures reflect differences in the significance of the main risks that arise from financial instruments.

The FRS requires specified numerical disclosures to be provided about: *FRS 13g*

(a)   interest rate risk;
(b)   currency risk;
(c)   liquidity risk (except for banks and similar institutions, which are covered by existing requirements);
(d)   fair values;
(e)   financial instruments used for trading (including, for banks and some other financial institutions, information on the market price risk of their trading book);
(f)   financial instruments used for hedging;
(g)   certain commodity contracts.

To avoid the numerical disclosures becoming so detailed that their message is obscured, the FRS encourages, and in some cases requires, a high degree of aggregation.   *FRS 13h*

8.4   Payments received on account

Payments received on account, in so far as they are not shown as deductions from stocks/work in progress, must be disclosed separately.   *SSAP 9, 30(b)*

This will normally only give rise to a creditor where the payments are in excess of the amount at which the relevant work in progress is stated.

8.5   Amounts owed to (or by) associated undertakings

An 'associated undertaking' means an undertaking in which the investing company has a long-term participating interest, but is not a subsidiary undertaking, or a joint venture. The investing company must exercise significant influence over the operating and financial policy of the undertaking. Representation on the board of directors is indicative of such participation but will neither necessarily give conclusive evidence of it nor be the only method by which the investing company may participate in policy decisions. An undertaking will be presumed to be an associate if the investing company holds 20 per cent or more of the voting rights unless the contrary is shown.   *FRS 9, 4*   *20, Sch 4A*

8.6   Accruals and deferred income

Accruals and deferred income must be shown either as a separate heading in the balance sheet or as a sub-heading of creditors. If there are significant amounts of non-current deferred income (e.g., the deferred credit in respect of regional development grants) it may be appropriate to segregate such amounts and show them under item H9 *8(10), Sch 4* or item J, rather than E9 where balance sheet Format 1 is adopted.

The liability for services completed and goods received but uninvoiced at the balance sheet date should be treated as an accrual.

8.7 Proposed dividends

The Companies Act 1985 requires that the amount of proposed dividends must be *51(3), Sch 4* disclosed, and that the dividends proposed (or declared and not yet payable) should be *SSAP 8, 32* included without the addition of the attributable ACT.

In addition, the notes to the accounts must state: *49, Sch 4*

(a)   the amount of any arrears in the payment of fixed cumulative dividends on the company's shares;
(b)   the period for which these dividends are in arrears. Where there is more than one class in arrears, this information must be given in respect of each class.

Where the entitlement to dividends in respect of non-equity shares is calculated by *FRS 4, 43* reference to time, the dividends should be accounted for on an accruals basis except in those circumstances (for example, where profits are insufficient to justify a dividend and dividend rights are non-cumulative) where ultimate payment is remote. All dividends should be reported as appropriations of profit.

8.8 Net current assets

This heading is preceded by a letter of the alphabet in Format 1 in CA 1985 and therefore has to be disclosed on the face of the balance sheet. There is no equivalent disclosure in Format 2 as the format is based on a total of assets and a total of liabilities. The narrative should be amended to 'net current liabilities' or 'net current assets/(liabilities)' as appropriate. It should be noted that 'prepayments and accrued *8(11), Sch 4* income', which may be disclosed in one of two places in the Format 1 balance sheet (CII 6 and D) must be taken into consideration in arriving at net current assets.

8.9 Total assets less current liabilities

This heading is preceded by a letter of the alphabet in Format 1 in CA 1985 and therefore has to be disclosed on the face of the balance sheet. There is no equivalent disclosure in Format 2 as the format is based on the total of assets and a total of liabilities.

8.10 Creditors: amounts falling due after more than one year

Refer to **8.1**.

8.11 Loan from a former director

There is no statutory requirement to disclose this loan as a result of it being from a former director. There is also no requirement to disclose details unless the loan falls within the categories described in **8.1** above (all or part falling due after five years) but when a material item is described as a 'loan' then good accounting practice requires that information is given as to the terms of repayment and the rate of interest paid.

8.12 Provisions for liabilities and charges

A provision for liabilities and charges is defined as an amount retained as reasonably necessary for the purpose of providing for any liability or loss which is either likely to be incurred, or certain to be incurred but uncertain as to the amount or as to the date on which it will arise.

89, Sch 4

In respect of any item included under the heading 'provisions for liabilities and charges', CA 1985 requires that where any amount is transferred to those provisions for liabilities or charges or is transferred from any such provision otherwise than for the purpose for which it was created, a reconciliation must be given between the opening and closing balances of the provision with explanations of transfers to or from the provision. Corresponding figures for the previous year are not required for this reconciliation.

46, Sch 4

58(3d), Sch4

This requirement only relates to those provisions listed in CA 1985, namely, pensions and similar obligations, taxation including deferred taxation and other provisions. In respect of other provisions the individual provisions included under this heading may be combined and the reconciliation given in respect of the total figures rather than for each provision included in the total so long as no one provision is material.

46(3), Sch 4

8.12.1 Objective of FRS 12

FRS 12 has established detailed criteria for the recognition of provisions. The introduction of this standard marks the end of general provisions for uncertain future events as provisions must now reflect obligations which are likely to lead to an out flow of funds. The standard includes detailed disclosures which explain the purpose of provisions and their movement during the year. As a result of the introduction of FRS 12, the opportunities for earnings management have been significantly reduced.

8.12.2 Recognition of provisions

A provision should be recognised when:

FRS 12, 14

(a)   an entity has a present obligation (legal or constructive) as a result of a past event;
(b)   it is probable that a transfer of economic benefits will be required to settle the obligation; and
(c)   a reliable estimate can be made of the amount of the obligation.

If these conditions are not met, no provision should be recognised.

8.12.3   Obligations – definitions

Legal obligation   *FRS 12, 2*

A legal obligation derives from:

(a)   a contract (through explicit or implicit terms), or from
(b)   legislation, or an
(c)   other operation of law.

Constructive obligation

A constructive obligation is one that derives from an entity's actions where by an   *FRS 12, 2*
established pattern of past practice, published policies or a sufficiently specific current
statement, the entity has indicated to other parties that it will accept certain
responsibilities, and as a result, the entity has created a valid expectation on the
part of those other parties that it will discharge those responsibilities.

Present obligation

A present obligation arises if, taking account of all the available evidence, it is more   *FRS 12, 15–16*
likely than not that an obligation exists at the balance sheet date.

In almost all cases it will be clear whether a past event has given rise to a present
obligation. In rare cases, for example in a lawsuit, it may be disputed whether certain
events have occurred or whether those events result in a present obligation. In such a
case, an entity determines whether a present obligation exists at the balance sheet date
by taking account of all available evidence, including, for example, the opinion of
experts. The evidence considered includes any additional evidence provided by events
occurring after the balance sheet date.

On the basis of such evidence:

(a)   where it is more likely than not that a present obligation exists at the balance
      sheet date, the entity recognises a provision (if the recognition criteria are met);
      and
(b)   where it is more likely that no present obligation exists at the balance sheet date,
      the entity discloses a contingent liability, unless the possibility of a transfer of
      economic resources is remote.

Past event

A past event – an obligating event – is an event that creates a legal or constructive   *FRS 12, 17*
obligation that results in an entity having no realistic alternative to settling that
obligation.

This is the case only:

(a)   where the settlement of the obligation can be enforced by law; or
(b)   in the case of a constructive obligation, where the event (which may be an
      action of the entity) creates valid expectations in other parties that the entity
      will discharge the obligation.

Financial statements deal with the financial position of an entity at the end of its   *FRS 12, 18* reporting period and not its possible position in the future. Therefore no provision is recognised for costs that need to be incurred to operate in the future. The only liabilities recognised in an entity's balance sheet are those that exist at the balance sheet date.

It is only those obligations arising from past events existing independently of an *FRS 12, 19* entity's future actions (i.e., the future conduct of its business) that are recognised as provisions. Examples of such obligations are penalties or clean-up costs for unlawful environmental damage, both of which would lead to a transfer of economic benefits in settlement regardless of the future actions of the entity. Similarly, an entity recognises a provision for the decommissioning costs of an operation to the extent that the entity is obliged to rectify damage already caused. In contrast, because of commercial pressures or legal requirements, an entity may intend or need to carry out expenditure to operate in a particular way in the future (for example, by fitting smoke filters in a certain type of factory). Because the entity can avoid the future expenditure by its future actions, for example by changing its method of operation, it has no present obligation for that future expenditure and no provision is recognised.

8.12.4 Probable transfer of economic benefits

A transfer of economic benefits is regarded as probable if the event is more likely than *FRS 12, 23* not to occur – the probability that the event will occur is greater than the probability that it will not.

8.12.5 Reliable estimate of the obligation

An estimate of the obligation, based upon a range of possible outcomes is acceptable. *FRS 12, 25*

Where no reliable estimate can be made, the liability cannot be recognised and should *FRS 12, 26* be disclosed as a contingent liability.

The amount recognised as a provision should be the best estimate of the expenditure *FRS 12, 36* required to settle the present obligation at the balance sheet date.

The estimates of outcome and financial effect are determined by the judgement of the *FRS 12, 38* entity's management, supplemented by experience of similar transactions and, in some cases, reports from independent experts. The evidence considered will include any additional evidence provided by events after the balance sheet date.

Uncertainties surrounding the amount to be recognised as a provision are dealt with by *FRS 12, 39* various means according to the circumstances. Where the provision being measured involves a large population of items, the obligation is estimated by weighting all possible outcomes by their associated probabilities.

Example

An entity sells goods with a warranty under which customers are covered for the cost of repairs of any manufacturing defects that become apparent within the first six months after purchase. If minor defects were detected in all products sold, repair costs of £1 million would result. If major defects were detected in all products sold, repair costs of £4 million would result. The entity's past experience and future expectations indicate that, for the coming year, 75 per cent of the goods sold will have no defects, 20 per cent of the goods sold will have minor defects and 5 per cent of the goods sold will have major defects.

The expected value of the cost of repairs is:

(75% of nil) + (20% of £1m) + (5% of £4m) = £400,000

Where a single obligation is being measured, the individual most likely outcome may be the best estimate of the liability. However, even in such a case, the entity considers other possible outcomes. Where other possible outcomes are either mostly higher or mostly lower than the most likely outcome, the best estimate will be a higher or lower amount. For example, if an entity has to rectify a serious fault in a major plant that it has constructed for a customer, the individual most likely outcome may be for the repair to succeed at the first attempt at a cost of £1 million but a provision for a larger amount is made if there is a significant chance that further attempts will be necessary. *FRS 12, 40*

8.12.6 Reimbursements

Where some or all of the expenditure required to settle a provision is expected to be reimbursed by another party, the reimbursement should be recognised only when it is virtually certain that reimbursement will be received if the entity settles the obligation. The reimbursement should be treated as a separate asset. The amount recognised for the reimbursement should not exceed the amount of the provision. *FRS 12, 56*

In the profit and loss account, the expense relating to a provision may be presented net of the amount recognised for a reimbursement. *FRS 12, 57*

8.12.7 Changes in provisions

Provisions should be reviewed at each balance sheet date and adjusted to reflect the current best estimate. If it is no longer probable that a transfer of economic benefits will be required to settle the obligation, the provision should be reversed. *FRS 12, 62*

Where discounting is used, the carrying amount of a provision increases in each period to reflect the passage of time. This increase is recognised as an interest expense. *FRS 12, 63*

8.12.8 Use of provisions

A provision should be used only for expenditures for which the provision was originally recognised. *FRS 12, 64*

Only expenditures that relate to the original provision are set against it. Setting expenditures against a provision that was originally recognised for another purpose would conceal the impact of two different events. *FRS 12, 65*

8.12.9 Disclosures

For each class of provision, an entity should disclose: *FRS 12, 89*

(a)   the carrying amount at the beginning and end of the period;
(b)   additional provisions made in the period, including increases to existing provisions;

Figure 8.1   Decision tree

This decision tree summarizes the approach of FRS 12

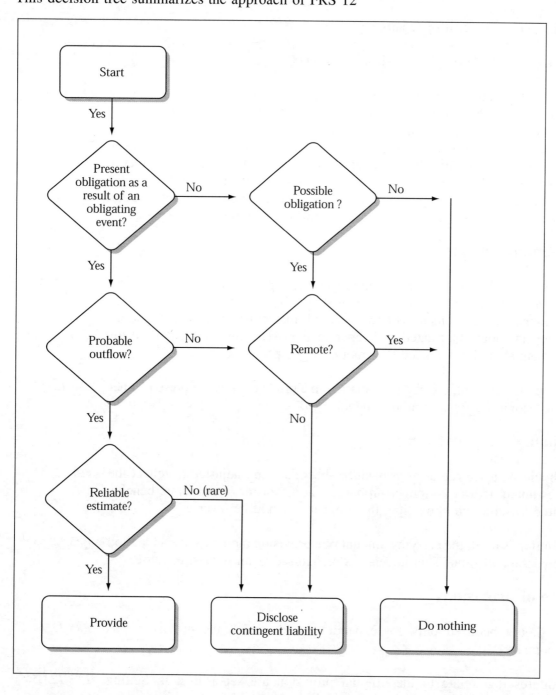

Note: in rare cases it is not clear whether there is a present obligation. In these cases, a past event is deemed to give rise to a present obligation if, taking account of all available evidence, it is more likely than not that a present obligation exists at the balance sheet date.

(c)   amounts used (i.e., incurred and charged against the provision) during the period;

(d)   unused amounts reversed during the period; and

(e)   the increase during the period in the discounted amount arising from the passage of time and the effect of any change in the discount rate.

Comparative information is not required.

An entity should disclose the following for each class of provision: *FRS 12, 90*

(a) a brief description of the nature of the obligation, and the expected timing of any resulting transfers of economic benefits;
(b) an indication of the uncertainties about the amount or timing of those transfers of economic benefits. Where necessary to provide adequate information, an entity should disclose the major assumptions made concerning future events; and
(c) the amount of any expected reimbursement, stating the amount of any asset that has been recognised for that expected reimbursement.

In determining which provisions may be aggregated to form a class, it is necessary to consider whether the nature of the items is sufficiently similar for a single statement about them to fulfil the requirements of the FRS. Thus it may be appropriate to treat as a single class of provision amounts relating to warranties of different products, but it would not be appropriate to treat as a single class amounts relating to normal warranties and amounts that are subject to legal proceedings. *FRS 12, 92*

Where a provision and a contingent liability arise from the same set of circumstances, the disclosures should be given in a way that shows the link between the provision and the contingent liability. *FRS 12, 93*

In extremely rare cases, where disclosure of some or all of the information required by the FRS can be expected to prejudice seriously the position of the entity in a dispute with other parties on the subject matter of a provision, contingent liability or contingent asset, an entity need not disclose the information, unless its disclosure is required by law. The entity should, however, disclose the general nature of the dispute, together with the fact that, and reason why, the information has not been disclosed. *FRS 12, 97*

8.12.10 Application of FRS 12

Future operating losses

Provisions should not be recognised for future operating losses. Future operating losses do not meet the general recognition criteria set out for provisions given above. *FRS 12, 68–69*

Onerous contracts

If an entity has a contract that is onerous, the present obligation under the contract should be recognised and measured as a provision. *FRS 12, 71*

Many contracts (e.g., some routine purchase orders) can be cancelled without paying compensation to the other party, and therefore there is no obligation. Other contracts (e.g., leases) establish both rights and obligations for each of the contracting parties. Where events make such a contract onerous, the contract falls within the scope of the FRS and a liability exists which is recognised. Executory contracts that are not onerous fall outside the scope of the FRS. *FRS 12, 72*

The FRS defines an onerous contract as a contract in which the unavoidable costs of meeting the obligations under it exceed the economic benefits expected to be received under it. The unavoidable costs under a contract reflect the least net cost of exiting *FRS 12, 73* from the contract i.e., the lower of the cost of fulfilling it and any compensation or penalties arising from failure to fulfil it.

Before a separate provision for an onerous contract is established, an entity recognises any impairment loss that has occurred on assets dedicated to that contract.

FRS 12, 74

Restructuring

The following are examples of events that may fall under the definition of restructuring: sale or termination of a line of business:

FRS 12, 75

- the closure of business locations in a country or region or the relocation of business activities from one country or region to another;
- changes in management structure, for example, eliminating a layer of management; and
- fundamental reorganisations that have a material effect on the nature and focus of the entity's operations.

A constructive obligation to restructure arises only when an entity:

FRS 12, 77

(a) has a detailed formal plan for the restructuring identifying at least:
    (i) the business or part of a business concerned;
    (ii) the principal locations affected;
    (iii) the location, function, and approximate number of employees who will be compensated for terminating their services;
    (iv) the expenditures that will be undertaken; and
    (v) when the plan will be implemented; and
(b) has raised a valid expectation in those affected that it will carry out the restructuring by starting to implement that plan or announcing its main features to those affected by it.

A management or board decision to restructure taken before the balance sheet date does not give rise to a constructive obligation at the balance sheet date unless the entity has, before the balance sheet date:

FRS 12, 80

(a) started to implement the restructuring plan; or
(b) announced the main features of the restructuring plan to those affected by it in a sufficiently specific manner to raise a valid expectation in them that the entity will carry out the restructuring.

In some cases the entity starts to implement the restructuring plan, or announces its main features to those affected by it, only after the balance sheet date. Disclosure may be required under SSAP 17 *Accounting for post balance sheet events* if the restructuring is of such importance that its non-disclosure would affect the ability of the users of the financial statements to make proper evaluations and decisions.

A restructuring provision should include only the direct expenditures arising from the restructuring, which are those that are both:

FRS 12, 85

(a) necessarily entailed by the restructuring and
(b) not associated with the ongoing activities of the entity.

A restructuring provision does not include such costs as: *FRS 12, 86*

- retraining or relocating continuing staff;
- marketing; or
- investment in new systems and distribution networks.

These expenditures relate to the future conduct of the business and are not liabilities for restructuring at the balance sheet date. Such expenditures are recognised on the same basis as if they arose independently of a restructuring.

Identifiable future operating losses up to the date of a restructuring are not included in a provision, unless they relate to an onerous contract. *FRS 12, 87*

Dilapidations and future repairs

The issue of how provisions for future repairs and dilapidations should be accounted for was a matter of some controversy when FRS 12 was issued. An appendix to FRS 15 makes it clear that such provisions are not permitted.

> 'Before FRS 12 became applicable, some entities recognised as a provision significant costs of future repairs, maintenance, inspections or overhauls of their tangible fixed assets. Under FRS 12, such future costs are not present obligations of the entity resulting from past events, and therefore no provision should be made for them, even if they are required by legislation if the asset is to continue to be used. In these circumstances, an entity should charge such expenditure to the profit and loss account as it is incurred.

FRS 15 Appendices IV, 15

> 'Alternatively, the entity may depreciate the relevant part of the asset that is declining in service potential to reflect the need for future repairs, maintenance, inspections or overhauls (ie to take account of the actual consumption of the asset's economic benefits) and to capitalise the subsequent expenditure because it results in the restoration of the asset or replacement of some of its components. This latter approach results in a charge being recognised in the profit and loss account that is similar to what would have been recognised under previous (pre-FRS 12) practices. However, the charge takes the form not of a provision for future expenditure but of depreciation, in recognition of the fact that economic benefits of the asset have been consumed at a different rate from that applicable to the remainder of the asset.'

FRS 15 Appendices IV, 16

Examples

Appendix III to FRS 12 contains a series of examples of the application of the principles of the standard. A number of these examples are reproduced below as illustrations.

Example 1: Warranties

A manufacturer gives warranties at the time of sale to purchasers of its product. Under the terms of the contract for sale the manufacturer undertakes to make good, by repair or replacement, manufacturing defects that become apparent within three years from the date of sale. On past experience, it is probable (i.e., more likely than not) that there will be some claims under the warranties.

- *Present obligation as a result of a past obligating event.* The obligating event is the sale of the product with a warranty, which gives rise to a legal obligation.
- *Transfer of economic benefits in settlement.* Probable for the warranties as a whole.
- *Conclusion.* A provision is recognised for the best estimate of the costs of making good under the warranty products sold before the balance sheet date.

Example 5A: Closure of a division – no implementation before balance sheet date

On 12 December 2000 the board of an entity decided to close down a division. Before the balance sheet date (31 December 2000) the decision was not communicated to any of those affected and no other steps were taken to implement the decision.

- *Present obligation as a result of a past obligating event.* There has been no obligating event and so there is no obligation.
- *Conclusion.* No provision is recognised.

Example 5B: Closure of a division – communication/implementation before balance sheet date

On 12 December 2000 the board of an entity decided to close down a division making a particular product. On 20 December 2000 a detailed plan for closing down the division was agreed by the board; letters were sent to customers warning them to seek an alternative source of supply and redundancy notices were sent to the staff of the division.

- *Present obligation as a result of a past obligating event.* The obligating event is the communication of the decision to the customers and employees, which gives rise to a constructive obligation from that date because it creates a valid expectation that the division will be closed.
- *Transfer of economic benefits in settlement.* Probable.
- *Conclusion.* A provision is recognised at 31 December 2000 for the best estimate of the costs of closing the division.

Example 11: Repairs and maintenance

Some assets require, in addition to routine maintenance, substantial expenditure every few years for major refits or refurbishment and the replacement of major components.

Example 11A: Refurbishment costs – no legislative requirement

A furnace has a lining that needs to be replaced every five years for technical reasons. At the balance sheet date, the lining has been in use for three years.

- *Present obligation as a result of a past obligating event.* There is no present obligation.
- *Conclusion.* No provision is recognised.

The cost of replacing the lining is not recognised because, at the balance sheet date, no obligation to replace the lining exists independently of the entity's future actions – even the intention to incur the expenditure depends on the entity deciding to continue operating the furnace or to replace the lining. Instead of a provision being recognised, the depreciation of the lining takes account of its consumption, i.e., it is depreciated over five years. The relining costs then incurred are capitalised with the consumption of each new lining shown by depreciation over the subsequent five years.

Example 11B: Refurbishment costs – legislative requirement

An airline is required by law to overhaul its aircraft once every three years.

- *Present obligation as a result of a past obligating event.* There is no present obligation.
- *Conclusion.* No provision is recognised.

The costs of overhauling aircraft are not recognised as a provision for the same reasons as the cost of replacing the lining is not recognised as a provision in example 11A. Even a legal requirement to overhaul does not make the costs of overhaul a liability because no obligation exists to overhaul the aircraft independently of the entity's future actions – the entity could avoid the future expenditure by its future actions, for example by selling the aircraft. Instead of a provision being recognised, the depreciation of the aircraft takes account of the future incidence of maintenance costs, i.e., an amount equivalent to the expected maintenance costs is depreciated over three years.

8.13 Deferred taxation

Any provision for deferred taxation would have to be shown in the balance sheet formats under 'provisions for liabilities and charges'. For such a provision there is a statutory requirement to disclose movements on the provision (see **8.12**).

Subject to the above statutory requirement the disclosure provisions relating to deferred taxation are included in SSAP 15. *SSAP 15, 24*

Profits assessable to taxation normally differ from those disclosed in the accounts because: *SSAP 15, 25*

(a) certain types of income may be non-taxable or certain expenditure is disallowable. These differences are referred to as 'permanent differences';

(b) certain types of income and expenditure may fall to be taxed (or be tax allowable) in periods different from those in which they have been accounted for. These differences are referred to as 'timing differences'.

Timing differences generally arise under five main headings:

(a) short-term timing differences which are expected in reverse in the following period (e.g., interest receipts, pensions payments);

(b) availability of capital allowances;

(c) revaluation surpluses;

(d) surpluses on disposal of fixed assets which are subject to rollover relief;

(e) losses which are available to relieve future profits from tax.

8.13.1 Disclosures

The standard requires that provision be made in respect of such timing differences for deferred taxation on the liability method and to the extent that it is probable that a liability or asset will crystallise. A provision should not be made to the extent that it is probable that a liability or asset will not crystallise. The assessment of whether deferred tax liabilities or assets will or will not crystallise should be based upon reasonable assumptions. The standard sets out assumptions which should be taken into account. *SSAP 15, 26 & 27*

Transfers to and from deferred taxation should be disclosed in a note. *SSAP 15, 28*
SSAP 15, 38

Where amounts of deferred taxation arise which relate to movements on reserves (e.g., resulting from a revaluation of assets) the amounts transferred to or from deferred taxation should be shown separately as part of such movements. *SSAP 15, 39*

Where only part of the full potential deferred tax liability is provided, the amount and the major elements of the provided and unprovided balance and the unprovided profit and loss charge should be stated, as should the amount of any potential deferred tax arising from the revaluation of an asset which does not constitute a timing difference. *SSAP 15, 35, 37 & 40*

SSAP 15, 41

Deferred tax relating to the ordinary activities of the enterprise should be shown separately as part of the tax on profit on ordinary activities and deferred tax relating to any extraordinary items should be shown separately as part of the tax on extraordinary items. *SSAP 15, 33*

SSAP 15, 34

If deferred tax is not provided on earnings retained overseas, that fact should be disclosed. *SSAP 15, 44*

8.13.2 Limitations on recoverable ACT set-off

Recoverable ACT can be deducted from the deferred taxation account providing the whole amount can be set off against deferred tax available for this purpose. If there is insufficient or no deferred tax available for set-off then the ACT should be shown as a deferred asset. *SSAP 15, 29*

SSAP 8, 27

It is of fundamental importance that the following set-off restrictions are understood:

(a) ACT relief cannot reduce the mainstream corporation tax liability below 13 per cent (or 5 per cent for a company enjoying the full small companies rate) as ACT set-off cannot exceed 20 per cent of chargeable profits. For example, where the UK corporation tax charge, after relief for overseas tax and excluding franked investment income and assuming two associated companies was based on an income of £1,000,000 at 33 per cent, then £330,000 would be the total tax liability and the minimum amount of mainstream corporation tax payable would be £130,000. The difference of £200,000 is, therefore, the maximum amount of ACT which may be recovered in respect of distributions during the chargeable accounting period to which the corporation tax liability relates.

(b) Any surplus ACT can be carried back against corporation tax paid in the previous six years (subject to the normal rates of offset applying for those years). Surplus ACT may also, in normal circumstances, be carried forward indefinitely, but for accounts purposes regard must be had to the likelihood of utilisation in the foreseeable future. SSAP 15 suggests: *SSAP 15, 31–32*

    (i) ACT on dividends proposed at the balance sheet date can be carried forward if it can be utilised in the following accounting period.

    (ii) other ACT should normally be written off if it cannot be utilised in the following accounting period without replacement by equivalent debit balances in respect of the following period's ACT.

8.14   Accruals and deferred income

This category of creditor may be disclosed in creditors, either as an amount due within one year or after one year, as appropriate, or as a separate item on the face of the balance sheet at position J in Format 1. Whilst CA 1985 states that these are alternatives it is suggested that any accrual or deferred income which falls due within one year should be disclosed under creditors due within one year. Unless this is done the net current assets (item F in Format 1) will be overstated to the extent that a current liability has been included under item J.

As government grants should not be deducted from the cost of the related asset the deferred credit must be included as deferred income.   *SSAP 4, 25*

8.15   Balance sheet totals

Format 1 of the balance sheet as prescribed in CA 1985 does not indicate at which points the balance sheet should be totalled. It has been argued that when using this format the balance sheet could be totalled to 'nil' but this is neither considered to be meaningful nor the intention of the Act. It is suggested that net assets are equated to shareholders' funds.

9 Hire purchase and lease transactions

9.1 Definitions

SSAP 21 *Accounting for leases and hire purchase contracts* requires all leases to be classified as finance leases or operating leases. The distinction between a finance lease and an operating lease will usually be evidenced from the terms of the contract between the lessor and lessee. The definitions of a finance lease and an operating lease are: *SSAP 21, 6*

(a) A finance lease is a lease that transfers substantially all the risk and rewards of *SSAP 21, 15* ownership of an asset to the lessee. It should be presumed that such a transfer of risks and rewards occurs if at the inception of a lease the present value of the minimum lease payments, including any initial payment, amounts to substantially all (normally 90 per cent or more) of the fair value of the leased asset. The present value should be calculated by using the interest rate implicit *SSAP 21, 24* in the lease. If the fair value of the asset is not determinable, an estimate thereof should be used.

(b) An operating lease is a lease other than a finance lease. *SSAP 21, 17*

A hire purchase contract is defined as one for the hire of an asset which contains a *SSAP 21, 18* provision giving the hirer an option to acquire legal title to the asset upon fulfilment of certain conditions stated in the contract.

9.2 Accounting principles

The standard requires that a finance lease should be capitalised by the lessee, that is, *SSAP 21, 10* accounted for as the purchase of rights to the use and enjoyment of the asset with simultaneous recognition of the obligation to make future payments. Hire purchase is normally accounted for in a similar way. Under an operating lease, only the rental will be taken into account by a lessee.

The amount due from a lessee under a finance lease should be recorded in the balance *SSAP 21, 38* sheet of a lessor as a debtor at the amount of the net investment (minimum lease payments and any unguaranteed residual value accruing to the lessor less gross earnings allocated to future periods) in the lease after making provisions for doubtful debts and rentals. The total gross earnings under a finance lease should normally be *SSAP 21, 39* allocated to accounting periods to give a constant periodic rate of return on the lessor's net cash investment in the lease in each period. Generally, interest is calculated on a straight-line basis for convenience. However, this is not consistent with showing a constant periodic rate of return, and, if the values are material, the interest should be calculated using either the implicit rate in the lease or the sum of digits method.

An asset held for use in operating leases by the lessor should be recorded as a fixed asset and depreciated over its useful life. Rental income from operating leases should be recognised on a straight-line basis over the period of the lease.

SSAP 21, 42

SSAP 21, 43

9.3 Disclosures

The disclosure requirements of the standard are set out in paras 49–57 for lessees and paras 58–60 for lessors. Equivalent information should be provided in respect of hire purchase contracts which have characteristics similar to finance leases.

9.3.1 Lessees

Lessees should disclose the following:

(a) the gross amount of assets held under finance leases; *SSAP 21, 49*

(b) the accumulated depreciation relating to finance leases. *SSAP 21, 49*

(c) the depreciation charge relating to finance leases; *SSAP 21, 49*

(d) the amount of obligations related to finance leases, shown separately from other obligations and liabilities, analysed among: *SSAP 21, 51 & 52*
    (i) amount payable in the next year;
    (ii) amounts payable in the second to fifth year inclusive;
    (iii) amounts payable after more than five years. In this case, the interest repayment terms must also be disclosed;

(e) the aggregate finance charges allocated for the period; *SSAP 21, 53*

(f) commitments existing at the balance sheet date in respect of finance leases entered into but for which inception occurs after the year end; *SSAP 21, 54*

(g) total operating lease rentals analysed between hire of plant and machinery and other operating leases; *SSAP 21, 55*

(h) the operating lease payments for land and buildings and other operating leases, separately, for which there is a commitment at the balance sheet date to pay during the next year analysed among those in which the commitment expires: *SSAP 21, 56*
    (i) within one year;
    (ii) in the second to fifth year inclusive;
    (iii) over five years;

(i) the accounting policies for operating and finance leases. *SSAP 21, 57*

The information in (a)–(c) above must be given for each category of leased asset. If leased assets are integrated with owned fixed assets then the net amount of assets held under finance leases and depreciation charge relating to them, and included in the overall total, must be disclosed. *SSAP 21, 50*

9.3.2 Lessors

Lessors should disclose the following:

(a) the net investment in: *SSAP 21, 58*
    (i) finance leases;
    (ii) hire purchase contracts;

(b) the gross amount of assets held for use in operating leases and the related accumulated depreciation charge; *SSAP 21, 59*

(c)   the accounting policy adopted for operating leases, finance leases and finance lease income;   *SSAP 21, 60a*

(d)   the aggregate rentals receivable in respect of: *SSAP 21, 60b*
  (i)   finance leases;
  (ii)   operating leases;

(e)   the cost of assets acquired, whether by hire purchase or finance lease for the purpose of letting under finance leases;   *SSAP 21, 60c*

(f)   the effect of tax-free grants on profit and the tax charge.   *SSAP 21, 41*

9.4   Rental expenses

The total of operating lease rentals charged as an expense in the profit and loss account should be disclosed, analysed between amounts payable in respect of hire of plant and machinery and in respect of other operating leases.   *SSAP 21, 55*

9.5   Lessee accounting for reverse premiums and similar incentives

A lessee may receive incentives to enter into an operating lease, particularly with regard to property transactions. Any benefits receivable by a lessee as an incentive to sign the lease should be spread by the lessee on a straight-line basis over the lease term or, if shorter than the full lease term, over the period to the first review date.   *UITF 12, 8*

Where, exceptionally, the presumption can be rebutted that an incentive is in substance part of the lessor's market return, another systematic and rational basis can be used, with disclosure of: *UITF 12, 8*

(a)   an explanation of the specific circumstances that render the standard treatment specified by the UITF misleading;

(b)   a description of the basis used and the amounts included;

(c)   a note of the effect on the results for the current and corresponding period of any departure from the standard treatment.

If in exceptional circumstances another method of spreading is considered more accurately to adjust the rents paid to the prevailing market rate, that method may be used, with the disclosure detailed above.   *UITF 12, 9*

10 Capital and reserves

10.1 Presentation

The Companies Act 1985 requires that capital and reserves should be analysed under the following headings:

8, Sch 4

(a) called-up share capital (**10.3** and **10.4**);
(b) share premium account (**10.5**);
(c) revaluation reserve (**10.6**);
(d) other reserves (**10.5**);
(e) profit and loss account (**10.5**).

As each of the above is preceded by a Roman numeral in the prescribed formats and to the extent that an amount falls to be disclosed under one of the five headings, it must be shown on the face of the balance sheet and cannot be relegated to the notes.

Other reserves must be analysed as to:

8, Sch 4

(a) capital redemption reserve;
(b) reserve for own shares;
(c) reserves provided for by the articles of association;
(d) other reserves.

To the extent that these reserves exist, they may be shown individually on the face of the balance sheet or in aggregate, with the analysis being shown by way of note.

10.2 Shareholders' funds

FRS 4 *Accounting for capital instruments* requires the amount of shareholders' funds to be identified on the face of the balance sheet and further analysis in the notes to the accounts between those amounts attributable to equity interests and other amounts, for example, attributable to preference shareholders, subdivided as to the different classes of non-equity shares.

FRS 4, 40
FRS 4, 55

Where there is only the one class of share, normally ordinary shares, this matter may be dealt with by a phrase such as 'shareholders' funds are fully attributable to equity interests' within the appropriate note or the description 'equity shareholders' funds' on the face of the balance sheet.

Where there is a deficiency of shareholders' funds and preference shares in addition to ordinary shares, the analysis should show the amount attributable to preference shareholders as a positive figure and the amount attributable to ordinary shareholders as a correspondingly greater negative figure.

FRS 3 also requires a reconciliation of movements in shareholders' funds to bring together the performance of the period, as shown in the statement of total recognised gains and losses, with all the other changes in shareholders' funds in the period, including capital contributed by or repaid to shareholders. *FRS 3, 28*

The net proceeds of an issue of shares or warrants in the period must be included in the reconciliation. *FRS 4, 37*

10.3   Share capital

The notes to the accounts must show the amount of a company's authorised share capital and, where shares of more than one class have been allotted, the number and the aggregate nominal value of the shares of each class that have been so allotted must be disclosed. See **10.4** for the disclosures relating to allotted shares which have been only part paid. *38(1), Sch 4*

Where different classes of share are in issue, such that there are both equity and non-equity shares, a brief summary of the class rights should be given. This should include details of: *FRS 4, 56*

(a)   their rights to dividends;
(b)   the dates at which the shares are redeemable and the amounts payable in respect of redemption;
(c)   their priority and amounts receivable on a winding-up;
(d)   their voting rights;
(e)   any other information necessary to explain the classification and a note if these vary according to circumstances.

The foregoing disclosures are not required for equity shares that have all the following features: *FRS 4, 57*

(a)   no rights to dividends other than as may be recommended by the auditors;
(b)   no redemption rights;
(c)   unlimited rights to share in the surplus remaining on a winding-up;
(d)   one vote per share.

10.3.1   Redeemable shares

Where any part of the allotted share capital consists of redeemable shares, the notes must disclose: *38(2), Sch 4*

(a)   the earliest and the latest dates on which the company may redeem those shares;
(b)   whether the company is obliged to redeem those shares or merely has an option to do so;
(c)   the amount of any premium payable on redemption, or the fact that no such premium is payable.

Prior to CA 1989, redeemable preference shares were the only shares capable of redemption. The amended CA 1985 now contains provisions that permit companies to allot redeemable equity shares. *ss159–160*

10.3.2 Allotment of shares

Where a company has allotted any shares during the financial year, the notes must also disclose: *39, Sch 4*

(a) the classes of shares allotted;
(b) the number allotted, the aggregate nominal value and the consideration received in respect of each class of shares allotted.

In addition, certain information must be given in respect of 'contingent rights to the allotment of shares'. These rights are either options to subscribe for shares, or any other rights under which a person may require the allotment of shares (whether, in the latter case, the rights arise on conversion of any other type of security or otherwise). The information to be given is: *40, Sch 4*

(a) the number, the description and the amount of the shares in respect of which the right is exercisable;
(b) the period during which the right is exercisable;
(c) the price to be paid for the shares allotted.

If a company has issued any debentures during the financial year, refer to **8.2** above.

10.3.3 Fixed rate cumulative shares

The Companies Act 1985 requires the following information to be shown by way of note, if not otherwise disclosed, in the case of fixed rate cumulative shares: *49, Sch 4*

(a) where any fixed cumulative dividends are in arrears, the amount of such arrears;
(b) the period for which these dividends are in arrears. Where there is more than one class, this information must be given in respect of each class.

Any dividend right established before 6 April 1973 on all fixed rate shares has been reduced to 70 per cent of the former gross rate. *SSAP 8, 18 & 28*

10.4 Called-up share capital

Note 12 to the prescribed balance sheet formats in CA 1985 requires that the amount of allotted share capital and the amount of paid-up capital must be shown separately under this heading. Called-up share capital means: *8(12), Sch 4*

s737(1)

(a) so much of a company's share capital as equals the aggregate amount of the calls on its shares (whether or not those calls have been paid);
(b) any share capital that has been paid up without being called;
(c) any share capital that is to be paid on a specific future date under the articles of association, the terms of allotment or any other arrangements for paying for those shares.

Capital and reserves

To illustrate these requirements, consider the following example.

Example

On 29 March 1999 a company allots 10,000 ordinary shares of £1 each. By 31 July 1999 the company has made calls amounting to 75p per share. At 31 July 1999 the holders of 1,000 shares have not paid the last call of 25p per share. In the financial statements at 31 July 1999 the company would have to make the following disclosures:

Called-up share capital	£7,500
Allotted share capital	£10,000
Paid-up share capital	£7,250
Called-up share capital not paid	£250

10.5   Reserves

The Companies Act 1985 requires that reserves be shown under specific headings, namely, share premium, revaluation reserve, other reserves and profit and loss account. These are laid down in both balance sheet formats and being preceded by a Roman numeral must be disclosed on the face of the balance sheet. Other reserves must be sub-analysed among capital redemption reserve, reserve for own shares, reserves provided for by the articles of association and other reserves, but the detail in respect of these reserves may be disclosed in the notes to the accounts.

In respect of each reserve certain information must be included in the notes to the accounts: *46(1)(2), Sch 4*

(a)   the aggregate amount of the reserve at both the beginning and the end of the year;
(b)   any amounts transferred either to or from the reserve during the year;
(c)   the source and application of amounts so transferred.

Reserves should not include any amount which falls within the definition of a provision (see **8.12**). Reserves are not defined in law, except in the case of companies covered by Schedule 9 to CA 1985, but may be taken to be that part of shareholders' funds not accounted for by the nominal value of issued share capital or by the share premium account.

The notes to the accounts should give details of reserves which the company does not regard as distributable where this is not apparent from the accounting heading. This disclosure is not a statutory obligation but in view of the restriction on dividends being paid from non-distributable reserves it is considered good accounting practice to make the disclosure.

FRS 9 requires disclosure in the notes of significant restrictions on the ability of an   *FRS 9, 54*
associate or joint venture to distribute its retained earnings. Similarly FRS 2 requires
the disclosure of the extent of the restrictions on the company's ability to distribute   *FRS 2, 53*
group profits.

Reserves not set aside for a specific purpose should normally be combined, in so far as they are properly regarded as distributable, with the balance on the profit and loss account and included in item KV (Format 1) or AV (Format 2). Any other non-distributable reserves not specifically mentioned in the formats (e.g, reserves arising on consolidation) could be included in other reserves – item KIV4 (Format 1) or AIV (Format 2).

No corresponding figures are required to be disclosed for movements on reserves. *58(3d), Sch 4*

The balance on the profit and loss account must be shown in the position laid down by the formats, even in the case of a debit balance.

10.6   Revaluation reserve

Any difference between the amount of any item determined according to one of the *34(1)(2), Sch 4* alternative accounting rules and the amount that would have been disclosed if the historical cost convention had been adhered to, must be credited or debited (as applicable) to a 'revaluation reserve'. In determining the amount of this difference, account should be taken, where appropriate, of any provisions for depreciation or diminution in value that were made otherwise than by reference to the value determined under the alternative accounting rules. Account should also be taken of any adjustments of any such provisions that were made in the light of that determination.

10.6.1   Reporting gains and losses on revaluation

Revaluation gains should be recognised in the profit and loss account only to the *FRS 15, 63* extent (after adjusting for subsequent depreciation) that they reverse revaluation losses on the same asset that were previously recognised in the profit and loss account. All other revaluation gains should be recognised in the statement of total recognised gains and losses.

Where a revaluation gain reverses a revaluation loss that was previously recognised in *FRS 15, 64* the profit and loss account, the gain recognised in the profit and loss account is reduced by the amount of depreciation that would have been charged had the loss previously taken to the profit and loss account not been recognised in the first place. This is to achieve the same overall effect that would have been reached had the original downward revaluation reflected in the profit and loss account not occurred.

All revaluation losses that are caused by a clear consumption of economic benefits *FRS 15, 65* should be recognised in the profit and loss account. Other revaluation losses should be recognised:

(a)   in the statement of total recognised gains and losses until the carrying amount reaches its depreciated historical cost; and

(b)   thereafter, in the profit and loss account unless it can be demonstrated that the recoverable amount of the asset is greater than its revalued amount, in which case the loss should be recognised in the statement of total recognised gains and losses to the extent that the recoverable amount of the asset (as calculated in accordance with the requirements of FRS 11) is greater than its revalued *FRS 15, 66* amount.

In determining in which performance statement gains and losses on revaluation should *FRS 15, 67*

Capital and reserves

be recognised, material gains and losses on individual assets in a class of asset should not be aggregated.

A downward revaluation may comprise, at least in part, an impairment loss. When it is obvious that there has been a consumption of economic benefits (e.g., physical damage or a deterioration in the quality of the service provided by the asset), the asset is clearly impaired and the loss recognised in the profit and loss account, as an operating cost similar to depreciation. *FSR 15, 68*

Other revaluation losses may be due in part to a general fall in prices (e.g., a general slump in the property market) and in part to a consumption of economic benefits. Unless there is evidence to the contrary, it is assumed that the fall in value from the asset's previous carrying amount to depreciated historical cost is due to a general fall in prices (which is recognised in the statement of total recognised gains and losses, as a valuation adjustment) and the fall in value from depreciated historical cost to the revalued amount is due to a consumption of economic benefits (and therefore recognised in the profit and loss account). However, where it can be demonstrated that the recoverable amount is greater than the revalued amount, the difference between the recoverable amount and the revalued amount is clearly not an impairment and should therefore be recognised in the statement of total recognised gains and losses as a valuation adjustment, rather than in the profit and loss account. *FRS 15, 69* *FRS 15, 70*

Example

Assumptions

A non-specialised property costs £1 million and has a useful life of 10 years and no residual value. It is depreciated on a straight-line basis and revalued annually. The entity has a policy of calculating depreciation based on the opening book amount. At the end of years 1 and 2 the asset has an EUV of £1,080,000 and £700,000 respectively. At the end of year 2, the recoverable amount of the asset is £760,000 and its depreciated historical cost is £800,000. There is no obvious consumption of economic benefits in year 2, other than that accounted for through the depreciation charge.

Accounting treatment under modified historical cost

	Year 1 £000	Year 2 £000
Opening book amount	1,000	1,080
Depreciation	(100)	(120)*
Adjusted book amount	900	960
Revaluation gain (loss)		
recognised in the STRGL	180	(220)
recognised in the profit and loss account	–	(40)
Closing book amount	1,080	700

*As the remaining useful economic life of the asset is nine years, the depreciation change in year 2 is $\frac{1}{9}$th of the opening book amount (£1,080,000 ÷ 9 = £120,000).

In year 1, after depreciation of £100,000, a revaluation gain of £180,000 is recognised in the statement of total recognised gains and losses, in accordance with para 63.

In year 2, after a depreciation charge of £120,000, the revaluation loss on the property is £260,000. According to para 65, where there is not a clear consumption of economic benefits, revaluation losses should be recognised in the statement of total recognised gains and losses until the carrying amount reaches its depreciated historical cost. Therefore, the fall in value from the adjusted book amount (£960,000) to depreciated historical cost (£800,000) of £160,000 is recognised in the statement of total recognised gains and losses.

The rest of the revaluation loss, £100,000 (i.e., the fall in value from depreciated historical cost of £800,000 to the revalued amount of £700,000), should be recognised in the profit and loss account, unless it can be demonstrated that recoverable amount is greater than the revalued amount. In this case, recoverable amount of £760,000 is greater than the revalued amount of £700,000 by £60,000. Therefore £60,000 of the revaluation loss is recognised in the statement of total recognised gains and losses, rather than the profit and loss account – giving rise to a total revaluation loss of £220,000 (£60,000 + £160,000) that is recognised in the statement of total recognised gains and losses. The remaining loss (representing the fall in value from depreciated historical cost of £800,000 to recoverable amount of £760,000) of £40,000 is recognised in the profit and loss account.

10.6.2 Disclosures

The revaluation reserve must be shown on the face of the balance sheet as a separate amount, although it need not be shown under that name. Any amount attributable to investment properties should be stated separately.
34(2), Sch 4

SSAP 19, 15

In the case of investment properties, changes in the market value should be taken to the statement of total recognised gains and losses unless a deficit (or its reversal) on an individual investment property is expected to be permanent, in which case it should be charged (or credited) in the profit and loss account of the period.
SSAP 19, 13

Where the directors are of the opinion that any amount standing to the credit of the revaluation reserve is no longer necessary for the purpose of the accounting policies that the company has adopted, then the reserve must be reduced accordingly. This would be the case if a surplus in relation to an asset had been credited to the revaluation reserve and subsequently there was a fall in the value of that asset. The revaluation reserve may also be reduced where the permissible capital payment (together with any new issue proceeds) for shares in a company that have been purchased or redeemed by that company exceeds their nominal value.
34(3), Sch 4

s171(5b)

10.6.3 Restrictions

The Companies Act 1985 restricts the circumstances in which an amount can be transferred from the revaluation reserve to the profit and loss account. This can be done where one of the following circumstances exists:
34(3), Sch 4

(a) the amount in question had previously been charged to the profit and loss account;
(b) the amount in question represents a realised profit;
(c) on capitalisation.

So as not to inhibit companies from revaluing their assets, CA 1985 permits, for dividend purposes, an amount equal to the additional depreciation charge arising from an upward revaluation of a depreciable asset to be treated as a realised profit.
s275(2)

10.6.4 Treatment for taxation purposes

Where any amount has been either credited or debited to the revaluation reserve, its treatment for taxation purposes must be disclosed in a note to the financial statements. This does not mean that there must be a statement of whether the amount is taxable or   *34(4), Sch 4* allowable under tax legislation. It means that there must be an explanation for the tax effect of the revaluation. An example of this might be an indication of the tax that would be payable if the revalued asset was sold at its revalued amount.

11 Other matters

11.1 Signing the balance sheet

The Companies Act 1985 requires that every balance sheet of a company shall be signed on behalf of the board by a director of the company. Previously, if the company had more than one director, two had to sign. There is nothing to prevent two directors continuing to sign the balance sheet. *s233*

SSAP 17 requires that the date on which the accounts were approved by the board of directors should be disclosed in the accounts. Some companies indicate this by making a positive statement in the notes to the accounts. The preferred treatment is for the date to be noted immediately above the director's signature on the balance sheet. *SSAP 17, 26*

11.2 Capital expenditure

The Companies Act 1985 requires disclosure, where practicable, of the aggregate amount or estimated amount of contracts for capital expenditure not provided for in the accounts. *50(3), Sch 4*

The amount disclosed should include any irrecoverable VAT. *SSAP 5, 6*

11.3 Contingent liabilities

The Companies Act 1985 requires that in respect of any contingent liability that has not been provided for in the accounts, there must be disclosed in the notes: *50(2), Sch 4*

(a) the amount, or the estimated amount of that liability;
(b) its legal nature (this disclosure is expanded by FRS 12, see **11.3.2**);
(c) whether any valuable security has been provided by the company in connection with that liability. Where this is so, details of the security must be given.

11.3.1 Definition

FRS 12 defines a contingent liability as: *FRS 12, 2*

(a) a possible obligation that arises from past events and whose existence will be confirmed only by the occurrence of one or more uncertain future events not wholly within the entity's control; or
(b) a present obligation that arises from past events that is not recognised because:
   (i) it is not probable that a transfer of economic benefits will be required to settle the obligation; or

(ii)   the amount of the obligation cannot be measured with sufficient reliability.

11.3.2   Treatment of contingent liabilities

Contingent liabilities should not be recognised in the accounts but should be disclosed in the notes, unless the possibility of a transfer of economic benefits is remote.   *FRS 12, 27–28*

At the balance sheet an entity should disclose for each class of contingent liability a brief description of the nature of the contingent liability and, where practicable: *FRS 12, 91*

(a)   an estimate of its financial effect;
(b)   an indication of the uncertainties relating to the amount or timing of any outflow; and
(c)   the possibility of any reimbursement.

11.4 Contingent assets

A contingent asset is a possible asset that arises from past events and whose existence will be confirmed ony by the occurrence of one or more uncertain future events not wholly within the entity's control.   *FRS 12, 2*

Where an inflow of economic benefits is probable, an entity should disclose a brief description of the nature of the contingent asset at the balance sheet date and, where practicable, an estimate of its financial effect.   *FRS 12, 94*

It is important that disclosures for contingent assets avoid giving misleading indications of the likelihood of a profit arising.   *FRS 12, 95*

Contingent assets should not be recognised in the accounts.   *FRS 12, 31*

11.5   Pension commitments

In respect of pensions, CA 1985 requires that the notes to the accounts must disclose particulars of: *50(4), Sch 4*

(a)   pension commitments that have been provided for;
(b)   pension commitments that have not been provided for.

To the extent that either (a) or (b) relate to a company's former director the commitment must be separately disclosed.   *50(4), Sch 4*

One problem that CA 1985 does not attempt to answer relates to the basis to be used to measure pension commitments that have not been provided for. It is presumed that the Act is intended to require disclosure of the company's policy in respect of pension costs, because the mere disclosure of pension commitments that have not been provided for will, on its own, be meaningless.

This section of the Act has been largely superseded by SSAP 24 (see **4.18**).

11.6   Financial commitments

The Companies Act 1985 requires that any other financial commitments (not referred to in **11.2**, **11.3**, **11.4** and **11.5** above) that have not been provided for must be disclosed in the notes to the extent that they are relevant to a proper understanding of the company's affairs.

50(5), Sch 4

An example of such a commitment might be where a company has agreed to enter into a major joint venture with another company. In such a case, the company would have to disclose the amount of money that it had agreed in principle to put into the venture. It is not envisaged that this provision would normally require disclosure of financial commitments that relate to the ongoing trading operations, such as commitments under supply contracts, a company's liability to continue to pay wages or match foreign exchange commitments.

This disclosure referred to above and in **11.2**, **11.3**, **11.4** and **11.5** must include separate details of commitments on behalf of, or for the benefit of:

(a)   any parent undertaking or fellow subsidiary undertaking;
(b)   any subsidiary undertaking of the company.

An example which might involve disclosure under the above paragraph is the existence of cross-guarantees under a group banking arrangement.

50 & 59A, Sch 4

11.7   Post balance sheet events

This is explained in **1.4**.

11.8   Parent company

Details of the parent company's name and location must be given for the smallest and largest group for which group accounts are drawn up and, if different, similar details of the ultimate parent company.

11 & 12, Sch 5

The address must be disclosed of where the above group accounts can be obtained, if available to the public.

11.9   Accounting policies

The notes to the accounts must set out the accounting policies the company has adopted and for large companies, as defined, state whether the accounts have been prepared in accordance with applicable accounting standards, together with particulars of and reasons for any material departures.

36 & 36A, Sch 4

15, Sch 4
SSAP 2, 17

Where this statement is given, it must include either the full disclosure required by UITF 7 in respect of any invoking of the true and fair override in the preparation and presentation of the financial statements, or a cross-reference to where their disclosure can be found.

UITF 7, 7

In particular, CA 1985 stipulates that the accounting policies must include:

(a)   the method of determining the provision for depreciation and diminution in value of assets;
36, Sch 4

(b)   the method of translating foreign currency amounts into sterling (refer to **4.26** above).
58(1), Sch 4
SSAP 20, 59

SSAP 2 defines accounting policies as the specific accounting bases selected and consistently followed by a business enterprise as being, in the opinion of the management, appropriate to its circumstances and best suited to present fairly its results and financial position.
SSAP 2, 16

SSAP 2 requires disclosure, by way of a note, of the accounting policies followed for dealing with items which are judged material or critical in determining profit or loss for the year and in stating the financial position. The explanations should be fair, clear, and as brief as possible.
SSAP 2, 18

Individual accounting standards also require that relevant accounting policies are stated.

11.10   Basis of accounting

SAS 600 does not specifically require that the auditor should refer in his report to the particular convention used in preparing the accounts. However, as reference to the convention used is included in all of the examples given in SAS 600, it is considered good practice to refer to the convention used in preparing the accounts in the opening paragraph of the audit report. It is important to amend the standard wording as necessary when items such as properties are included at a valuation.

The Companies Act 1985 permits all companies to prepare accounts on the current cost basis (see **5.4.3** above). At the present time there is no accounting standard in place on current cost accounting following the withdrawal of SSAP 16 in 1988.
29–34, Sch 4

11.11   Reporting the substance of transactions

FRS 5 requires an entity's financial statements to report the substance of the transactions into which it has entered. The standard sets out how to determine the substance of a transaction (including how to identify its effects on the assets and liabilities of the entity), whether any resulting assets and liabilities should be included in the balance sheet, and what disclosures are appropriate.
FRS 5, 1

The standard does not change the accounting treatment and disclosure of the vast majority of transactions. Where transactions are straightforward and the substance and commercial effect are readily apparent, applying established accounting practices will usually be sufficient to ensure that such transactions are appropriately reported in the accounts. The standard mainly affects more complex transactions whose substance may not be readily apparent. The true commercial effect of these transactions may not be adequately expressed by their legal form and, where this is the case, it will not be sufficient to account for them by merely recording that form.

FRS 5 contains application notes specifying how to apply the standard's principles to transactions involving the following:

(a)   consignment stock;
(b)   factoring of debts;
(c)   sale and repurchase agreements;
(d)   securitised assets;
(e)   loan transfers.

The areas most likely to be encountered in practice are consignment stocks, most particularly in connection with motor traders, and the factoring of debts.

11.11.1   Consignment stocks

Consignment stock is stock held by one party (dealer) but legally owned by another (manufacturer), on terms that give the dealer the right to sell the stock in the normal course of its business or, at its option, to return it unsold to the legal owner. *FRS 5, A1*

The stock should be included on the dealer's balance sheet if it has access to the principal benefits and risks of the stock. Indications that the benefits and risks have passed to the dealer include: *FRS 5, A5–A10*

(a)   the manufacturer cannot require the dealer to return or transfer stock, or financial incentives have to be given to persuade the dealer to transfer stock at the manufacturer's request;
(b)   dealer has no right to return stock or is commercially compelled not to exercise its right of return;
(c)   dealer bears obsolescence risk;
(d)   stock transfer price charged by manufacturer is based on manufacturer's list price at time of delivery;
(e)   dealer bears slow movement risk.

Indications that the risk and benefits have not passed to the dealer and hence that the stock is not an asset of the dealer include: *FRS 5, A5–A10*

(a)   the manufacturer can require the dealer to return or transfer stock without compensation, or a penalty is paid by the dealer to prevent returns/transfers of stock at the manufacturer's request;
(b)   the dealer has unfettered right to return stock to the manufacturer without penalty and in practice exercises the right;
(c)   the manufacturer bears obsolescence risk;
(d)   stock transfer price charged by the manufacturer at date of transfer of legal title;
(e)   the manufacturer bears slow movement risk.

11.11.2   Factoring of debts

There are three possible treatments of factoring transactions in the seller's (the recipient of finance from the factor) financial statements: *FRS 5, C3*

(a)   to remove the factored debts from the balance sheet and show no liability in respect of any proceeds received from the factor 'derecognition';
(b)   to show the proceeds received from the factor deducted from the factored debts

on the face of the balance sheet within a single asset caption (a 'linked presentation');

(c)   to continue to show the factored debts as an asset, and show a corresponding liability within creditors in respect of the proceeds received from the factor (a 'separate presentation').

The accounting treatment is determined by whether the seller has access to the benefits of the factored debts and exposure to the risks inherent in these benefits and whether the seller has a liability to repay amounts received from the factor. The benefits attaching to the debts are further cash flow from payment and the risks are slow payment and bad debts.

FRS 5, C4–C5

Indications that derecognition is appropriate (debts are not an asset of the seller) include:

FRS 5, C11–C14

(a)   transfer is for a single, non-returnable fixed sum;

(b)   there is no recourse to the seller for losses;

(c)   the factor is paid all amounts received from the factored debts (and no more); the seller has no rights to further sums from the factor.

Indications that a linked presentation is deemed appropriate include:

FRS 5, C15–C16

(a)   some non-returnable proceeds received, but the seller has rights to further sums from the factor (or vice versa) whose amount depends on whether or when debtors pay;

(b)   there is either no recourse for losses, or such recourse has a fixed monetary ceiling;

(c)   the factor is paid only out of amounts collected from the factored debts, and the seller has no right or obligation to repurchase debts.

Indications that a separate presentation is appropriate (debts are an asset of the seller):

FRS 5, C17

(a)   finance cost varies with speed of collection of debts;

(b)   there is full recourse to the seller for losses;

(c)   seller is required to repay amounts received from the factor on or before a set date, regardless of timing or amounts of collections from debtors.

11.11.3   Goods sold subject to reservation of title

The issue of recognising the commercial substance of a transaction as opposed to its legal form also arises in respect of goods sold subject to a reservation of title.

Where goods are sold subject to reservation of title the seller retains title to the goods sold, and in some cases, the right to other goods produced from them and the ultimate sale proceeds, until payment has passed. The reservation of title may have no economic relevance to either party to the transaction, except in the event of the insolvency of the purchaser, and the goods are supplied and payment is due on an identical basis to other goods which are sold without reservation of title. In these circumstances, the sale should be recognised as revenue immediately, unless there is significant doubt about the collectability of the amount due.

AR 2.404

Although Accounting Recommendation 2.404 suggests several disclosures regarding transactions which are subject to reservation of title, these disclosures are usually not given because of the routine usage of these clauses and the preparation of financial statements on a going concern basis.

11.12 Fair values of assets and liabilities acquired

FRS 7 requires that when a business entity is acquired by another, all the assets and liabilities that existed in the acquired entity at the date of acquisition are recorded at fair values reflecting their condition at that date, and that all changes to the acquired assets and liabilities, and the resulting gains and losses, that arise after control of the acquired entity has passed to the acquirer are reported as part of the post-acquisition financial performance of the acquiring group. *FRS 7, 1*

The FRS is framed in terms of the acquisition of a subsidiary undertaking by a parent company that prepares consolidated financial statements. However, it also applies where an individual company acquires a business other than a subsidiary undertaking. *FRS 7, 4*

The FRS considers that the following do not affect fair values at the date of acquisition and should be treated as post-acquisition items: *FRS 7, 7*

(a) changes resulting from the acquirer's intentions or further action;
(b) impairments, or other changes, resulting from events subsequent to the acquisition;
(c) provisions or accruals for future operating losses or for reorganisation and integration costs expected to be incurred as a result of the acquisition.

FRS 7 contains detailed explanations applying its principles to specific classes of assets and liabilities. *FRS 7, 9–22*

11.13 Revised annual financial statements and directors' reports

Sections 245 and 245A of the Companies Act 1985, which were introduced by the Companies Act 1989, give company directors the authority to revise annual financial statements or directors' reports which do not comply with the Act.

The Act also gives the Secretary of State for Trade and Industry or any person authorised by him power to apply to the court for an order requiring the directors to revise defective accounts. Procedures for the voluntary revision of financial statements by the directors are set out in the Companies (Revision of Defective Accounts and Report) Regulations 1990 (SI 1990 No. 2570). The only revisions permitted are those which are deemed necessary to correct errors in the original financial statements and directors' reports. *s245B & C*

s245 (2)

The correction of annual financial statements and directors' report may be by complete replacement or by the issue of a supplementary note. The regulations contain no conditions which require one form or the other of revision to be used. The directors *SI 1990 No. 2570, 1* may therefore use the form that is most appropriate to the circumstances leading to the revision. In both instances the financial statements or directors' report are to be prepared as if prepared and approved by the directors as at the date of the original financial statements or directors' report. The auditors' opinion on the view given by the revised financial statements is also given as at the date on which the original financial statements were approved.

SI 1990 No. 2570, 4 & 5
SI 1990 No. 2570, 6

If the company has prepared and filed abbreviated accounts, the directors must also consider the effect of the revision on these abbreviated accounts. They must file either a revised version of the abbreviated accounts or a statement that the revision of the full financial statements does not affect the abbreviated accounts.

SI 1990 No. 2570, 13

11.13.1 Revision by replacement

The revised financial statements must include, in a prominent position, a statement by the directors concerning the revision. This should state:

SI 1990 No. 2570, 4

(a) that the revised accounts replace the original annual accounts for the financial year (specifying it);

(b) that they are now the statutory accounts of the company for that financial year;

(c) that they have been prepared as at the date of the original annual accounts and not as at the date of revision and accordingly do not deal with events between those dates;

(d) the respect in which the original annual accounts did not comply with the requirements of the Act; and

(e) any significant amendments made consequential upon the remedying of those defects.

11.13.2 Revision by supplementary note

SI 1990 No. 2570, 5

If the defect has been corrected by a supplementary note, the note should provide adequate information concerning the defect in the original financial statements and any consequential amendments, and should state the following:

(a) that the note revises in certain respects the original annual accounts of the company and is to be treated as forming part of those accounts; and .

(b) that the annual accounts have been revised as at the date of the original annual accounts and not as at the date of revision and accordingly do not deal with events between those dates.

11.14 Transactions with related parties

11.14.1 Background and definition

FRS 8 requires that reporting entities should disclose transactions with related parties. A related party transaction is a transfer of assets or liabilities or the performance of the services by, to or for a related party irrespective of whether a price is charged. The definition of a 'related party' is complex and is set out in full in FRS 8. A summary of the definition is set out below:

FRS 8, 1
FRS 8, 25

(a) Two or more parties are related when for all or part of the period:

(i) one party has either direct or indirect control of the other party;

(ii) the parties are subject to common control from the same source;

(iii) one party has influence over the financial and operating policies of the other party to an extent that the other party might be inhibited from pursuing at all times its own separate interests; or

(iv) the parties, in entering a transaction, are subject to influence from the same source to such an extent that one of the parties to the transaction has subordinated its own separate interests.

(b) For the avoidance of doubt the following are deemed to be related parties of the reporting entity:

(i) its ultimate or intermediate parent undertaking or undertakings, subsidiary undertakings, and fellow subsidiary undertakings;

(ii) its associates and joint ventures;

(iii) the investor or venturer in respect of which the reporting entity is an associate or a joint venture;

(iv) directors of the reporting entity and the directors of its ultimate and intermediate parent undertaking;

(v) pension funds for the benefit of the employees of the reporting entity or of any entity that is a related party of the reporting entity.

(c) The following are presumed to be related parties of the reporting entity unless it can be demonstrated that neither party has influenced the financial and operating policies of the other in such a way as to inhibit the pursuit of separate interests:

(i) the key management of the reporting entity and the key management of its parent undertaking or undertakings;

(ii) a person owning or able to exercise control over 20 per cent or more of the voting rights of the reporting entity, whether directly or through nominees;

(iii) each person acting in concert in such a way as to be able to exercise control or influence over the reporting entity;

(iv) an entity managing or managed by the reporting entity under a management contract.

(d) The following are presumed to be related parties of the reporting entity, by nature of their close relationship with other related parties:

(i) members of the close family of any individual falling under parties mentioned in (a)–(c) above;

(ii) partnerships, companies, trusts or other entities in which any individual or member of the close family in (a)–(c) has a controlling interest.

FRS 8 does *not* require disclosure: *FRS 8, 3*

(a) in consolidated financial statements, of any transactions or balances between group entities that have been eliminated on consolidation;

(b) in a parent's own financial statements when those statements are presented together with its own consolidated financial statements;

(c) in the financial statements of subsidiary undertakings, 90 per cent or more of whose voting rights are controlled within the group, of transactions with entities that are part of the group or investees of the group qualifying as related parties, provided that the consolidated financial statements in which that subsidiary is included are publicly available;

(d) of pension contributions paid to a pension fund;

(e) of emoluments in respect of services as an employee of the reporting entity.

Reporting entities taking advantage of the exemption in (c) above are required to state the fact.

FRS 8 does *not* require disclosure of the relationship and transactions between the reporting entity and the parties listed below simply as a result of their role as: *FRS 8, 4*

(a) providers of finance in the course of their business in that regard;
(b) utility companies;
(c) government departments and their sponsored bodies;

even though they may circumscribe the freedom of action of an entity or participate in its decision-making progress; and

(d) a customer, supplier, franchiser, distributor or general agent with whom an entity transacts a significant amount of business.

11.14.2 Disclosure of transactions

Material transactions with a related party should be disclosed irrespective of whether a price is charged. The disclosure should include: *FRS 8, 6*

(a) the names of the transacting related parties;
(b) a description of the relationship between the parties;
(c) a description of the transactions;
(d) the amounts involved;
(e) any other elements of the transactions necessary for an understanding of the financial statements;
(f) the amounts due to or from related parties at the balance sheet date and provisions for doubtful debts from such parties at that date;
(g) amounts written off in the period in respect of debts due to or from related parties.

Transactions with related parties may be disclosed on an aggregated basis (aggregation of similar transactions by type of related party) unless disclosure of an individual transaction, or connected transactions, is necessary for an understanding of the impact of the transactions on the financial statements of the reporting entity or is required by law. *FRS 8, 6*

When the reporting entity is controlled by another party (including individuals), the relationship and name of that party must be disclosed and, if different, the name of the ultimate controlling party. If neither is known, that fact must be disclosed. This disclosure is required irrespective of whether any transactions have taken place between the controlling parties and the reporting entity. *FRS 8, 5*

12 Cash flow statements

FRS 1 (Revised 1996) replaced the original FRS 1 for accounting periods ending on and after 23 March 1997. The revised standard shows only movements in cash and the concept of 'cash equivalents' has been dropped. The revised FRS clarifies the link between cash flows and balance sheet movements by requiring a reconciliation between the cash flow statement and components of 'net debt', a widely used tool of financial analysis. This complements the links between the profit and loss account and other balance sheet movements, which were shown by the original FRS 1 cash flow statement.

12.1   Main changes from original FRS 1

The main changes may be summarised as:

(a)   the statement now deals purely with cash flows – the concept of cash equivalents has been dropped;
(b)   the original five standard headings have been replaced by eight:
    (i)   operating activities;
    (ii)   returns on investments and servicing of finance;
    (iii)   taxation;
    (iv)   capital expenditure and financial investment;
    (v)   acquisitions and disposals;
    (vi)   equity dividends paid;
    (vii)   management of liquid resources (which will include cash flows relating to items previously treated as cash equivalents);
    (viii) financing;
(c)   the reconciliation to the balance sheet is now required to focus on the movement in net debt.

12.2   Definitions

FRS 1, 2

12.2.1   Cash

Cash includes cash in hand and deposits *repayable on demand* with any qualifying financial institution, less overdrafts from any qualifying financial institution.

12.2.2   Liquid resources

Liquid resources are current asset investments held as readily disposable stores of value.

A readily disposable investment is disposable by the reporting entity without curtailing or disrupting its business and is either:

(a)   readily convertible into known amounts of cash at or close to its carrying amount, or

(b)   traded in active market.

12.3   Scope

FRS 1 (Revised 1996) applies to all financial statements intended to give a true and fair few except the following: *FRS 1, 5*

(a)   Subsidiary undertakings where 90 per cent or more of the voting rights are controlled within the group, provided that consolidated financial statements are publicly available. (This exemption applies where the parent is foreign, provided that its consolidated financial statements are filed with a public registration body of similar access and nature to Companies House);

(b)   mutual life assurance companies;

(c)   pension funds;

(d)   open ended investment funds;

(e)   building societies;

(f)   companies which are entitled to small company filing exemptions;

(g)   other entities which would be eligible for small companies filing exemptions if they were companies.

12.4   Preparation of cash flow statements

The cash flow statement should include: *FRS 1, 6*

(a)   all inflows of cash;

(b)   all outflows of cash.

Transactions that do not result in cash flows of the reporting entity should not be reported in the cash flow statement.   *FRS 1, 6*

An entity's cash flow statement should list its cash flows for the period classified under the following standard headings: *FRS 1, 7*

(a)   operating activities;

(b)   dividends from joint ventures and associates;

(c)   returns on investments and servicing of finance;

(d)   taxation;

(e)   capital expenditure and financial investment;

(f)   acquisitions and disposals;

(g)   equity dividends paid;

(h)   management of liquid resources;

(i)   financing.

The first seven headings should be in the sequence set out above.   *FRS 1, 7*

Operating cash flows can be presented by either: *FRS 1, 7*

(a) direct method, showing the relevant constituent cash flows, or
(b) indirect method, calculating operating cash flows by adjustment to the operating profit reported in the profit and loss account.

Normal practice is for the indirect method to be used.

Cash flows relating to the management of liquid resources and financing can be *FRS 1, 7*
combined under a single heading provided that the cash flows relating to each are
shown separately and separate subtitles are given.

12.5 Classification of cash flows

Except for cash inflows and outflows that are shown net (as permitted by the FRS), the *FRS 1, 8*
individual categories of inflows and outflows under the standard headings should be
disclosed separately, where material, in the cash flow statement or in a note.

The cash flow classifications may be further subdivided to give a fuller description of *FRS 1, 8*
the activities or to provide segmental information.

The requirement to show cash inflows and outflows separately does not apply to cash *FRS 1, 9*
flows relating to operating activities.

Cash inflows and outflows within management of liquid resources or financing may be *FRS 1, 9*
netted against each other if they either:

(a) relate in substance to a single financing transaction; or
(b) are due to short maturities and high turnover.

12.6 Operating activities

Cash effects of transactions and other events relating to operating or trading activities, *FRS 1, 11*
normally shown in the profit and loss account in arriving at operating profit, should be
shown under 'operating activities'.

Cash flows in respect of operating items relating to provisions should be included *FRS 1, 11*
whether or not the provision was included in operating profit.

Dividends received from joint ventures and associates should be included as separate *FRS 1, 12A*
items between operating activities and returns on investments and servicing of
finance.

A reconciliation between the operating profit reported in the profit and loss account *FRS 1, 12*
and the net cash flow from operating activities should be given either adjoining the
cash flow statement or as a note.

The reconciliation should disclose separately: *FRS 1, 12*

(a) movements in stocks, debtors and creditors related to operating activities;
(b) other differences between cash flows and profits;

12.7 Returns on investments and servicing of finance costs

These are: *FRS 1, 13*

(a)   receipts resulting from the ownership of an investment;
(b)   payments to providers of finance, non-equity shareholders and minority interests.

Cash inflows   *FRS 1, 14*

- Interest received, including any related tax recovered.
- Dividends received, net of any tax credits (except dividends from equity accounted entities whose results are included as part of operating profit).

Cash outflows   *FRS 1, 15*

- Interest paid (even if capitalised), including any tax deducted and paid to the relevant tax authority.
- Cash flows that are treated as finance costs under FRS4 (this will include issue costs on debt and non-equity share capital).
- The interest element of finance lease rental payments.
- Dividends paid on non-equity shares of the entity.
- Dividends paid to minority interests.

12.8 Taxation

Cash flows to or from taxation authorities in respect of the reporting entity's revenue and capital profits should be shown under 'taxation'.   *FRS 1, 16*

For a subsidiary undertaking, cash flows relating to group relief should be included.   *FRS 1, 17*

Cash flows in respect of other taxation, including value added tax, other sales taxes, property taxes and other taxes not assessed on profits should not be included in this section.   *FRS 1, 16*

Cash inflows   *FRS 1, 17*

- Tax rebates.
- Claims or returns of overpayments.

Cash outflows   *FRS 1, 18*

- Cash payments to the relevant tax authority of tax, including payments of advance corporation tax.

12.9   Capital expenditure and financial investment

This category includes cash flows related to the acquisition or disposal of any fixed asset unless it is required to be classified under 'acquisitions and disposals' and any current asset investments not included in liquid resources. *FRS 1, 19*

If there are no cash flows relating to financial investment, the caption may be reduced to 'capital expenditure'. *FRS 1, 19*

Cash inflows

- Receipts from sales or disposals of property, plant or equipment. *FRS 1, 20*
- Receipts from the repayment of loans or sales of debt instruments.

Cash outflows

- Payments to acquire property, plant or equipment. *FRS 1, 21*
- Loans given and payments to acquire debt instruments.

12.10   Acquisitions and disposals

This category shows cash flows relating to the acquisition or disposal of any trade or business, or of an investment in an entity that is or, as a result of the transaction, becomes or ceases to be an associate, joint venture, or subsidiary undertaking. *FRS 1, 22*

Cash inflows

- Receipts from sales of investments in subsidiary undertakings, showing separately any balances of cash and overdrafts transferred as part of the sale. *FRS 1, 23*
- Receipts from sales of investments in associates or joint ventures.
- Receipts from sales of trades or businesses.

Cash outflows

- Payments to acquire investments in subsidiary undertakings, showing separately any balances of cash and overdrafts acquired. *FRS 1, 24*
- Payments to acquire investments in associates and joint ventures.
- Payments to acquire trades or businesses.

12.11   Equity dividends paid

Cash outflows *FRS 1, 25*

- Dividends paid on the equity shares, excluding any advance corporation tax.

12.12 Management of liquid resources

Each entity should explain what it includes as liquid resources and any changes in its policy. *FRS 1, 26*

Cash flows in this section can be shown in a single section with those under 'financing' provided that separate subtitles for each are given. *FSR 1, 26*

Cash inflows

- Withdrawals from short-term deposits not qualifying as cash.
- Inflows from disposal or redemption of any other investments held as liquid resources. *FRS 1, 27*

Cash outflows

- Payments into short-term deposits not qualifying as cash. *FRS 1, 28*
- Outflows to acquire any other investments held as liquid resources.

12.13 Financing

Cash flows comprising receipts or payments of principal from or to external providers of finance should be shown under 'financing'. *FRS 1, 29*

Cash inflows

FRS 1, 30

- Proceeds from issuing shares or other equity instruments.
- Receipts from issuing debentures, loans, notes, and bonds and from other long-term and short-term borrowings (other than overdrafts).

Cash outflows

- Repayment of amounts borrowed (other than overdrafts). *FRS 1, 31*
- Capital element of finance lease payments.
- Payments to re-acquire or redeem the entity's shares.
- Payments of expenses or commissions on any issue of equity shares.

The amounts of any financing cash flows received from or paid to equity accounted entities should be disclosed separately. *FRS 1, 32*

12.14 Reconciliation to net debt

A note reconciling the movement of cash in the period with the movements in net debt should be given either adjoining the cash flow statement or in a note. *FRS 1, 33*

The changes in net debt should be analysed from the opening to the closing components showing separately, where material, changes resulting from: *FRS 1, 33*

(a)   the cash flows of the entity;

(b) the acquisition or disposal of subsidiary undertakings;
(c) other non-cash changes;
(d) the recognition of changes in market value and exchange rate movements.

Where several balance sheet amounts or parts thereof have to be combined to form the components of opening and closing net debt, sufficient detail should be shown to enable the cash and other components of net debt to be respectively traced back to the amounts shown under the equivalent captions in the balance sheet. *FRS 1, 33*

12.15 Exceptional items

Cash flows which relate to items that are classified as exceptional in the profit and loss account should be shown under the appropriate standard headings, according to the nature of each item. *FRS 1, 37*

Cash flows relating to exceptional items should be identified in the cash flow statement or a note to it and the relationship between the cash flows and the originating exceptional item should be explained. *FRS 1, 37*

Where cash flows are exceptional because of their size or incidence but are not related to items that are treated as exceptional in the profit and loss account, sufficient disclosure should be given to explain their cause and nature. *FRS 1, 38*

12.16 Acquisitions and disposals of subsidiaries undertakings

A note to the cash flow statement should show a summary of the effects of acquisitions and disposals of subsidiaries undertakings indicating how much of the consideration comprised cash. *FRS 1, 45*

Material effects on amounts reported under each of the standard headings reflecting the cash flows of a subsidiary undertaking acquired or disposed of in the period should be disclosed, as far as practicable. This information could be given by dividing cash flows between continuing and discontinued operations and acquisitions. *FRS 1, 45*

12.17 Restrictions on remittability

A note to the cash flow statement should identify the amounts and explain the circumstances where restrictions prevent the transfer of cash from one part of the business or group to another. *FRS 1, 47*

12.18 Comparative figures

Comparative figures should be given for all items in the cash flow statement and such notes thereto. Exceptions would be in: *FRS 1, 48*

(a) note that analyses changes in the balance sheet amounts making up net debt;

(b)   note of the material effects of acquisitions and disposals of subsidiary undertakings on each of the standard headings.

12.19   Material non-cash transactions

The notes to the cash flow statement should also provide details of material non-cash   *FRS 1, 46* transactions, for example the inception of finance leases and bonus issues of shares, if disclosure is necessary for an understanding of the underlying transactions.

13 Notice of annual general meeting

13.1 Annual general meeting

The directors must lay copies of the annual accounts, together with the auditors' report and directors' report, before the company at an annual general meeting. Such reports and accounts must be sent to members and debenture holders not less than 21 days before the date of the meeting. At least 21 days' notice of the meeting must be given in writing. Timetables for the publication of financial statements must take into consideration in this statutory requirement, particularly where the notice of meeting is published with the accounts. *s241* *s238*

13.2 Elective regime

Members of a private company may elect not to lay accounts at the annual general meeting. Where this election is made, every member must be sent a copy of the accounts not less than 28 days before the end of 10 months after the balance sheet date, together with a notice informing the member of his right to require the laying of the accounts before a general meeting. *s252* *s253*

14 Year 2000 and the euro

14.1 Year 2000

14.1.1 Accounting for software modification costs

The costs of rendering existing software year 2000 compliant should be written off to the profit and loss account except in those cases where: *UITF 20, 9*

(a)   an entity already has an accounting policy for capitalising software costs; and
(b)   to the extent that the expenditure clearly represents an enhancement of an asset beyond that originally assessed rather than merely maintaining its service potential: that is, its useful economic life is extended and/or its specification or capability is improved.

14.1.2 Disclosures

Exceptional items

Consideration should be given as to whether year 2000 software costs meet the existing definition of exceptional items given by FRS 3. If the costs are exceptional, then the disclosures required by FRS 3 should be given. *UITF 20, 10*

Commitments

Significant commitments at the balance sheet date in respect of year 2000 software modification costs should also be disclosed, when they are considered to fall within the existing CA 1985 requirement to give particulars of financial commitments which are relevant to assessing the company's state of affairs. *UITF 20, 10*

Impact of year 2000

Reporting entities should also consider the potential impact and extent of the year 2000 problem on the business and operations and should make the following disclosures: *UITF 20, 11*

(a)   The risks and uncertainties associated with the year 2000 problem. If the entity has not made an assessment of this problem or has not determined its materiality, that fact should be stated.
(b)   The entity's general plans to address year 2000 issues relating to its business and operations and, if material, its relationships with customers, suppliers and other relevant parties.
(c)   Whether the total estimated costs of these plans, including amounts to be spent in future periods, have been quantitifed and, where applicable, an indication of the total costs likely to be incurred, with an explanation of the basis on which the figures are calculated.

As part of the impact analysis, directors need to consider whether the issue year 2000 raises any uncertainty as to the continuing applicability of the underlying going concern assumption and make appropriate disclosures regarding any doubts which arise. For example, the magnitude of the cost of the replacements and rectifications required to address the year 2000 problem may be beyond the resources of the business.

The most appropriate location for the series of disclosures regarding the impact of year 2000 is likely to be the directors' report or the operating and financial review, if one is presented.

UITF 20, 12

14.1.3 Other accounting implications

Other accounting issues which arise, and which should be addressed using normal accounting principles include:

(a) considering the write-down of assets such as software or computer-controlled equipment that cannot be used after 31 December 1999, because the equipment cannot be rectified or is not economical to repair;

(b) considering the write-down to net realisable value of stocks of goods for resale or component stocks which contain programmed processes which are not year 2000 compliant;

(c) disclosure of contingent liabilities in respect of warranties, litigation or compensation which might arise from manufacturing or supplying equipment which proves not to be year 2000 compliant.

Another accounting implication is the possibility that account balances have been misstated because the year 2000 system issue can, in some cases, cause error in systems at an earlier stage. An example is where the system carries out calculations involving future dates, such as a stock ageing system or the generation of a debtors ageing analysis.

14.2 Accounting for the euro

Initial guidance in respect of accounting for the implication of the introduction of the euro was developed by the UITF in 1998. This guidance is relatively straightforward and reflects the fact that for most UK reporting entities the euro is a foreign currency and accounts will continue to be presented in sterling. However, many businesses are likely to incur some costs as a result of the euro's introduction even if the UK does not join. This is because of the impact upon European markets and trading partners. UK companies which wish to prepare and file accounts in euros are entitled to do so, as the Companies Act contains no restrictions on the use of foreign currencies, including the Euro, for financial reporting. Clearly, prominent disclosure would need to be made of the reporting currency.

In Abstract 21 the UITF reached a consensus that the costs of making the necessary modifications to assets to deal with the euro should be written off to the profit and loss account except in those cases where:

UITF 21, 17

(a) an entity already has an accounting policy to capitalise assets of the relevant type; and

(b) to the extent that the expenditure clearly results in an enhancement of an asset beyond that originally assessed rather than merely maintaining its service potential.

Other costs associated with the introduction of the euro should also be written off to the profit and loss account. *UITF 21, 17*

The approach adopted is therefore similar to that adopted for accounting for year 2000 related modification costs.

Expenditure incurred in preparing for the changeover to the euro and regarded as exceptional should be disclosed in accordance with FRS 3. Particulars of commitments at the balance sheet date in respect of costs to be incurred (whether to be treated as capital or revenue) should be disclosed where they are regarded as relevant to assessing the entity's state of affairs. Where the potential impact is likely to be significant to the entity, the UITF recommends that other information and discussion should be given, including an indication of the total costs likely to be incurred. This information may be more appropriately located in the directors' report or any operating and financial review or other statement included in the annual report published by the entity. *UITF 21, 18*

Following the principle set out in FRS 3, cumulative foreign exchange translation differences recognised in the statement of total recognised gains and losses in accordance with SSAP 20 should remain in reserves after the introduction of the euro and should not be reported in the profit and loss account. *UITF 21, 19*

Where gains and losses on financial instruments used as anticipatory hedges are at present deferred and matched with the related income or expense in a future period, the introduction of the euro should not alter this deferral and matching treatment. *UITF 21, 20*

14.2.1 Date from which effective

This consensus was effective for accounting periods ending on or after 23 March 1998. *UITF 21, 21*

14.2.2 Further guidance

In August 1998 the UITF issued a number of technical questions and answers relating to the first use of the euro as the accounts presentational currency. These were intended mainly for Irish users and the two issues which private companies are more likely to come into contact with are commented on below. *UITF 21, Appendix*

- What translation rate should be used where an entity chooses to provide a convenient translation of its financial statements, including comparative amounts in respect of accounting periods before the introduction of the euro?

The accounts that are translated into euros should be the ones previously translated into the local currency. The trends that existed due to the exchange rate movements prior to the introduction of the euro should not be lost on translation.

- Does the introduction of the euro and the fixing of exchange rates mean that exchange gains on unsettled items (in respect of currencies of countries in participating member states) become realised?

SSAP 20 requires continuous recognition of gains and losses on all monetary items, even long-term ones, whether realised or not. There is no cause to recognise any further gain or loss when realisation takes place.

15 Abbreviated accounts

15.1 Entitlement to file abbreviated accounts

For a company to be eligible to file abbreviated accounts, it must satisfy the qualifying conditions for small or medium-sized companies set out in CA 1985.

ss247 & 249

The qualifying conditions for an individual company are as follows:

	Small	*Medium*
Turnover	£2.8m	£11.2m
Gross assets	£1.4m	£5.6m
Number of employees	50	250

Those for a group are as follows:

	Small	*Medium*
Aggregate turnover	£2.8m net or £3.36m gross	£11.2m net or £13.44m gross
Aggregate gross assets	£1.4m net or £1.68m gross	£5.6m net or £6.72m gross
Aggregate number of employees	50	250

'Net' means after consolidation adjustments, 'gross' means a simple total of all of the companies in the group.

The Department of Trade and Industry is proposing to raise the turnover and balance sheet thresholds by up to 40 per cent. It is anticipated that a Statutory Instrument will be presented to Parliament during the autumn of 1999 and that the new threshold will be applicable by early 2000.

If a company or group meets (i.e., is less than or equal to) at least two of the above three criteria in its first financial year, it will be entitled to file abbreviated accounts for that year and the following year. A company other than a newly formed company, is entitled to file abbreviated accounts if it satisfies the above criteria for two consecutive years. If the company fails to meet the criteria in the third year, it may continue to file abbreviated accounts. However, if it fails to meet the criteria again in the fourth year, it must then file full accounts (or medium abbreviated accounts if it previously satisfied the 'small' criteria and now satisfies the 'medium' criteria).

If a company is, or was at any time during the financial year: *s246*

(a)   a public company;
(b)   a banking or insurance company;
(c)   an authorised person under the Financial Services Act 1986; or
(d)   a member of a group containing one or more of the above;

it is not entitled to file abbreviated accounts.

A parent company only qualifies as a small or medium-sized company if the group   *s246(5)*
headed by it likewise qualifies as a small or medium-sized group. There is no statutory
provision for a small or medium-sized parent company to file abbreviated group
accounts instead of individual accounts.

15.2   Advantage of filing abbreviated accounts

The advantage of filing abbreviated accounts is to limit the information made
available to competitors, the general public, credit rating agencies and other analysts.
For a small company the reduction in information made available (compared with full
accounts) is considerable; however, for a medium-sized company very little
information is permitted to be omitted. Details are given below.

15.3   Disclosure requirements for abbreviated accounts

15.3.1   Small companies

A small company must file an abbreviated balance sheet showing at least those   *1, Sch 8A*
headings to which a letter or Roman numeral is attached. The company does not
have to file a profit and loss account or a directors' report. The format of the balance
sheet is presented in Appendix III.

Details of accounting policies must be disclosed, including policies with respect to the   *4, Sch 8A*
depreciation and diminution in value of assets. If the accounts include amounts   *9, Sch 8A*
translated from foreign currencies, then the basis of translation should be disclosed.

Notes to the financial statements

Disclosures in the notes should include the following: *2 & 5–8,*
Sch 8A

(a)   cost or valuation and depreciation of each class of fixed asset (intangible,
      tangible and investments) at the beginning and end of each year together with
      the movements during the year;
(b)   details concerning investments;
(c)   amount of debtors falling due after more than one year must be stated whether
      on the face of the balance sheet or in the notes to the abbreviated accounts;
(d)   the amount of secured liabilities;
(e)   total creditors falling due after more than one year must be shown either on the
      face of the balance sheet or in the notes to the accounts;
(f)   for each item included in creditors show:

(i) total amount falling due after more than five years and not repayable by instalments;

(ii) total amount payable by instalments, any part of which is payable after five years, together with total amount of instalments falling due after more than five years;

(g) details of share capital;

(h) comparative figures for the preceding year;

(i) details of any loans or transactions concerning directors;

(j) if the company is a subsidiary undertaking within a group not preparing group accounts, details of the ultimate parent company;

(k) details of any departures from the true and fair view requirement incorporated in the full financial statements or any additional information given to fulfil the true and fair requirement;

(l) company's registered number.

15.3.2 Medium-sized companies

s246A

Abbreviations apply only to the profit and loss account.

Disclosures which may be omitted are:

(a) turnover, cost of sales and other operating income;

(b) turnover, change in stocks, own work capitalised, other operating income, raw materials and consumables and other external charges.

These items may be combined under one heading of 'gross profit or loss'.

Segmental analysis of turnover is not required, but a full balance sheet and directors' report must be filed.

15.4 Directors' statement

s246(8)

The directors must make a statement above the director's signature on the balance sheet stating that advantage has been taken of the exemptions conferred by the relevant provisions of CA 1985 on the grounds that, in their opinion, the company is entitled to those exemptions as a small or medium-sized company.

s246A(4)

15.5 Special auditors' report

The practice of presenting a report which contains the full text of the auditors' report on the full financial statements has now ended and current practice is set out in *Audit Bulletin 1997/1*.

The auditors' report is addressed to the company. Its scope is limited to confirming:

(a) that the company is entitled to deliver abbreviated accounts prepared in accordance with the relevant provision;

(b) that the abbreviated accounts have been properly prepared in accordance with the relevant provision from the full financial statements.

If the audit report on the full financial statements is qualified then the following should be presented:

(a)   the text of the report in full;

(b)   further material necessary to understand the qualification.

Consideration should be given as to whether any qualification included in the audit report on the full financial statements would cast doubt on compliance with the exemption criteria.

If the audit report on the full financial statements contains a fundamental uncertainty, the APB recommends that details should be given in the report on the abbreviated accounts, as illustrated by the example on page 204.

15.5.1   Example auditors' reports

Example of a report on the abbreviated accounts of a small company

Auditors' report to XYZ Limited under section 247B of the Companies Act 1985

We have examined the abbreviated accounts set out on pages . . . to . . ., together with the financial statements of the company for the year ended . . . . prepared under section 226 of the Companies Act 1985.

Respective responsibilities of directors and auditors
The directors are responsible for preparing the abbreviated accounts in accordance with section 246 of the Companies Act 1985. It is our responsibility to form an independent opinion as to whether the company is entitled to deliver abbreviated accounts prepared in accordance with sections 246(5) and (6)* of the Act to the registrar and whether the accounts to be delivered are properly prepared in accordance with those provisions and to report our opinion to you.

Basis of opinion
We have carried out the procedures we consider necessary to confirm, by reference to the financial statements, that the company is entitled to deliver abbreviated accounts and that the abbreviated accounts to be delivered are properly prepared. The scope of our work for the purpose of this report did not include examining or dealing with events after the date of our report on the financial statements.

Opinion
In our opinion the company is entitled to deliver abbreviated accounts prepared in accordance with sections 246(5) and (6) of the Companies Act 1985, and the abbreviated accounts on pages . . . to . . . are properly prepared in accordance with those provisions.

Other information
[*If relevant*]

Registered auditors   Address
Date

Example of a report on the abbreviated accounts of a medium-sized company

Auditors' report to XYZ Limited under section 247B of the Companies Act 1985

We have examined the abbreviated accounts set out on pages . . . to . . ., together with the financial statements of the company for the year ended . . . . prepared under section 226 of the Companies Act 1985.

Respective responsibilities of directors and auditors

The directors are responsible for preparing the abbreviated accounts in accordance with section 246A of the Companies Act 1985. It is our responsibility to form an independent opinion as to whether the company is entitled to deliver abbreviated accounts prepared in accordance with section 246A(3) of the Act to the registrar and whether the accounts to be delivered are properly prepared in accordance with that provision and to report our opinion to you.

Basis of opinion

We have carried out the procedures we consider necessary to confirm, by reference to the financial statements, that the company is entitled to deliver abbreviated accounts and that the abbreviated accounts to be delivered are properly prepared. The scope of our work for the purpose of this report did not include examining or dealing with events after the date of our report on the full financial statements.

Opinion

In our opinion the company is entitled to deliver abbreviated accounts prepared in accordance with section 246A(3) of the Companies Act 1985, and the abbreviated accounts on pages   to   are properly prepared in accordance with that provision.

Other information

[*If relevant*]

Registered auditors   Address
Date

Example of a report on the abbreviated accounts of a small company including other information – explanatory paragraph regarding a fundamental uncertainty (going concern)

Auditors' report to XYZ Limited under section 247B of the Companies Act 1985

We have examined the abbreviated accounts set out on pages . . . to . . ., together with the financial statements of the company for the year ended . . . . prepared under section 226 of the Companies Act 1985.

Respective responsibilities of directors and auditors

The directors are responsible for preparing the abbreviated accounts in accordance with section 246 of the Companies Act 1985. It is our responsibility to form an independent opinion as to whether the company is entitled to deliver abbreviated accounts prepared in accordance with sections 246(5) and (6) of the Act to the registrar and whether the accounts to be delivered are properly prepared in accordance with those provisions and to report our opinion to you.

Basis of opinion

We have carried out the procedures we consider necessary to confirm, by reference to the financial statement, that the company is entitled to deliver abbreviated accounts and that the abbreviated accounts to be delivered are properly prepared. The scope of our work for the purpose of this report did not include examining or dealing with events after the date of our report on the financial statements.

Opinion

In our opinion the company is entitled to deliver abbreviated accounts prepared in accordance with sections 246(5) and (6) of the Companies Act 1985, and the abbreviated accounts on pages . . . to . . . are properly prepared in accordance with those provisions.

Other information

On . . .* we reported as auditors to the members of the company on the financial statements prepared under section 226 of the Companies Act 1985 and our report included the following paragraph:

> '*Going concern*
> In forming our opinion, we have considered the adequacy of the disclosures made in note 1 of the financial statements concerning the uncertainty as to the continuation and renewal of the company's bank overdraft facility. In view of the significance of this uncertainty we consider that it should be drawn to your attention but our opinion is not qualified in this respect.'

Registered auditors   Address
Date

15.6   Companies exempt from audit

If the directors propose to deliver abbreviated accounts to the Registrar of Companies no special report by independent accountants on the accounts is required.

However, to avoid any possible confusion, the Audit Faculty of the ICAEW *IS 3.907, 21* recommends that a non-statutory accountant's report is presented on the full accounts. The directors should then append to the copy of the report that is to be delivered to the Registrar the accountant's report prefixed by some explanatory words, such as

> 'The following reproduces the text of the accountants' report in respect of the company's annual financial statements, from which the abbreviated accounts (set out on pages . . . to . . .) have been prepared.'

The accountants' report on the full financial statements would usually take the format recommended by the Audit Faculty which is reproduced on page 220.

16 Simplified accounts

Simplified accounts may be prepared by companies or groups which meet with the CA 1985 definition of a small company or group. Simplified accounts, which are the full accounts prepared for shareholders, contain a reduced level of statutory disclosures and are prepared in accordance with Schedule 8 of the Act, rather than Schedule 4, the full reporting schedule. The statutory profit and loss account and balance sheet in a set of simplified accounts are largely the same as for full accounts and therefore the main reduction in disclosure requirements is seen in the detailed notes to the accounts.

16.1 Disclosure requirements for simplified accounts

The disclosures in the notes of a set of simplified accounts are detailed below.

16.1.1 Formats

The balance sheet and profit and loss account formats contained in Schedule 8 are *1, Sch 8* presented in Appendix 2. The general rules for applying the formats are the same as those described in Chapters 4 and 5 for Schedule 4. However, the level of supporting analysis, usually given in the notes, is reduced by application of these less detailed formats.

16.1.2 Disclosure of accounting policies   *36, Sch 8*

(a)   Accounting policies adopted by the company in determining the amounts to be included in respect of items shown in the balance sheet and in determining the profit or loss should be stated.
(b)   Disclosure must include policies with respect to the depreciation and diminution in value of assets.

16.1.3 Disclosures

Fixed assets, including totals for additions and disposals, and the depreciation   *40–41, Sch 8*
charge for the year

(a)   Opening balance and movements during the year.
(b)   Date of last valuation.
(c)   Details of revaluations during the year.
(d)   Name/particulars of valuer.
(e)   Bases of valuation.

Simplified accounts

Investments

(a) The amount of ascribable to listed investments.
(b) Aggregate market value of those investments where it differs from the amount stated market.
(c) Market value and stock exchange value if the former is higher than the latter.

42, Sch 8

Debtors

The amount falling due after more than one year shall be shown separately for each item included under debtors unless the aggregate amount of debtors falling due after more than one year is disclosed in the notes to the accounts.

8, Sch 8

Creditors

The following must be shown separately:

8, Sch 8

(a) The amount of any convertible loans.
(b) The amount for creditors in respect of taxation and social security.

Reserves and provisions

(a) Details of transfers to or from any reserves and to any provisions for liabilities and charges.
(b) Details of any transfer from the provision for liabilities and charges otherwise than for the purpose for which the provision was established.
(c) The amount of reserves or provisions at the beginning and end of the period.

43, Sch 8

44, Sch 8

Details of indebtedness

(a) Aggregate amounts of any creditors which are payable or repayable otherwise than by instalments and fall due for payment or repayment after five years.
(b) In respect of creditors which are payable or repayable by instalments, the aggregate amount of any instalments which fall due for payment after five years.
(c) Aggregate amount of creditors for which security has been given.

If any fixed cumulative dividends are in arrears

45, Sch 8

(a) The amount of the arrears.
(b) The period for which the dividends are in arrears.

Guarantees and other financial commitments

46, Sch 8

(a) Details of any charge on the assets of the company to secure the liabilities of any other person.
(b) Contingent liabilities not provided for:
    (i) amount or estimated amount;
    (ii) legal nature;
    (iii) whether any valuable security has been provided and if so, what.
(c) Aggregate amount or estimated amount of contracts for capital expenditure not provided for.
(d) Details of pension commitments provided in the balance sheet and other pension commitments for which no provision has been made. (Give separate details if the particulars relate to past directors.)
(e) Particulars of any other financial commitments which either:

      (i)   have not been provided for; or

      (ii)   are relevant to assessing the company's state of affairs.

(f)   State separately details of commitments given in respect of other members of the group.

(g)   Details for parent and fellow subsidiaries must be separate from those in respect of the company's own subsidiaries.

Share capital *38–39, Sch 8*

(a)   Authorised.

(b)   Number and aggregate nominal value of each class.

(c)   Description of redeemable shares.

(d)   Details of allotments during the year.

Profit and loss account supporting disclosures

The following information should be disclosed to support the profit and loss account.

(a)   Particulars of turnover – percentage of turnover attributable to geographical   *48–51, Sch 8* markets outside the UK.

(b)   Details of exceptional items by virtue of size or incidence.

(c)   Details of prior year adjustments.

(d)   Basis of translation of sums originally denominated in foreign currencies.

16.2   Directors' report

The directors' report of a company preparing simplified accounts is required only to   *s246(4)* provide the following information:

(a)   names of directors;

(b)   principal activities;

(c)   directors' share interests;

(d)   directors' share options;

(e)   political and charitable gifts (exceeding £200).

16.3   Directors' statement *s246(8)*

If a company is preparing simplified accounts the directors must state:

(a)   in the directors' report above the secretary's signature, 'the above report is prepared in accordance with the special exemptions available to small companies';

(b)   on the balance sheet, above the director's signature, ' the company's financial statements are prepared in accordance with the special exemptions eligible to small companies'.

17 The Financial Reporting Standard for Smaller Entities (FRSSE)

The FRSSE was first issued in November 1997 and a revised version was published in December 1998. The revised FRSSE reflects developments in accounting standards that have taken place since the publication of the original FRSSE. The revised FRSSE is effective for accounting periods ending from 23 March 1999. In July 1999, an exposure draft for a second revision was issued.

The Financial Reporting Standard for Smaller Entities (FRSSE) prescribes the basis, for those entities within its scope that have chosen to adopt it, for preparing and presenting their financial statements. The definitions and accounting treatments are consistent with the requirements of companies legislation and, for the generality of small entities, are the same as those required by existing accounting standards or a simplified version of those requirements. The disclosure requirements exclude a number of those stipulated in other accounting standards.

Reporting entities that apply the FRSSE are exempt from complying with other accounting standards (Statements of Standard Accounting Practice and Financial Reporting Standards) and Urgent Issues Task Force (UITF) Abstracts, unless preparing consolidated financial statements, in which case certain other accounting standards apply, as set out in para 16.1 of the FRSSE.

Financial statements will generally be prepared using accepted practice and, accordingly, for transactions or events not dealt with in the FRSSE, smaller entities should have regard to other accounting standards and UITF Abstracts not as mandatory documents but as a means of establishing current practice.

The FRSSE is not a mandatory standard – small companies may continue to apply the full reporting standards if they wish. For most small companies, the differences between a set of accounts prepared under the FRSSE and under the full standards are marginal, as the FRSSE's disclosure reductions relate mainly to detailed or complex matters not found in the typical set of small company accounts. The FRSSE is also not an 'all or nothing' standard and companies may apply as much, or as little, of it as they please.

17.1 Scope

The FRSSE may be applied to all financial statements intended to give a true and fair view of the financial position and profit or loss (or income and expenditure) of all entities that are:

FRSSE 1.1

(a) small companies or groups as defined in companies legislation;
(b) entities that would also qualify if they had been incorporated under companies legislation.

The FRSSE does not apply to the following:

(a) large or medium-sized companies, groups and other entities;
(b) public companies;
(c) banks or insurance companies;
(d) authorised persons under the Financial Services Act 1986.

Reporting entities that are entitled to adopt the FRSSE, but choose not to do so, should apply Statements of Standard Accounting Practice (SSAPs), other Financial Reporting Standards (FRSs) and UITF Abstracts when preparing financial statements intended to give a true and fair view of the financial position and profit or loss of the entity.

FRSSE, Scope

17.2 Small groups

Small groups which adopt the FRSSE and choose to prepare consolidated financial statements should follow accounting standards and UITF Abstracts relating to the accounting practices and disclosures required in respect of consolidated financial statements.

17.3 Main disclosure reductions

The main disclosure reductions permitted by the FRSSE are as follows.

FRSSE,
Appendix VI

FRS 3 requirements

(a) No analysis of turnover and profits into continuing and discontinued activities.
(b) No reconciliation of movements in shareholders' funds.
(c) No requirement for a note of historical cost profits and losses.

FRS 4 requirements

(a) Elimination of most disclosure requirements, unless the company has a complex form of capital (refer to FRS 4 direct).
(b) Arrangement fees can generally be taken direct to the profit and loss account – the balance sheet will reflect outstanding capital only.

FRS 8 requirements

Related party transactions that are material to the related party, but not the reporting entity do not have to be disclosed. For example, the gift of a secondhand car worth £2,000 to the daughter of a director would probably not need to be disclosed, as the car is unlikely to be material to the giving company.

17.4   True and fair view

Financial statements should present a true and fair view of the results for the period *FRSSE 2.1* and of the state of affairs at the end of the period. As with the preparation of any set of financial statements, regard should be had to the substance of any arrangement or transaction. Where there is any doubt as to whether applying any provisions of the *FRSSE 2.2* FRSSE would be sufficient to give a true and fair view, adequate explanation should be given in the notes to the accounts of the transaction or arrangement concerned and the treatment adopted.

17.5   Accounting principles and policies

Financial statements should state that they have been prepared in accordance with the *FRSSE 2.3* FRSSE.

Accounting policies followed for dealing with items that are judged material or critical *FRSSE 2.5* in determining profit or loss for the year and in stating the financial position should be disclosed by way of note.

17.6   Disclosure of changes in accounting policy

Following a change in accounting policy, the amounts for the current and corresponding *FRSSE 2.8* periods should be restated on the basis of the new policies. The disclosures necessary when a change of accounting policy is made should include, in addition to those for prior period adjustments, an indication of the effect on the current period's results. In those cases where the effect on the current period is immaterial, or similar to the quantified effect on the prior period, a simple statement saying this suffices. Where it is not practicable to give the effect on the current period, that fact, together with the reasons, should be stated.

17.7   True and fair override disclosures   *FRSSE 2.9*

In cases where the true and fair view override is being invoked this should be stated clearly and unambiguously. To this end the followng should be given:

- a statement of the treatment that would normally be required in the circumstances and a description of the treatment actually adopted;
- a statement explaining why the treatment prescribed would not give a true and fair view; and
- a description of how the position shown in the financial statements is different as a result of the departure, normally with quantification, except (i) where quantification is already evident in the financial statements themselves or (ii) whenever the effect cannot be reasonably quantified, in which case the directors should explain the circumstances.

Where a departure continues in subsequent financial statements, the disclosures should be made in all subsequent statements and should include corresponding amounts for the previous period.

17.8   Profit and loss account

All gains and losses recognised in the financial statements for the period should be included in the profit and loss account or the statement of total recognised gains and losses.   *FRSSE 3.1*

Gains and losses may be excluded from the profit and loss account only if they are specifically permitted or required to be taken direct to reserves by the FRSSE or by companies legislation.   *FRSSE 3.1*

17.9   Exceptional items

Exceptional items should be credited or charged in arriving at a profit or loss on ordinary activities by inclusion under the statutory format headings to which they relate.   *FRSSE 3.2*

The amount of each exceptional item should be disclosed separately by way of note, or on the face of the profit and loss account if that degree of prominence is necessary to give a true and fair view.   *FRSSE 3.2*

An adequate description of each exceptional item should be given to enable its nature to be understood.   *FRSSE 3.2*

The following items should be shown separately on the face of the profit and loss account after operating profit and before interest: *FRSSE 3.3*

(a)   profits or losses on the sale or termination of an operation;
(b)   costs of a fundamental reorganisation or restructuring;
(c)   profits or losses on the disposal of fixed assets.

17.10   Prior period adjustments

Prior period adjustments should be accounted for by restating the comparative figures for the preceding period in the primary statements and notes and adjusting the opening balance of reserves for the cumulative effect. The cumulative effect of the adjustments should also be noted at the foot of the statement of total recognised gains and losses of the current period. The effect of prior period adjustments on the results for the preceding period should be disclosed where practicable.   *FRSSE 2.7*

17.11   Statement of total recognised gains and losses

This should have the same prominence as the profit and loss account. It should contain the gains and losses that are recognised in the period in so far as they are attributable to shareholders. Where the only recognised gains and losses are the results included in the profit and loss account, no separate statement to this effect need be made.   *FRSSE 4.1*

17.12 Foreign currency translation

Each asset, liability, revenue or cost arising from the transaction denominated in a foreign currency should be translated at the exchange rate in operation on the date on which the transaction occurred. *FRSSE 13.1*

At the balance sheet date, monetary assets and liabilities denominated in a foreign currency should be translated using the closing rate. *FRSSE 13.3*

All exchange gains or losses on settled transactions and unsettled monetary items should be reported as part of the profit or loss for the year from ordinary activities. *FRSSE 13.4*

17.13 Taxation

The following items should be included in the taxation charge and, where material, should be separately disclosed: *FRSSE 9.1*

(a)   amount of UK corporation tax specifying:
   (i)   charge for corporation tax on the income of the year;
   (ii)   tax attributable to franked investment income;
   (iii) irrecoverable advance corporation tax;
   (iv)   relief for overseas taxation;
(b)   total overseas taxation, relieved and unrelieved, specifying that part of the unrelieved overseas taxation which arises from the payment or proposed payment of dividends.

17.14 Deferred tax

The approach taken to accounting for deferred tax is the same as that taken by SSAP 15 and therefore:

(a)   deferred tax should be computed under the liability method; *FRSSE 9.3*
(b)   tax deferred or accelerated by the effect of timing differences should be accounted for to the extent that it is probable that a liability or asset will crystallise; *FRSSE 9.4*
(c)   disclose the deferred tax balance, and its major components and details of transfers to and from deferred tax. *FRSSE 9.12–13*
(d)   the total accumulated amount of any deferred tax unprovided for at the balance sheet date, and unprovided in respect of the period, should be disclosed, analysed into their major components. *FRSSE 9.15–16*

17.15 Goodwill and intangible assets

The FRSSE has been revised to reflect the accounting treatment for goodwill and intangible assets introduced in FRS 10. This means that positive purchased goodwill and purchased intangible assets should be capitalised and depreciated over their useful economic lives. The useful economic life should not exceed 20 years. Useful economic lives should be reviewed at the end of each reporting period. Goodwill *FRSSE 5.9– 5.14* and intangible assets should not be revalued and internally generated goodwill and intangible assets should not be capitalised.

If negative goodwill arises, the balance arising should be recognised on the face of the profit and loss account, and should be released to the profit and loss account over the period that benefit is expected.   *FRSSE 5.15*

Goodwill written off directly to reserves under former standard practice, need not be reinstated.

17.16   Investment properties

Investment properties should not be subject to periodic charges for depreciation except   *FRSSE 5.32*
for properties held on lease, which should be depreciated at least over the period when
the unexpired term is 20 years or less. Investment properties should be included in the   *FRSSE 5.33*
balance sheet at open market value.

The names of the persons making the valuation, or particulars of their qualifications,   *FRSSE 5.34*
should be disclosed together with the bases of valuation used by them. If the valuation
is performed by an officer or an employee, that fact should be disclosed.

Changes in market value should not be taken to the profit and loss account but should
be taken to be statement of total recognised gains and losses unless the deficit (or its   *FRSSE 5.35*
reversal) is expected to be permanent.

17.17   Depreciation

All assets having a finite useful economic life should be depreciated. The FRSSE   *FRSSE 5.17*
considers that buildings have a limited useful economic life and should be depreciated.   *FRSSE 5.23*

Disclosures for (1) land and buildings and (2) other tangible fixed assets in aggregate   *FRSSE 5.24*
should include:

(a)   depreciation methods used;
(b)   useful economic lives or depreciation rates used;
(c)   total depreciation charged for the period;
(d)   gross amount of depreciable assets and the related accumulated depreciation.

The exposure draft issued in July 1999, proposes to bring the core requirements of
FRS 15 into the FRSSE.

17.18   Government grants

Grants should be recognised in the profit and loss account so as to match them with the   *FRSSE 5.37*
expenditure towards which they are intended to contribute. Grants received as a
contribution towards expenditure on a fixed asset should be treated as deferred income.

The effect of government grants on the results for the period and/or the financial   *FRSSE 5.40*
position should be dislcosed.

Where the results are affected materially by the receipt of forms of government *FRSSE 5.40* assistance other than grants, the nature of that assistance and an estimate of the effect on the financial statements.

17.19   Stocks and long-term contracts

Stocks should be stated at the lower of cost and net realisable value of the separate *FRSSE 8.1* items of stock or of groups of similar items.

17.9.1   Long-term contracts

Long-term contracts are accounted in accordance with the approach of SSAP 9(R). *FRSSE 8.2* Contracts should be assessed on a contract-by-contract basis and reflected in the profit and loss account by recording turnover and related costs as contract activity progresses.

Where it is considered that the outcome can be assessed with reasonable certainty, *FRSSE 8.3* attributable profit should be recognised in the profit and loss account.

Balance sheet disclosures (SSAP 9(R) approach) are: *FRSSE 8.4*

(a)   amounts recoverable on contracts;
(b)   payments on account;
(c)   long-term contract balances;
(d)   provision for foreseeable losses.

17.20   Debt factoring

Accounting treatment is determined by whether all significant benefits and all *FRSSE 8.6–8* significant risks relating to the debts have been transferred to the factor or continue to rest in the entity. The treatment broadly follows FRS 5.

17.21   Consignment stock

The approach of FRS 5 is followed, although there is no reference in the FRSSE to *FRSSE 8.5* disclosures. If consignment stocks are material, then disclosure would be expected to show a true and fair view.

17.22   Leasing

Accounting for hire purchase contracts, finance leases and operating leases follows the *FRSSE 6* principles of SSAP 21, and the general disclosure requirements are unchanged.

17.23   Pensions

The accounting objective is that the employer should recognise the expected cost of *FRSSE 10.1* providing pensions and other post-retirement benefits on a systematic and rational basis over the period during which it derives benefit from the employees' services. The FRSSE significantly reduces the disclosures required in respect of defined benefit schemes. However, defined benefit schemes are very rare in small companies.

In respect of defined contribution schemes the charge against profits should be the amount *FRSSE 10.3* of contributions payable to the pension scheme in respect of the accounting period. The disclosures required are straightforward and the following is given as an example:

> *The company operates a defined contribution pension scheme. The assets of the scheme are held separately from those of the company in an independently administered fund. The pension cost charge represents contributions payable by the company to the fund and amounted to £50,000 (1998 – £45,000). Contributions totalling £2,500 (1998 – £1,500) were payable to the fund at the year end and are included in creditors.*

17.24   Capital instruments

Capital instruments other than shares should be classified as liabilities as they contain *FRSSE 12.1* an obligation to transfer economic benefits. Instruments that do not contain an obligation to transfer economic benefits should be reported within shareholders' funds.

The finance costs of debt should be allocated to periods over the term of the debt at a *FRSSE 12.2* constant rate on the carrying amount. All finance costs should be charged in the profit *FRSSE 12.4* and loss account. Where an arrangement fee is such as to represent a significant additional cost of finance when compared with the interest payable over the life of the instrument, the treatment set out above should be followed. Where this is not the case it should be charged in the profit and loss account immediately it is incurred.

Where the entitlement to dividends in respect of shares is calculated by reference to *FRSSE 12.5* time, dividends should be accounted for on an accruals basis except in those circumstances where ultimate payment is remote.

All dividends should be reported as appropriations of profit in the profit and loss *FRSSE 12,5* account

17.25   Contingencies

In addition to amounts accrued under the accounting principle of prudence, a material *FRSSE 11.1* contingent loss should be accrued in financial statements where it is probable that a future event will confirm a loss that can be estimated with reasonable accuracy at the date on which the financial statements are approved by the board of directors.

In respect of each contingency that is required to be disclosed, the following *FRSSE 11.4* information should be stated by way of note to the financial statements:

(a)   the nature of the contingency;
(b)   the uncertainties that are expected to affect the ultimate outcome; and
(c)   a prudent estimate of the financial effect, made at the date on which the financial statements are approved by the board of directors, or a statement that it is not practicable to make such an estimate.

Where there is disclosure of an estimate of the financial effect of a contingency, the amount disclosed should be the potential financial effect. In the case of a contingent loss, this should be reduced by: *FRSSE 11.5*

(a)   any amount accrued; and
(b)   the amount of any components where the possibility of loss is remote.

Only the net amount need be disclosed.

17.26   Provisions

The version of the FRSSE issued in December 1998 makes no reference to the principles of how provisions should be recognised in the accounts, as FRS 12 was issued after the commencement of the first set of revisions to the FRSSE. Therefore, in theory, the requirements of FRS 12 could be avoided by applying the FRSSE. This 'benefit' will, however, be short-lived as the July 1999 exposure draft, setting out the second set of revisions to the FRSSE, contains the main requirements of FRS 12.

17.27   Post balance sheet events

The accounting treatment and disclosure follows SSAP17.   *FRSSE 14*

17.28   Related party disclosures

Only those related party transactions that are material to the reporting entity (that is, no need to disclose those that are material only to the related party) should be disclosed. The disclosures should comprise the following: *FRSSE 15.1*

(a)   names of the transacting parties;
(b)   description of the relationship between the parties;
(c)   description of the transactions;
(d)   amounts involved;
(f)   any other elements of the transactions necessary for an understanding of the
         financial statements;
(g)   amounts due to or from related parties at the balance sheet date and provisions
         for doubtful debts due from such parties at that date;
(h)   amounts written off in the period.

The materiality of a related party transaction should be judged not only in terms of its significance to the reporting entity but also in relation to the other related party.   *FRSSE 15.1*
   (footnote)

Personal guarantees given by directors in respect of borrowings should be disclosed in the notes.   *FRSSE 15.2*

18 Exemptions from audit

Companies are exempt from audit if their annual turnover is less than £350,000 and their balance sheet total (gross assets) is less than £1,400,000. The statutory accountants' report (the s249A(2) report) was abolished for most companies for periods ending on and after 15 June 1997. Therefore, for the majority of smaller companies there is now no reporting distinction between having a turnover of less than £350,000 and having a turnover of less than £90,000. Consequently, there is no statutory requirement for an independent report to be given on the accounts of a company which is exempt from audit. *SI 1997/936*

The types of companies which are not permitted by the legislation to be exempt from audit are: *s249B*

(a)   public companies;
(b)   parent companies or subsidiaries;
(c)   special register bodies and employers' associations under the Trade Union and Labour Relations (Consolidation) Act 1992;
(d)   banks;
(e)   insurance companies;
(f)   insurance brokers enrolled under the Insurance Brokers (Registration) Act 1977;
(g)   authorised persons and appointed representatives under the Financial Services Act 1986.

Charitable companies are also exceptions. The income threshold for an audit is reduced to £250,000 and the statutory accountants' report must still be presented on accounts where the income falls in the range £90,000 to £250,000. Where income is less than £90,000 no statutory report is required. *s249A(2)*

In 1997, provisions were introduced allowing the members of small groups to be exempt from audit. This provision applies to both parent undertakings and subsidiary undertakings provided that the aggregate turnover of the group for the year is not more than £350,000 net (or £420,000 gross) and that the group's aggregate balance sheet total is not more than £1.4 million net (or £1.68 million gross). As with the statutory definition of small or medium sized group 'net' means after consolidation adjustments, and 'gross' means a simple total of all the members of the group. *SI 1997/936*

The Audit Faculty of the ICAEW recommends that where the accounts of a company exempt from audit are prepared by an independent accountant and are presented in a manner which creates an association with the accountant, a report by the accountants should be attached to the accounts. An 'association' could be created by presenting the accounts on the accountants' paper or by the accounts containing the accountants' name and address. The presentation of a report prevents any confusion arising as to the duties of the accountants employed to prepare the accounts and, in particular, indicates *IS 3.907, 17* that the accounts have not been audited. Therefore this report should be attached to the set of accounts which is filed with the Registrar of Companies.

The suggested form of accountants' report is:

IS 3.907,
Appendix 2

Accountants' Report on the Unaudited Financial Statements to the Directors of XYZ Limited

As described on the balance sheet you are responsible for the preparation of the financial statements for the year ended . . . ., set out on pages . . . to . . . . You consider that the company is exempt from an audit.

In accordance with your instructions, we have compiled thse unaudited financial statements in order to assist you to fulfil your statutory responsibilities, from the accounting records and information and explanations supplied to us.

Chartered Accountants
Date

Appendix I   Schedule 4 Companies Act 1985 accounts formats – full accounts

Balance sheet format 1

A   **Called-up share capital not paid**

B   **Fixed assets**

I   **Intangible assets**
1   Development costs
2   Concessions, patents, licences, trade marks and similar rights and assets
3   Goodwill
4   Payments on account

II   **Tangible assets**
1   Land and buildings
2   Plant and machinery
3   Fixtures, fittings, tools and equipment
4   Payments on account and assets in the course of construction

III   **Investments**
1   Shares in group undertakings
2   Loans to group undertakings
3   Participating interests
4   Loans to undertakings in which the company has a participating interest
5   Other investment other than loans
6   Other loans
7   Own shares

C   **Current assets**

I   **Stocks**
1   Raw materials and consumables
2   Work in progress
3   Finished goods and goods for resale
4   Payments on account

II   **Debtors**
1   Trade debtors
2   Amounts owed by group undertakings

    3   Amounts owed by undertakings in which the company has a participating interest

    4   Other debtors

    5   Called-up share capital not paid

    6   Prepayments and accrued income

III   Investments

    1   Shares in group undertakings

    2   Own shares

    3   Other investments

IV   Cash at bank and in hand

D   Prepayments and accrued income

E   Creditors: amounts falling due within one year

    1   Debenture loans

    2   Bank loans and overdrafts

    3   Payments received on account

    4   Trade creditors

    5   Bills of exchange payable

    6   Amounts owed to group undertakings

    7   Amounts owed to undertakings in which the company has a participating interest

    8   Other creditors including taxation and social security

    9   Accruals and deferred income

F   Net current assets/(liabilities)

G   Total assets less current liabilities

H   Creditors: amounts falling due after more than one year

    1   Debenture loans

    2   Bank loans and overdrafts

    3   Payments received on account

    4   Trade creditors

    5   Bills of exchange payable

    6   Amounts owed to group undertakings

    7   Amounts owed to undertakings in which the company has a participating interest

    8   Other creditors including taxation and social security

    9   Accruals and deferred income

I   Provisions for liabilities and charges

    1   Pensions and similar obligations

    2   Taxation, including deferred taxation

    3   Other provisions

J   Accruals and deferred income

K   Capital and reserves

    i   Called-up share capital

    ii   Share premium account

    iii   Revaluation reserve

        iv   Other reserves
              1   Capital redemption reserve
              2   Reserve for own shares
              3   Reserves provided for by the articles of association
              4   Other reserves
        v   Profit and loss account

Profit and loss account formats

Format 1

1   Turnover
2   Cost of sales
3   Gross profit or loss
4   Distribution costs
5   Administrative expenses
6   Other operating income
7   Income from shares in group undertakings
8   Income from participating interests
9   Income from other fixed asset investments
10   Other interest receivable and similar income
11   Amounts written off investments
12   Interest payable and similar charges
13   Tax on profit or loss on ordinary activities
14   Profit or loss on ordinary activities after taxation
15   Extraordinary income
16   Extraordinary charges
17   Extraordinary profit or loss
18   Tax on extraordinary profit or loss
19   Other taxes not shown under the above items
20   Profit or loss for the financial year

Format 2

1   Turnover
2   Change in stocks of finished goods and in work in progress
3   Own work capitalised
4   Other operating income
5   (a)   Raw materials and consumables
     (b)   Other external charges
6   Staff costs
     (a)   Wages and salaries
     (b)   Social security costs
     (c)   Other pension costs
7   (a)   Depreciation and other amounts written off tangible and intangible fixed
           assets
     (b)   Exceptional amounts written off current assets
8   Other operating charges
9   Income from shares in group undertakings
10   Income from participating interests
11   Income from other fixed asset investments

12 Other interest receivable and similar income
13 Amounts written off investments
14 Interest payable and similar charges
15 Tax on profit or loss on ordinary activities
16 Profit or loss on ordinary activities after taxation
17 Extraordinary income
18 Extraordinary charges
19 Extraordinary profit or loss
20 Tax on extraordinary profit or loss
21 Other taxes not shown under the above items
22 Profit or loss for the financial year

Appendix 2   Schedule 8 Companies Act 1985 accounts formats – simplified accounts

Balance sheet format 1

A   **Called-up share capital not paid**

B   **Fixed assets**

I   **Intangible assets**
- 1   Goodwill
- 2   Other intangible assets

II   **Tangible assets**
- 1   Land and buildings
- 2   Plant and machinery etc.

III   **Investments**
- 1   Shares in group undertakings and participating interests
- 2   Loans to group undertakings and undertakings in which the company has a participating interest
- 3   Other investment other than loans
- 4   Other investments

C   **Current assets**

I   **Stocks**
- 1   Stocks
- 2   Payments on account

II   **Debtors**
- 1   Trade debtors
- 2   Amounts owed by group undertakings and undertakings in which the company has a participating interest
- 3   Other debtors

III   **Investments**
- 1   Shares in group undertakings
- 2   Other investments

IV   **Cash at bank and in hand**

D **Prepayments and accrued income**

E **Creditors: amounts falling due within one year**
1   Bank loans and overdrafts
2   Trade creditors
3   Amounts owed to group undertakings and undertakings in which the company has a participating interest
4   Other creditors

F **Net current assets (liabilities)**

G **Total assets less current liabilities**

H **Creditors: amounts falling due after more than one year**
1   Bank loans and overdrafts
2   Trade creditors
3   Amounts owed to group undertakings and undertakings in which the company has a participating interest
4   Other creditors

I **Provisions for liabilities and charges**

J **Accruals and deferred income**

K **Capital and reserves**
i   Called-up share capital
ii   Share premium account
iii Revaluation reserve
iv   Other reserves
v   Profit and loss account

Profit and loss account formats

Format 1

1   Turnover
2   Cost of sales
3   Gross profit or loss
4   Distribution costs
5   Administrative expenses
6   Other operating income
7   Income from shares in group undertakings
8   Income from participating interests
9   Income from other fixed asset investments
10   Other interest receivable and similar income
11   Amounts written off investments
12   Interest payable and similar charges
13   Tax on profit or loss on ordinary activities
14   Profit or loss on ordinary activities after taxation
15   Extraordinary income
16   Extraordinary charges

17 Extraordinary profit or loss
18 Tax on extraordinary profit or loss
19 Other taxes not shown under the above items
20 Profit or loss for the financial year

Format 2

1   Turnover
2   Change in stocks of finished goods and in work in progress
3   Own work capitalised
4   Other operating income
5   (a) Raw materials and consumables
    (b) Other external charges
6   Staff costs
    (a) Wages and salaries
    (b) Social security costs
    (c) Other pension costs
7   (a) Depreciation and other amounts written off tangible and intangible fixed assets
    (b) Exceptional amounts written off current assets
8   Other operating charges
9   Income from shares in group undertakings
10 Income from participating interests
11 Income from other fixed asset investments
12 Other interest receivable and similar income
13 Amounts written off investments
14 Interest payable and similar charges
15 Tax on profit or loss on ordinary activities
16 Profit or loss on ordinary activities after taxation
17 Extraordinary income
18 Extraordinary charges
19 Extraordinary profit or loss
20 Tax on extraordinary profit or loss
21 Other taxes not shown under the above items
22 Profit or loss for the financial year

Appendix 3   Small company abbreviated accounts

Balance sheet format 1

A   Called-up share capital not paid

B   Fixed assets
    i   Intangible assets
    ii   Tangible assets
    iii   Investments

C   Current assets
    i   Stocks
    ii   Debtors
    iii   Investments
    iv   Cash at bank and in hand

D   Prepayments and accrued income

E   Creditors: amounts falling due within one year

F   Net current assets (liabilities)

G   Total assets less current liabilities

H   Creditors: amounts falling due after more than one year

I   Provisions for liabilities and charges

J   Accruals and deferred income

K   Capital and reserves
    i   Called-up share capital
    ii   Share premium account
    iii   Revaluation reserve
    iv   Other reserves
    v   Profit and loss account

INDEX